CW00691392

Victimhood, Memory, and Consumerism

Victimhood, Memory, and Consumerism

Profiting from Pablo

KATJA FRANKO AND DAVID R. GOYES

University of Oslo, Norway

OXFORD
UNIVERSITY PRESS

Great Clarendon Street, Oxford, OX2 6DP,
United Kingdom

Oxford University Press is a department of the University of Oxford.
It furthers the University's objective of excellence in research, scholarship,
and education by publishing worldwide. Oxford is a registered trade mark of
Oxford University Press in the UK and in certain other countries

First Edition published in 2023

Published in the United States of America by Oxford University Press
198 Madison Avenue, New York, NY 10016, United States of America

British Library Cataloguing in Publication Data

Data available

Library of Congress Control Number: 2023942385

ISBN 978–0–19–287411–5

DOI: 10.1093/oso/9780192874115.001.0001

Printed and bound in the UK by
TJ Books Limited

Preface

'Colombian? Oh, Pablo Escobar, cool', European and North Americans often exclaim when David introduces himself. A man from whom he bought a second-hand keyboard praised Escobar's brilliance, while a female cashier at Western Union confessed her attraction to the drug lord and explained how Escobar inspired her to learn Spanish. A married couple admitted to their fascination with the Netflix's popular show *Narcos*, through which they learned about Colombia's history. Yet, others who wonder what it *really* was like to live in Colombia in the 1980s and 1990s amidst the well-documented drug violence—violence that David had lived through. Casual comments and questions notwithstanding, Escobar casts a shadow over many conversations between a Colombian and someone from the Global North. This is, in large part, due to *Narcos*, whose larger-than-life representation of Pablo Escobar has brought Colombia into the thrall of the drug lord's legend.

When Katja visited Colombia for the first time, her impression of the country was coloured in advance not only by her fondness for the work of Gabriel Garcia Márquez, whom she had read as a teenager growing up in Slovenia, but also by several seasons of *Narcos* that she had watched in the evenings with her partner. The guide book she had bought before her journey invited her to visit Medellín and get to know better the life of the drug lord. Although she had studied issues of crime and global inequality for a number of years, her encounter with dark tourism in the city elicited not only discomfort, but a very visceral reaction that challenged her own position as a Northern media consumer and awoke the desire for a better understanding.

This book explores what happens to a society when trauma becomes a commodity and to a city, Medellin, when it is haunted by the image of a man responsible for its mass victimization. The book is motivated by our shared, long-standing interest in issues of crime and global inequality. In our everyday life as academic criminologists, we examine how the Global North–Global South relations affect the patterns of ecological destruction, migration, and border control, as well as our knowledge of these phenomena. In some ways, the subject of this book lies outside our usual spheres of interest. However, it had touched us on a personal level. The book's findings challenge the practices of media consumption, cultural symbols, and knowledge paradigms that underlie our daily lives, not only as academics, but also as citizens and consumers. On an ordinary quiz night at a pub in Oslo, for example, we might face an opposing team called 'Pablo Quizcobar'. The cover design of this book is based on a Google maps search result for 'Escobar pub'. And although not every 'Escobar pub' is named after the drug lord, the number of those that are is astounding, as is their proliferation around the world. One of the aims of this book is to show how such everyday practices open up important ethical questions. The insight that the type of show we choose to watch on television at night might impact individuals in another part of the world, inspired us to embark on a project that we had no funding for. The writing of this book developed as a side project outside our other tasks. It was driven by curiosity and the belief that the stories we began to uncover matter and deserve to be heard.

Both of us contributed equally to the making of this book. Short segments from chapters 2 and 4 have been previously published in an article in *The British Journal of Criminology* (Goyes and Franko, 2021). Chapter 8 is based on an article in *Social and Legal Studies* (Franko and Goyes, 2023). We are grateful to the journals' editors and the anonymous reviewers for their constructive feedback.

We also thank Angie Cuchimba and Sara Álvarez García, who transcribed the interviews, and Kamilla Kristiansen, who assisted us in contacting *Narcos*' producers. Sara also conducted a focus group interview with inhabitants of Medellín. Jan Christian Andersen, Cecilia Bailliet, Solveig Langerud, Kjersti Lohne, Jorge Nuñez, Eva Magdalena Stambøl, Thomas Ugelvik, Yvonne Yewkes, and Per Jørgen Ystehede commented on drafts of this text and provided invaluable feedback—we are grateful for their collegiality. We also owe great thanks to Rose Elisabeth Boyle, Susana Valdés Builes, and Tanya Wyatt for sending us some of the photos used in the book, and to Heloise Sverderup Lund for helping us with counting the Escobar pubs. Helen Sword gave us writing advice on how to try to capture some of the almost ineffable events in Colombia's recent history, while David D. Menilla and Ela Kotkowska provided excellent help with language editing and insightful comments about the text. A great thank you is also owed to Fiona Briden at Oxford University Press for her belief in the project and to Kezia Johnson for her assistance with the production. We thank Héctor Mauricio Rodríguez Sepúlveda for putting his skills to our service in designing a cover that we believe captures the core insight of this book.

First and foremost, however, we are indebted to the residents of Medellín, particularly the victims and survivors of drug violence who opened their hearts to us and shared their stories—many of them for the very first time in decades.

David wants to dedicate this book to Hernando and Gloria, and the Todd-Kvam family: John, Mari, Sofia, and Martin. Katja would like to dedicate this book to her daughters, as well as to the Department of Criminology and Sociology of Law at the University of Oslo, which not only provided the limited financial means that made this book possible, but which, for twenty-five years, has also provided her with a safe haven of collegiality, intellectual curiosity, and inspiration.

Contents

List of Figures xi

1. Introduction 1
   - Consumerism and the trauma economy 1
   - The trauma(tic) economy 6
   - Victimhood and cosmopolitan solidarity in a divided world 9
   - Framing drug violence 12
   - The Global North–Global South divide and the hierarchies of victimhood 15
   - Methodology 16
   - Outline of the book 20
2. A city at war 25
   - A long-standing conflict 25
   - Violent oppression, inequality, and colonialism 26
   - A war within a war 34
   - The war seen, heard, and felt 38
   - The trauma of war 45
3. Invisible victims in a commodified world 47
   - 'We don't talk about it much because it is painful' 47
   - Telling the story 49
   - Layers of silence 52
   - Unseen and unheard 57
   - Repressed individual and collective traumas 64
   - The advent of global media companies 67
4. Building a global brand 69
   - From trauma to entertainment 69
   - The birth of narco-telenovelas 70
   - Beautifying Escobar 73
   - Netflix: The business of entertainment 80
   - Why do we consume violence? 86
   - How violence as a spectacle hinders trauma healing 91

5. 'There are many uncomfortable dynamics in a production' 97
Toxic masculinity and violence 97
Living the Al Capone and James Bond life 98
Branding the macho conquistador 101
Hegemonic masculinity in the South 106
Exoticizing the post-colonial Other 109
Immortalizing macho men, submissive women, and exotic others 112

6. Dark consumerism and the trauma(tic) economy 117
'Kidnapped memory' 117
Dark tourism and the impossibility of forgetting 119
The trauma(tic) economy 127
Memory and branding in an unequal society 133

7. The quest for recognition 143
The battle to control memory 143
Netflix and the writing of history 143
Political profiting and local resistance 148
'Respect our pain, honour our victims' 154
The struggle for recognition and the cosmopolitan exclusion 157
The difficult path to recognition 160

8. Global hierarchies of victimhood 163
The Victims' Law 163
Hierarchies of victimhood 166
Mass drug violence: A civil war or an 'ordinary crime'? 169
A war seen 'from below', but not 'from above' 173
'An ignored death': The elusiveness of justice 177
Unequal victims and the obliteration of pain 183

9. Conclusion 187
Memory, voice, identity, and power in a global society 187
Narcos and the epistemic power of the North 192
Do no harm: Crime drama and the global consumer culture 195
The fear of oblivion 200

References 203
Index 223

List of Figures

1.1. A menu featuring Escobar-inspired drinks at a bar in Vienna 3

1.2. Pablo Escobar's T-shirt sold in Camden Market, London 4

2.1. The rubble of the Monaco building, demolished on the order of the Medellín's major in 2019 36

4.1. Pablo Escobar 75

4.2. Andrés Parra in his role as Pablo Escobar in *El Patrón del Mal* 76

4.3. Wagner Moura as Pablo Escobar and Paulina Gaitán (middle) as Escobar's wife in Narcos 78

4.4. Javier Bardem as Pablo Escobar and Penelope Cruz as Virginia Vallejo in *Loving Pablo* (2017) 79

4.5. A billboard for *Narcos* in Madrid, Spain 93

5.1. A replica of James Bond's jet ski at the Escobar Museum in Medellín 99

5.2. Wagner Moura (as Pablo Escobar) 'dominating' Stephanie Sigman (as Valeria Velez) in *Narcos*, season 1, episode 3 102

5.3. Brendan Fraser playing Pablo Escobar in the movie *Bedazzled* (2000) 107

6.1. Visitors to Escobar's grave, located next to the church 121

6.2. Pilgrims' offerings at Escobar's tomb. The epitaph reads: 'You were a conqueror of impossible dreams, beyond the legend that it symbolizes today, few know the true essence of your life.' 122

6.3. Visitors taking pictures at the entrance to the Napoles ranch, in front of the HK-617 Colombian airplane used by drug lord Pablo Escobar to transport his first shipment of cocaine to the United States 123

6.4. Mural in El Barrio Pablo Escobar in Medellín 124

6.5. A hairdresser's in El Barrio Pablo Escobar in Medellín 125

6.6. A mug shot of Pablo Escobar taken by the regional Colombian control agency in Medellín in 1976 130

6.7. Souvenirs with the image of Pablo Escobar at a shop in Comuna 13 in Medellín 131

6.8. A tourist in Comuna 13 in Medellín showing off his Escobar tattoo 131

6.9. The statue of a saint in El Barrio Pablo Escobar 139

6.10. Portraits of prominent members of the Medellín cartel in El Barrio Pablo Escobar 140
7.1. Parque Conmemorativo Inflexión 150
7.2. Museo Casa de la Memoria, Medellín 155
9.1. *Pablo Escobar Muerto* by Fernando Botero, 2006 199

1
Introduction

Consumerism and the trauma economy

At the height of its power, the Medellín cartel controlled 60 per cent of the world's cocaine trade, and made the city where it was based amongst the most violent in the world. During the 1980s, 375 homicides per 100,000 inhabitants were recorded annually in the city of Medellín, which is more than thirty-five times the World Health Organization's definition of epidemic violence (Maclean, 2015: 2). This considerably exceeded the already high levels of violence in Colombia at the time, earning Medellín the reputation of the 'murder capital of the world' (Brodzinsky, 2014). At the centre of Medellín's tragedy was Pablo Escobar, the charismatic and ruthless leader of the Medellín cartel. (Various sources credit Escobar with killing close to 5,000 people.[1]) The clash between the Medellín cartel and the state took an enormous toll on the city's civilian population and left long-lasting scars on social institutions and local communities. In 1993, after years of persecution, security forces from Colombia and the United States gunned down Escobar in a hail of bullets when he tried to escape.

Today, Medellín is a more peaceful city with a vibrant cultural and economic life, even when social inequality pervades the city and violence alarms inhabitants. Yet, the city also lives a parallel life in media and commercial networks where its identity and history are recast to satisfy consumer tastes. Such networks have made Medellín an attractive place to visit, whimsically defining its identity, while at the same time distorting its violent and traumatic past.

In Medellín's parallel life, Pablo Escobar—one of the main perpetrators of the bloodshed that took place more than three decades ago—has become a cultural icon. His life and violent 'achievements' are told

[1] For more information, see Wallace (2013).

Victimhood, Memory, and Consumerism. Katja Franko and David R. Goyes, Oxford University Press.
 DOI: 10.1093/oso/9780192874115.003.0001

and retold in books, movies, and TV series. Hollywood stars, like Javier Bardem and Wagner Moura, enact Escobar's life story in global blockbusters and the drug lord's grinning face features on T-shirts, coffee cups, and other memorabilia available worldwide on Amazon as well as locally in myriad retail outlets.

As a result of his newfound fame and commodification, Pablo Escobar has become an omnipresent consumer brand. During the process of writing of this book, colleagues and friends across the world sent us numerous pictures they took whenever they saw yet another Escobar image decorating cultural or commercial venues. Escobar-themed bars and restaurants—including the ones depicted on the cover of this book—can be located in numerous countries across the world, with as many as 120 in Europe. A Mexican restaurant in Norway offers Escobar-inspired dishes; an Australian pub called *Pablo's* sells *escoburgers* with a knife planted in the middle; and a Viennese cocktail bar pours *Columbian spirits* and has a menu decorated with Escobar's face (Figure 1.1). Escobar's likeness can also be found in the popular Camden Market in London, where Escobar-themed T-shirts are sold side by side with Nirvana and Maradona apparel (Figure 1.2). Even in online gaming platforms his name is used as a handle (a player named Pablo_Escobar419 popped up on chess.com).

These cultural artefacts testify to how Escobar's global image has gradually shifted from disgrace and notoriety to fame. In the process, the international perception of Colombia and Medellín has also metamorphosed.

Seeing these changes take place compels us to ask the question, what do these commercial and cultural practices tell us about contemporary culture and the way it relates to violence? Consumer objects and practices tell stories. They indicate how we, as a society, relate to violence and engage with the pain it inflicts. An Escobar T-shirt is not simply an item of clothing—it is also an emblem of cultural values: an endorsement of mischievousness and a symbol of nonchalant, violent masculinity. When clothing manufacturers put Escobar's image on a consumer product, they send a message, which the buyers of the product endorse and promote. The product signifies a way of relating to the world. When shoppers in Camden Market or elsewhere buy merchandise inspired by the drug lord and wear it on their bodies, they are both identifying with, and advertising, his image, values, and the views he represents. Escobar thus becomes part of their identity, however transiently. Although the spheres

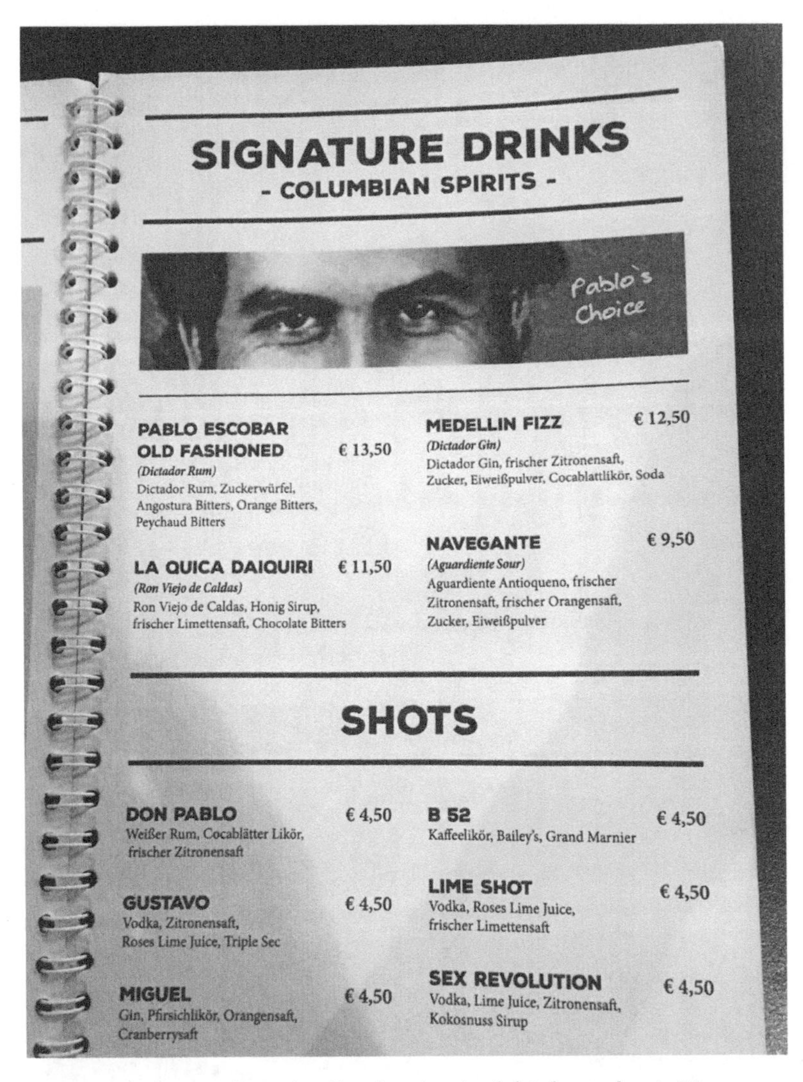

Figure 1.1. A menu featuring Escobar-inspired drinks at a bar in Vienna.
Source: © Tanya Wyatt.

in which Escobar's *fame* circulates and the *physical sphere* he inhabited are somewhat different, they do intersect. As Jean Baudrillard (2016) reminds us, there is an intimate connection between consuming (i.e., wearing) and being. Yet, practices of global consumerism trample upon the everyday lives of Medellín's inhabitants—particularly those who

Figure 1.2. Pablo Escobar's T-shirt sold in Camden Market, London.
Source: © Rose Elisabeth Boyle.

lived through Escobar's violence and lost loved ones to his clash with the state. Encountering casual consumers of Escobar T-shirts and tourists in search of Escobar's relics on the streets of their home city feels, as one survivor put it, akin to his resurrection. Escobar continues to haunt the scene of his crimes.

This is a book about haunting. To 'haunt' means 'to visit often', 'to recur constantly and spontaneously', and 'to have a disquieting or harmful effect on'.[2] All three definitions apply to Medellín. It is a haunted city. The wearers of Escobar T-shirts, the viewers of *Narcos*, and the visitors to Escobar's shrines might not think of their actions as haunting or intentionally distressing. Yet, these consumer practices are intimately connected to memories of the worst atrocities that the city ever experienced. Every consumer object brings the traumatic past back to life; it makes that violent past hauntingly real again. Haunting and ghost apparitions blur the boundaries between 'real and unreal, present and absent' (Klima, 2019: 19; see also Monleón, 1990). This is also true of Medellín: although its story is one of enormous resilience and entrepreneurial spirit, the city's present spatio-cultural identity also intersects with its traumatic memories. As Fiddler (2019: 463) observes, 'a given space's violent histories can become embedded in the texts that constitute it and the language that describes it'. The narratives about Medellín's violent past continue to 'haunt' its present.

This book describes the city's strategies for coping with and resisting Escobar's commercially fuelled resurrection. Observers of haunting as a sociological phenomenon point out that haunting is essentially about 'politics of memory, of inheritance, and of generations' (Klima, 2019: 20). Cities associated with past violence and illegality often 'struggle to cast off the shackles of their public image' (Fraser and Li, 2017: 218). The global economic influence of movies, documentaries, and works of fiction keep them tied to their violent past. When Fraser and Li studied the traumatic cultural memory of Kowloon Walled City, they found that it 'became untethered from the place itself, and recast in the realm of 'real virtuality'. The authors concluded that 'consumerism and commodification figure in memorialisation' (ibid.: 229). A similar phenomenon takes place in

[2] See 'haunt', *Merriam-Webster Dictionary*, https://www.merriam-webster.com/dictionary/haunt, accessed 15 February 2023.

Medellín. The stories of violence that circulate about the city in the global commercial networks shape its local texture and memory.

The haunting we describe in this book is shaped by the logics of commodification and consumer cultures. Money—like ghosts—is empty, marked by an absence of substance (Klima, 2019: 8). Yet, the consumerism that money allows is one of the most important cultural forces of our time (Miles, 1998). Few social phenomena today, including victimization and traumatic experiences, remain untouched by the joint forces of consumerism and globalization. Consumerism binds the world through a dense web of commercial networks that also impact society's understanding of victimhood. A large body of criminological scholarship shows that victimhood is never socially neutral. It involves powerful interests, diverse inequalities, and popular and media discourses that tend to privilege particular understandings of victims (White, 2015). In this book, we examine how the narrative power of global capitalism impacts the experiences and social understandings of victimhood. We argue that global commercial practices and media representations shape collective memories of societies to a degree we have not fully acknowledged. While we have intense public discussions about the ethical impact of consumerism in various social spheres, such as the fashion industry and food consumption, we currently lack the conceptual tools to discuss the effects of consumerism in portrayals of violence. Consumerism and commercialism affect the lives of individuals exposed to drug violence—particularly in societies of the Global South.

The trauma(tic) economy

The way societies understand themselves and are seen by others is shaped by processes of remembrance and memorialization (Brown and Rafter, 2013). The dynamics through which the violence that affected Medellín in the 1980s and 1990s is converted into collective memory are, therefore, vital for the city's identity. What kind of narratives are being told about Medellín? Who created them and how? In this book, we probe into the inability of Medellín's inhabitants to narrate their trauma and shape their collective identity. We demonstrate that the narrative power of global commercial media not only shapes the understanding of the past and the present of the city, but also silences other ways of remembering.

In Medellín, as elsewhere, the process of translating violent conflict into memory has been partly shaped by media and the mandates of popular culture. Collective pasts are 'narrated by the media, through the use of the media, and about the media' (Neiger, Meyers, and Zandberg, 2011: 1). As Nicole Rafter points out, film is 'one of the primary sources (albeit an unscientific one) through which people get their ideas about the nature of crime' (Rafter, 2007: 417). The images shown in documentaries, movies, and TV programmes give societies a mediated understanding of crime and become central to consumers' interpretation of past conflicts. In their analysis of genocide films, Brown and Rafter (2013: 1028) demonstrated that they were central in building the collective memories of the affected communities. Moreover, as various scholars have shown, the dynamics of 'celebrity, criminality, desire, fame, trauma and voyeurism' play a significant role in the production, consumption, and interpretation of mediated accounts of violence (Carrabine, 2014: 134–5; see also Greer and McLaughlin, 2017; Jewkes, 2015).

Traumatic memories are, moreover, also open to commodification. Mourning and consumerism are related in complex ways through the 'economic networks that emerge around historical events, including events of trauma' (Sturken, 2007: 4; see also Monleón, 1990). Because of its marketability, trauma intersects with capitalist power structures, ensuring that 'representations of trauma continually circulate, and in that circulation enable or disable awareness of particular traumatic experiences across space and time' (Tomsky, 2011: 49). Yet, while we have considerable knowledge on global media, the role of consumer practices and commercialism in building memories of crime and atrocities remains a virtually unexplored terrain. In this book, we address this knowledge gap by drawing on the concept of the *trauma economy*. Tomsky (ibid.) defined trauma economy as the media, information networks, and communicative capitalism that form the material framework for the movement of traumatic memory in a global age. The concept of trauma economy draws attention to the fact that *memory is determined by capitalism* and that the privilege of narrating and re-narrating trauma is determined by 'economic, cultural, discursive and political structures that guide, enable and ultimately institutionalize the representation, travel and attention to certain traumas' (ibid.: 53).

Traumatic memories do not escape the dominant global consumerist culture; they are shaped by it. Sturken's study about consumer practices surrounding events such as 9/11 and the Oklahoma bombing shows how commercial entrepreneurs offer consumers the opportunity to experience history from the position of tourists: as 'innocent outsiders, mere observers whose actions are believed to have no effect on what they see' (Sturken, 2007: 10). Consumerism provides a safe experience through the 'purchasing of souvenirs at sites of loss such as Ground Zero as a means of expressing sorrow at the lives lost there, without trying to understand the contexts of volatile world politics that produced the attacks' (ibid.: 10). In this book, however, we show that the intersections of trauma, consumerism, and tourism are safe and sanitized only for the tourists—not for the locals. For local inhabitants, the trauma economy brings about profoundly problematic material and symbolic effects. In this book, we narrate how Medellín has been transformed, through the commodification of its trauma, and branded in terms of its violent past (see Volcic, Erjavec, and Peak, 2013 for similar findings on the branding of post-war Sarajevo).

In the book, we also highlight the contrast between the traumatic sensory and emotional impact of those violent events on the survivors with the light and entertaining tone of narco-shows, Escobar tours, and memorabilia, which since the 2000s have been the dominant global narrative about the city's past. In addition to the journalistic entries written in the 1980s and 1990s by local reporters, we also bring together psychological and sensory memories of direct witnesses of drug violence in order to provide a sensory overview (McClanahan and South 2019) of events and to give readers a deeper understanding of the merciless conflict that transpired in Medellín (McClanahan and South, 2019). We also show how commercial actors frame the violence as a form of entertainment and nurture the fascination with Escobar's persona, accentuating the traumatic impact on victims and survivors.

Considering the profound impacts brought about by the commercialization of Medellín's violent past, we raise the question about whether the concept of trauma economy should be adjusted to take into account the transformations in the meaning of trauma. An Escobar T-shirt, bought in Camden Market or elsewhere, references a violent past. For someone who lost a family member to the conflict, meeting a wearer of that T-shirt can be traumatic. Yet, in the commercial exploitation of Escobar's story, victims' trauma is toned down, if not entirely erased from the narrative. The current profiting from Escobar focuses on the morbid fascination with the perpetrator and the excitement and entertainment it provides. When appropriating the privilege of narrating the traumatic events that took place in Medellín and distributing their narratives to global audiences, powerful commercial actors radically change the meaning of those events. Narratives of atrocious violence turn into entertainment.

In the eyes of the victims, what is being consumed and commercialized is their trauma. Yet, the product sold to consumers and tourists is detached from the suffering of those who lived through the violence. Paradoxically, in the trauma economy, trauma stops being trauma and rather becomes a *traumatic economy*. In consumer experiences, the trauma and pain caused by violence is restrained, neutralized, or even denied. Along the way, the city of Medellín lives a life, in the symbolic universe, of a transgressive and deviant city. These phenomena are the result of commercial actors exerting their symbolic and narrative power over Medellín's inhabitants. In this book, we explore the effects that this traumatic economy and the global commercial appropriation of history have on Escobar's victims, their possibilities for achieving justice, the identities of Medellín's inhabitants, and the city's strategies of resistance.

Victimhood and cosmopolitan solidarity in a divided world

Traumatic events are deeply embedded in everyday life and the language which societies use to articulate what trauma is. According to Jeffrey Alexander (2004: 8), cultural trauma is a product of 'a socially mediated attribution', where events become imagined as traumatic as they occur or through a post-hoc process of reconstruction. Cultural trauma is, therefore, primarily an empirical, scientific concept, as well as being fundamentally related to questions of social solidarity and social responsibility.

By identifying cultural trauma, societies also take responsibility for it, as Alexander also points out: 'Insofar as they identify the cause of trauma, and thereby assume such moral responsibility, members of collectivities define their solidarity relationships in ways that, in principle, allow them to share the suffering of others' (ibid.: 1).

Following Alexander's view, a large body of scholarship has recently argued that removing layers of repressed trauma and bringing greater visibility to victims can contribute to national and transnational justice and reconciliation processes (Brants and Klep, 2013; Karstedt, 2010). Globalization has been seen as conducive to the cosmopolitanization of memory (Beck, Levy, and Szneider, 2016). This argument suggests that by developing globally shared imaginaries of atrocity transnational agents not only develop institutional structures for bringing perpetrators to justice (Lohne, 2019), but also build global ethical communities around shared narratives of violence and mourning (Skillington, 2013). Commemorations of the Holocaust and the genocide in Rwanda, for instance, are argued to contribute to the 'moral instruction of global audiences' (ibid.: 502) and be conducive to building global solidarity.

The findings in this book, however, bring a more pessimistic reading of global interconnectedness and solidarity. They challenge the common assumption that (global) visibility is intrinsically positive for the acknowledgement of victims of violence. Instead, we suggest that the construction of collective memory, when embedded in the global capitalist economy, can erect barriers that prevent groups of victims from being included in the 'common we'. The capitalist co-option of memory can, furthermore, re-victimize those who have experienced atrocities. Our findings align with the scholarship that documents how only some experiences of trauma and some groups of victims evoke recognition, sympathy and aid, while others remain in the shadows (Tomsky, 2011; McGarry and Walklate, 2015). In other words, the recognition of trauma and victimhood is distributed inequitably around the world. As Caple James observes, the concept of trauma intersects with various 'linkages of power relations or forces from the local to international realms of social and political action' and 'the ability to participate in these debates [of trauma recognition] depends on positioning, whether geopolitical, communal, or individual' (2004: 128–9). Therefore, analysing collective trauma demands not only considering its socio-cultural and psychological impact, but also looking into the framework of tangible economic relations. Part of the focus should be on 'distinguishing who possesses the resources to "work through" traumas from those who do not' (Lerner, 2018: 551). This perspective makes it possible to discern which groups have the ability to get their story heard and how they achieve social recognition.

In this book, we address the question of why certain traumas get recognized while others do not. While some cities and communities achieve the acknowledgment of their loss and receive widespread solidarity, others do not. Medellín is among the latter. The linkages between trauma and the global media and commercial networks are an important reason why recognition is distributed unequally. Commercial forces turned Medellín's traumatic past into a source of entertainment and made Pablo Escobar a global icon. Meanwhile, the suffering of individual victims and an entire city has remained obscured. The concept of a trauma(tic) economy thus exposes global interconnectedness and cosmopolitan memory traditions as fraught with inequality, consumerism, and oblivion.

We also show how Medellín's authorities have tried to join the global traditions of atrocity remembrance, seeking to obtain acknowledgement and respect for the severity of the violence their city had suffered. Their efforts have been in vain. The city's traumatic past continues to be narrated in frameworks radically different from those used for mass atrocities elsewhere in the world. Therefore, we examine how geopolitical circumstances, particularly the impact of the United States-led war on drugs and the continued, pervasive impact of colonialism, shape the current understanding of victims of mass drug violence in countries of the Global South.

Collective memories of atrocities are a fractured and disputed terrain (Hearty, 2016)—a field where powerful actors are often able to impose their accounts to the detriment of local narratives. In this book, we explore why the trauma left by large-scale drug violence is not recognized despite the gravity of its impact on the civilian populations, but rather becomes open to commercial exploitation as entertainment. Global imaginaries of trade in narcotics have framed drug violence as an 'ordinary crime' rather than one associated with mass atrocities despite its casualties exceeding, particularly in Latin America, the conventional definitions of civil warfare (Lessing, 2018).

Framing drug violence

Geopolitically, policies related to the trade in criminalized narcotics have been an extremely contentious terrain dominated by powerful actors, particularly the United States. Andreas and Nadelmann point out that the debate about trade in narcotics has been 'one of the most important—and one of the most overlooked—dimensions of U.S. hegemony in world politics' (2006: 10). The models, methods, and priorities of international drug control have, historically, been determined and exported by the most powerful states in the international system (ibid.). The imposition of models of crime control, with respect to drug trafficking, are particularly visible in the history of Colombia. Through political, economic, and military coercion, the United States has enforced its 'war on drugs' policy in the South American country. The war-on-drugs entailed a governmentally sanctioned combative and militarized approach to narcotics, and elicited an equally violent response from the cartels. The dramatic bombing of a commercial flight from Bogotá to Cali, in which 107 civilian passengers died, was an example of the levels of violence connected to the efforts to get drug traffickers extradited and tried in U.S. courts. (We provide more details about this attack in chapter 2.)

When talking and writing about victims of drug violence, we therefore encounter considerable conceptual difficulties in terms of clarity, delineation, and etymology. What do we mean by 'drug violence'? Whose concepts are we using and how did they come about? Not only drug cartels perpetrate drug violence; state actors and paramilitary organizations are also responsible to a considerable extent. In Colombia, as in several other Latin American countries, the state has initiated vicious attacks under the excuse of combating drug trafficking, which has increased the numbers of casualties (Lessing, 2018). State actors often use the label 'drug violence' as part of their ideological campaign, seeking to (de)legitimize the actions of other actors. Another example of this political discourse used by the state is its use of the concept of 'narco-terrorism' to indicate that only a handful of illicit actors—but not the state—is responsible for the loss of lives in the war on drugs. As we discuss in chapter 2, the notions of 'drug violence' and 'narco-terrorism' are, therefore, an integral component of the political realm and activities of national and international political actors. The concept of 'drug violence' is thus not satisfactory as a scholarly term. One of the critiques of the narratives promoted by the entertainment industry regarding Medellín in the 1980s and 1990s is that the United States-led war on drugs escapes critical scrutiny. In fact, the story of *Narcos*—one of the most widely distributed narratives about violence in Colombia—is told through the eyes of two North American law enforcement agents.

Another reason why the term 'drug violence' has been contentious is that it might be interpreted to imply a causal relationship between drugs and violence. Although many, if not most, societies experience trade in illegal narcotics, levels of violence related to the trade vary considerably. Rather, violence depends on the political responses to the phenomenon. As Angelica Durán-Martínez (2018) shows in her study, drug violence is thoroughly intertwined with politics in terms of its causes and responses to it. As a result of this 'intimate connection between political change and large-scale criminal violence' in several Latin American countries (Trejo and Ley, 2020: 3), the term 'drug violence' demands thorough attention to the political context in which it is applied.

Mindful of these arguments, we use the term 'mass drug violence' to convey the scale of casualties among the civilian population and the role of the powerful in its perpetration. We use the term to highlight the violence that cartels perpetrate in connection and cooperation with political elites, state institutions, and international actors. The term borrows from a common definition of mass atrocities, which 'consist of extreme violence inflicted on a large scale or in a deliberate manner, particularly on civilians and non-combatants by State or non-State actors' (Khalfaoui, 2020). Victims of large-scale drug violence, as we show in this book, are usually excluded from consideration as victims of political violence. Yet, the information we provide about the violence that transpired in Medellín (including numbers of casualties, modi operandi, types of victims, and sensory experiences) reveals that the distinctions between political violence and drug violence are not based on objective differences but are first and foremost influenced by political convenience.

The challenge of finding the right terminology mirrors the difficulty victims of mass drug violence face when trying to have their voices heard. Victims and survivors of Medellín's violence, as we show in this book, face reluctance on the part of the state of Colombia when it comes to acknowledging the severity of their situation. They have also been generally neglected by national and international scholarship, even though several academic disciplines have in the past two decades taken a keen interest in how societies remember traumatic events, particularly mass atrocities. Yet, little has been written in scholarly literature about victims of mass drug violence. Even Colombian studies on collective memories of atrocities have focused on political violence, which generally excludes drug-related violence. As Giraldo (2011) points out, the main focus of such research is on the perpetrators (paramilitaries, guerrillas, and the state); certain groups of victims (vulnerable civil society groups, Indigenous peoples, and non-male persons); and the role of young people in the creation of collective memory of the conflict (see also Riaño-Alcalá, 2010). Of the 104 books published by the National Centre of Historical Memory between 2008 and 2021,[3] only one deals with drug violence in Medellín (Centro Nacional de Memoria Histórica, 2017). In sum, there is little research on the construction of collective memory of drug violence (for an exception, see Aristizábal Uribe, 2018).

Yet, during the past decade, scholars have become increasingly interested in the cultural legacy of drug violence in Colombia, particularly in the role of the media. Aldona Pobutsky (2013), professor of Latin American Studies at Oakland University, documented how the popularity of narco-shows has contributed to the mushrooming of Escobar-themed bestsellers, which provide anecdotal and intimate narratives about the drug lord and his lifestyle. Those bestsellers, explains Pobutsky, obstruct the national and local efforts to frame their experiences as a tragedy. Similarly, anthropologist Xavier Andrade and colleagues (2021: 213) argue that TV series such as *Pablo Escobar: El Patrón del Mal* [*Pablo Escobar, The Drug Lord*] help create a glamorous 'narco-aesthetic'. Andrade offers as an example the case of the Historical Museum of the Colombian National Police. The museum was established to commemorate the fight against drug trafficking but, ironically, instead became a temple of narco-relics. These and other academic contributions are valuable for understanding the creation of collective memory surrounding

[3] The Centro Nacional de Memoria Histórica is a product of the 2005 peace process with the paramilitaries and has been central to the researching and production of collective memory of political violence in Colombia. The Centro's publications are freely available at https://centrodememoriahistorica.gov.co/libros/, accessed 21 June 2021.

the violence that transpired in Medellín in the 1980s and 1990s, but the existent scholarship lacks a sustained focus on the victims.

This book seeks to fill social and academic gaps by bringing forth the voices of those who were (and still are) directly affected by mass drug violence. The book outlines the intricate dynamics of victim-silencing and perpetrator hyper-visibility that shape the present terrain of collective memories of violence in Medellín.

The Global North–Global South divide and the hierarchies of victimhood

One of our central arguments in this book is that the current framing of mass drug violence is marked by three inter-related phenomena: (i) the sidelining, particularly in commercial products, of the suffering of victims and survivors; (ii) the conceptual placing of mass drug violence outside the sphere of mass atrocities and political violence; and (iii) the structural obstacles experienced by victims and survivors in their efforts to obtain recognition, and their consequential sense of exclusion from the cosmopolitan community. Our interviewees often asked whether the commercialization of their suffering would have been possible if it had happened in a European or North American city. They wondered whether it would have been possible to erase the pain of those affected by violence from popular and historical narratives and replace it with excitement, exotic otherness, and fascination with the perpetrator. The questions our interviewees posed signal that, beyond the economic and commercial aspects, another important power dimension in processes of memory construction is the linkage of trauma with the unequal relations between the Global North and the Global South.

How have global inequality and the legacies of colonialism shaped the knowledge that we have, and the language that we use, about drug violence? The models we use for understanding violence, including drug violence, are mainly produced by scholars in the Global North, where this type of violence generally does not achieve such endemic proportions. What repercussions does the semi-monopoly on knowledge have for the victims of mass drug violence? Residents of Medellín remember bombs exploding in public spaces; public executions of civilians, judges, and police officers; kidnappings; and emergency school evacuations—events that closely resembled experiences of war. Yet, national and international scholarly and legal definitions do not include drug violence as warfare or political violence. Victims and survivors are thus excluded from truth, justice, and reparation programmes offered to victims of political violence. We argue, drawing on the previous scholarship on *hierarchies of victimhood*, that the global conceptualization of mass drug violence subordinates its victims and hinders their social and legal recognition.

We argue that a central constitutive element of hierarchies of victimhood is the victims' ability to have their voices heard in the public domain. *Epistemic injustice* (Santos, 2002; Fricker, 2007), the lack of recognition and interest of certain experiences and knowledge, determines to a large degree where the victims are placed in the hierarchy of victimhood (see also Franko, 2021). Survivors of violence in Medellín experience two of the forms of epistemic injustice described by Fricker (2007): testimonial injustice (less credibility given to their accounts) and hermeneutical injustice (a disadvantage in making sense of their experiences). Global inequalities and power imbalances, which give greater narrative power to certain actors and accounts, such as those offered by Netflix or close associates and relatives of Pablo Escobar, are at the core of the epistemic injustice experienced by victims and survivors. The continued hermeneutical influence of colonialism, which privileges global designs at the expense of local histories in the Global South (Mignolo, 2012; Quijano, 2007), also negatively affects victims' and survivors' search for recognition.

Methodology

Victimhood, Memory, and Consumerism: Profiting from Pablo explores the power relations and social structures that shape the national and global understandings of the violence that transpired in Medellín in the 1980s and 1990s and that resulted in an egregious loss of life. The term 'profiting' in our title refers to the complex web of local, national, and global actors that have turned Escobar's story into a profitable economy. By doing so, these actors have turned Medellín's traumatic past into a hyper-visible phenomenon, while simultaneously changing the very meaning of the city's trauma. Escobar's story has not only inspired TV series, documentaries, movies, and books, but also numerous commercial products, such as cocktails, clothing, memorabilia, and themed tours. 'Profiting' also refers to the political actors that have, in recent years, tapped into the local resentment of the commercial appropriation of the victims' suffering and turned it into an electoral issue. In this book, we offer an empirically grounded exploration of the many forms of social profiting from trauma and of the power relations that shape the collective narratives about the city's past.

In our attempt to examine and challenge the deep-seated economic, narrative, and knowledge imbalances, we employed a bottom-up empirical approach by presenting first-hand experiences of those who were directly affected by Medellín's violence. For some, the meeting with us was their first opportunity to tell their story. However, by no means do we imply that our own positionality escapes narrative power imbalances. Although one of us is a native Colombian, we both work at a Northern university and possess a narrative power that is not afforded to most individual victims or local historians. Unlike several of our interviewees who have, in vain, tried to get their stories published, we are able to publish our accounts with prestigious academic publishing houses and to convey our opinions to broad audiences of students and experts. We too 'profit' from Escobar's story. We hope, however, that our contribution opens up a debate about the commercial exploitation of violence and trauma and that, ultimately, victims and survivors benefit from this study.

Our positionality as researchers has also been shaped by our own individual trajectories. These have both enabled us to observe some things and prevented us from seeing others. One of us is Colombian, and for me, any mentions of Escobar and *Narcos* transport me back to my childhood in Bogotá under the constant threat of yet another car bomb. My background has allowed me to connect with victims and survivors and understand the violent context that all Colombians shared in the 1980s and 1990s as a result of the drug wars. For the other author, the fieldwork for this book presented the first meeting with Colombia and Medellín. As for most foreign visitors, my meeting with Medellín was intensely scripted before the encounter, not only through the viewing of *Narcos*, but also through the presentations of the city's image in guidebooks, online travel resources, and user commentaries on TripAdvisor. Escobar featured prominently in all available scripts of Medellín. Consequently, this book is the product of combining the view of a local with the view of a cosmopolitan visitor. It is, furthermore, an attempt to tell the story from the perspective of the locals while simultaneously tracing the complex global networks formed around Medellín's past and present.

We gathered the material for this book through a combination of diverse qualitative methods implemented in two stages. During the first stage of research, which spanned from March 2019 to August 2019, we undertook (i) participant observation of the dynamics of the city; (ii) interviews with taxi drivers; and (iii) media analysis. Our participant observation took place at sites of dark tourism and in locations connected to drug cartels and Pablo Escobar. The term *dark tourism* refers to the visits and the industry fashioned around sites of assassination, crime, genocide, holocaust, or incarceration (Lennon, 2017). Pablo Escobar tours take visitors to his various residences, to the prison he built for himself as a compromise with the government, to the museums locals and relatives have built in his honour, to the place where he was killed, and to his grave. The observations generated handwritten notes and a diversity of photographic material; both elements were useful to contextualize and describe the materiality of dark tourism in the city. Many of the pictures we took are powerful signifiers of the prominence of Escobar's story and simultaneous concealment of the victims' and survivors' experiences and suffering. We did not receive the permission to reproduce most of those pictures in the book, and they will probably never see the light of day. Commercial providers of dark tourism control the uses of those images, and through the existing legal regulations shape the visual narratives about the city.

One of our objectives with this study is to capture the stories about Medellín that are not the part of the 'official history' of the city, but that rather emerge through commercial and media practices. So, we approached the city, its buildings, and streets as a living archive (Rao, 2009). In this way, we recorded the contestations between commercial actors, inhabitants, and city authorities for the control of the infrastructure and its associated symbolism. Part of our ethnographic study of the city as an archive were twelve interviews with randomly chosen taxi drivers. These interviews helped us to chart the universe of discourses floating through Medellín. They also gave us information about the impact of narco-shows and dark tourism on Medellín's identity. Media analyses included a thematic analysis of *Narcos* (a Netflix-produced series that began to air in 2015) and a database with sixty-two news clips reporting violent events connected to drug cartels in Medellín from 1980 to 2001.

During the second stage of fieldwork (September 2019–November 2020), we gathered data to probe into the themes identified during the first stage. The material consists of interviews with (i) individuals involved in processes of memory construction, including the personal secretary of the mayor of Medellín (2016–2020), a journalist working for the programme *Medellín abraza su historia* [*Medellín Embraces its History*], a producer working for *Narcos*, two creators of the Colombian TV series *Pablo Escobar: El Patrón del Mal*, and the founder of NarcosLab, an independent initiative for remembering drug violence in Medellín. (ii) Twenty-six interviews with inhabitants of Medellín who were eighteen or older at the time the cartels were highly active in Medellín (*c.*1976–1993). Of the twenty-six interviewees, some fall into the blurry categories of direct victims and indirect victims (Walklate, 2007). There are significant differences in what they lived and how violence affected them. Eleven of the research participants witnessed violence in events such as car bombings or felt generally afraid. Fifteen of the interviewees were close to violence by having lost a relative (usually a parent or a spouse) or were directly victimized by being kidnapped. (iii) A database with information from the mayoralty of Medellín (2016–2020) regarding official communication on the phenomenon of dark tourism and official, but publicly unavailable, statistics.

This project was approved by the Norwegian Centre for Research Data, a national entity responsible for privacy and ethical approval of research activities of the two authors. Since data was collected in Colombia, we also complied with the Colombian legal requirements concerning research ethics established in Resolution 0843 of 1993. We obtained informed consent from all interviewees, having explained the purpose of the project in Spanish. During the interviews, interviewees were constantly reminded of their freedom not to respond to any questions they wanted to avoid. Additionally, the fieldwork was guided by a trauma-informed approach (described in depth in Todd-Kvam and Goyes, 2023), which entailed not only standard routines, such as debriefing and follow-up conversations, but also training in how to deal with trauma triggers, post-traumatic stress symptoms, and secondary trauma. Interviews were recorded and transcribed. Due to ethical considerations, we anonymized all the interviewees except for one with the personal secretary of the mayor of Medellín, and one of the victims Federico Arellano—whose father died in the HK-1803 bombing and whose name is highly recognizable as the first victim of drug violence who has managed to obtain official recognition by the state as a victim in 2013. Although some other victims and survivors have a degree of visibility through the books and blogs they have written, we chose to preserve their anonymity to avoid exposing personal details and compromising their safety.

Outline of the book

We start chapter 2 by offering readers a brief overview of the history of violence in Colombia and some reflection on how it engendered the mass drug violence that transpired in Medellín in the 1980s and 1990s. In the second part of the chapter, we map the damage that the clash between drug cartels and the state wracked on the daily life of the city, the local communities, and state institutions, particularly the legal system. We draw on a database of news reports of violent events connected to the activities of drug cartels in the city, along with historical studies of the events, to illustrate the deep structural damages inflicted by drug violence. By giving voice to Medellín's inhabitants with first-hand experiences of violence, the chapter then provides a sensorial account of what it was like to live in the city at the time the Medellín cartel was at the peak of its power. Our use of the sociology of the senses seeks to convey the 'bodily experience' of being in a city dominated by fear, uncertainty, and violence (Herrity, Schmidt, and Warr, 2021: xxv). That violence permeated all aspects of daily life, and its extreme cruelty created a pervasive sense of anxiety, powerlessness, and mistrust.

Chapter 3 delves deeper into the experiences of the victims and survivors and discusses the sense of injustice, voiceless-ness, and re-victimization they experienced. We begin by describing their search for a voice and a narrative that could convey their pain and would enable them to heal, participate in social memory creation, and remember their loved ones with dignity. We present a variety of victim initiatives, including intergenerational, orally transmitted narratives, and blog entries, low-cost documentaries, autobiographies, and lengthy legal proceedings. We then contrast these attempts to tell the stories of victimhood with the layers of silence under which many other victims of drug violence have buried their experiences. Even four decades later, some find it too painful to talk about their victimization. Silence also results from a broader cultural lack of interest in their experiences: for a long time, their stories were not part of the historical record.

The subdued nature of the victims' voices stands in stark contrast to the loud cacophony of stories focusing on Pablo Escobar, one of the main perpetrators of the violence on the inhabitants of the city. Chapter 4 therefore addresses the commercial appropriation of Escobar's story by Netflix and other national and international media producers. We first offer a media analysis of the narco-series genre, examining how it balances (or rather fails to do so) entertainment, factual accuracy, and acknowledgement of victims' experiences.

Drawing on interviews with informants involved in the Colombian and Netflix productions, we examine the rationales behind the media companies' approach to Medellín's history. In their efforts to attract viewers, and profoundly influenced by U.S. series such as *The Sopranos*, the genre makes full use of the appeal of the mafia-boss psyche. To Escobar's victims, however, that approach signifies an ode to violence. We also show that processes of memory creation, which ideally should lead to a communitarian understanding of social trauma, are adapted to attract a global viewership, turning the history of Medellín's violence into the story of Pablo Escobar.

Chapter 5 focuses on the gender and racial dynamics shaping the depiction of violence in narco-shows. We study both the working conditions in production sets and the gendered and racialized portrayals in the shows. Escobar's fascination with notorious figures such as Al Capone, and his conscious nurturing of a macho image through an ostentatious lifestyle replete with the exploitation of women and animals, has been an essential aspect of his iconization. Subsequently, narco-shows drew on gender, cultural, and racial stereotypes in the neo-colonial contexts to link violence with cultural identity. The chapter therefore highlights how the series and their creators draw on deeply gendered and racialized stereotypes that not only glorify male brutality but also portray white agents as saviours.

In chapter 6, we turn our attention to other forms of commercial exploitation of violence. The profitability of the trauma economy goes beyond *Narcos* and is present in the everyday economy of the city. The growth of dark tourism in Medellín in the aftermath of the commercial success of narco-series, added to a thriving business of souvenirs and T-shirts, forms a dark commercial web centred on the 'Escobar experience'. Tourists are supplied with everything from souvenirs and tours to drugs and sexual services. Drawing on statistical data provided by Medellín's authorities, interviews with taxi drivers, and ethnographic observations of narco-tours in the shrines dedicated to Escobar, the chapter explores the materiality of dark tourism and its impact on processes of collective memory creation.

Commercial developments that exploit Medellín's trauma have not gone unchallenged. Individual survivors, non-governmental organizations (NGOs), and city authorities have implemented strategies of resistance. In chapter 7, we examine the politics of resistance and discuss the phenomenon of political profiting from trauma. We describe a campaign initiated by a former mayor to inspire 'Medellín to embrace its history' and reclaim ownership of its memory. Local efforts attempt to challenge the stories imposed by commercial actors and to confront the narratives advanced by actors who exploit violence and the glorification of Escobar's persona. We show how Medellín's authorities have drawn inspiration from Holocaust-related processes of memory-creation and how, despite all these efforts, achieving recognition and global empathy has remained elusive.

The final two chapters offer a theoretical analysis of the position of victims and survivors of drug violence in Medellín and their struggle to access justice and make their voices heard in public discourses about violence. Taking Colombia's Victims' Law (2011) as a starting point, chapter 8 argues that the binary distinction between war and crime fails to address the needs of victims of mass drug violence and creates a hierarchy among victims. This has important symbolic, legal, and material implications for survivors of drug violence in Medellín, who find themselves in the less favoured category. We argue that the current understanding of mass drug violence as 'conventional crime' represents a Northern perspective on violence, which can be counterproductive when used uncritically in Southern contexts and deepens existing global inequalities among victims.

Our theoretical reflections in this book owe a great debt to the criminological scholarship on critical and cultural victimology and hierarchies of victimhood (McGarry and Walklate, 2015; McEvoy and McConnahie, 2012, 2013) as well as numerous other contributions in southern criminology and globalization studies that have put global inequality on the agenda (Franko, 2021). This book, however, is written with the explicit wish to engage in a conversation not only with our academic colleagues, but also with readers and students of varied backgrounds, and most of all, with residents and survivors of violence in Medellín. Corporate and commercial actors tend to keep inconvenient forms of victimization 'obscured from public view or hidden from plain sight' (McGarry and Walklate, 2015: 5). *Victimhood, Memory, and Consumerism* is an attempt to shine light on some of these dynamics.

2
A city at war

A long-standing conflict

On Monday, 27 November 1984, at 3:55 p.m., a car bomb exploded in front of the U.S. embassy in Bogotá, Colombia. The ambassador, the target of the bomb, was not in his office when the dynamite stored in a Fiat 125 detonated. A mother of five was the only fatal victim of the attack while six other persons were injured in the explosion. Police officers later found a book about drug dependence amidst the debris—it was a message from the perpetrators. The U.S. embassy had received repeated threats from the Colombian drug cartels ever since both governments had agreed to extradite four Colombian drug lords to the United States (*El Colombiano*, 1984). The intention of the bombers was to press the ambassador to reverse the agreement. While this was the fourth car bomb that had exploded in Bogotá in three years, it was just the beginning of a wave of bombings that hit major social institutions (and their representatives) in Colombia.

The bombings reached their peak on 27 November 1989 when domestic flight HK-1803 from Bogotá to Cali was blown up, killing all 107 civilian passengers on board. The bombing was also orchestrated by Pablo Escobar's cartel in a continued attempt to resist U.S. pressure on the Colombian government, which had decided to make drug lords stand trial in the United States on trafficking charges (Smyth, 1998). While the main target of the attack was the presidential candidate, César Gaviria, who had promised to extradite drug lords should he win the election, the assault intended to 'make visible the power of drug cartels, and their capacity to control and discipline the population through terror' (Solano Cohen, 2015: 87).

Both the attack on the U.S. embassy and the HK-1803 bombing were part of a greater, long-standing conflict. Violence connected to the trade

Victimhood, Memory, and Consumerism. Katja Franko and David R. Goyes, Oxford University Press.
 DOI: 10.1093/oso/9780192874115.003.0002

in criminalized narcotics is rooted in centuries of violent oppression and misery. The history of violence in Colombia has been, for centuries, the history of the powerful abusing and victimizing the powerless. From the colonial period until today, Colombia has been marked by extreme inequality and the existence of a small, exclusive ruling class. Inequality informs all aspects of the country's social life. The remarkable rise and power of the cartels should be, therefore, situated within centuries of abuse, marginalization, and inequality, which have induced the powerless to innovate and use alternative means to attaining power and wealth.

The violent drug trade has been, moreover, nourished not only by pervasive inequality within Colombia, but also by deep inequality between the Global North and the Global South. Illegalized drugs have, in past decades, been in great demand by consumers in countries of the Global North, opening the market for entrepreneurial actors from the Global South who lack access to legitimate market opportunities. The globally excluded, through trade in criminalized goods, have been able 'to find a space to be innovative, a space in which the rules of the game have not already been stacked against them'—albeit at a great cost to their local communities (Gilman, Goldhammer, and Weber, 2011: 274; Franko, 2019).

Violent oppression, inequality, and colonialism

The history of structural oppression in Colombia can be situated in the fifteenth century with the European invasion of the 'new continents'. The Spanish conquerors arrived in the Americas in 1492, conquered what is present-day Colombia in 1499, and began full-scale colonization in 1509 (Galeano, 1997). The shiny jewellery worn by the locals and their 'enormous treasures of gold ornaments' (Koning, 1993: 25) compelled the conquerors to go deeper into the new territories in search of gold and other treasures. Along the way, they left a trail of devastation and dispossession (Robertson, 2005). The diseases brought by the Europeans decimated most of the native population (Koch et al., 2019). The Spanish army, Catholic missions, and administrative authorities killed off much of the remaining Indigenous populations which had survived the pestilence (Goyes et al., 2021).

Uruguayan journalist Eduardo Galeano describes the three centuries of Spanish Colonial rule in the Americas (1492–1810) as a period in which

> Latin American silver and gold ... penetrated like a corrosive acid through all the pores of Europe's moribund feudal society, and, for the benefit of nascent mercantilist capitalism, the mining entrepreneurs turned Indians and black slaves into a teeming 'external proletariat'.... The price of the tide of avarice, terror, and ferocity bearing down on these regions was Indian genocide[.] ... The Indians of the Americas totalled no less than 70 million when the foreign conquerors appeared on the horizon; a century and a half later, they had been reduced to 3.5 million. (1997: 38)

The Spanish invasion of the Americas established a perennial dynamic in Colombia: powerful actors waging war against and dispossessed the vulnerable. Pablo Escobar would, five centuries later, use the abuse of the powerful over the poor to excuse and facilitate his acts of violence. 'Only when Escobar openly involved diverse excluded sectors in Medellín', explains political analyst Gustavo Duncan, 'did he become a relevant powerful actor' (2013: 250).

The power of the Spanish Crown in the Americas diminished by the beginning of the nineteenth century as the sons of the conquerors, the Creoles, gained increasing influence in local governments. The Creoles also amassed lands and resources, becoming more and more powerful (Villalba, 2016). When Spain was busy with the Napoleonic wars, the creoles took the opportunity to declare independence from the Crown. They led the independence with words. The dispossessed fought for it with spears and machetes:

> [However,] independence did not reward them; it betrayed the hopes of those who had shed their blood. Peace came, and with it, a new era of daily misery. Landowners and businessmen increased their fortunes while poverty grew among the masses. (Galeano, 1997: 115)

Independence brought about a new era of misery for most of the inhabitants of what today is Colombia. Freedom from Spain did not destroy the class system imposed by the colonizers (Jurado Jurado, 2015). The new leaders of the country were 'grandsons or great-grandsons of the conquerors … they were the offspring of the Spanish with some creole, they were "stained by the soil", but none of them creole of several generations. They were all relatives' (Caballero, 2014: 8). The political turmoil that followed, when the country gained independence in 1819, resulted in a conflict between the ruling classes—fought on the ground by the lower classes (Robayo, 2010). A soldier described one of the wars as '[a] thousand detonations, the whistles of the bullets, the clouds of smoke that hinder vision and almost suffocate, the bugle calls and the continuous drumming of the drums' (José María Espinosa, 1876, quoted in Caballero, 2014: 11–12). Continuous internal strife for power took place in Colombia after its independence—the elites fought the ideological battle while the poor paid for it with blood (Goyes, 2015).

Neither did independence from the Spanish Crown mean Colombia had escaped the colony status. As the European empire withdrew from Colombia, a Northern American one stepped in. U.S. president James Monroe declared in 1823 that every country in the Americas should be free from attacks from Europe, and that any European intervention in the Americas would be an attack on the United States (Bull, 2021). From there on, the United States 'developed its ambitions in Latin America from a wish to secure territorial control vis-à-vis European powers, to include a moral responsibility for the stability and wellbeing in the region' (ibid.: 29). The United States has treated Latin America (including Colombia) as its backyard: 'increasingly more actions evidenced a lack of respect for Latin America's own priorities' (ibid.). As we will see later, the role the United States would play in the drug wars fought in Colombia cannot be overstated (ibid.).

On 9 April 1948, the nature and form of the conflict in Colombia had changed. While earlier clashes were between political parties were directed by the upper classes who wanted to acquire the power to rule the state, this new phase of the conflict was characterized by the use of war to transform economic, social, and political relations within the country. War became a revolutionary tool (Medina Gallego, 2010). Five centuries of (external and internal) colonialism had left a divided country with growing inequality. The Gini index, which measures the distribution of income, property, and access to services, was at 0.52. In other words, '[i]f one person accumulates all the riches, the index would be 1; if all the people had the same, the index would be 0' (Ramírez R. and Rodríguez Bravo, 2002: 86). Colombia had passed the halfway point toward total inequality. Then, the assassination of the liberal presidential candidate Jorge Eliecer Gaitán on 9 April 1948 ignited the flame, inspiring disappointed Liberals to launch a guerrilla war (Offstein, 2003). Campesinos fought for their lands against the state, which defended the interests of the elites, while a culture of corruption and clientelism, which had existed before the guerrillas and would continue to exist after them, maintained inequality (Robinson, 2016). Elite families, heirs of the colonizers, helped each other to remain in power. Politicians exploited people's precariousness to buy their votes, without ever helping their constituents to gain a foothold in the political process. In a highly undemocratic system, the poor never got access to the kind of political power required to change the structures of society. The fundamental needs of a significant portion of the population therefore remained neglected. The elites amassed riches while the Indigenous, 'mestizos', and 'mulattos' fought for the crumbs.

When, in the course of the civil war, the guerrillas were growing stronger, the government became desperate to resist them, and in 1968 gave wide latitude to the possession of self-defence weapons (formerly only permitted for the army) and approved the formation of self-defence militias—also known as the paramilitaries. This relaxation of law was largely taken advantage of by the increasingly fearful and insecure Colombian oligarchy (Ballvé, 2012; Grajales, 2013; Leal Buitrago, 2011). As time passed by, the guerrilla groups initiated a stronger confrontation strategy: they began to use force for offensive, rather than just defensive, purposes. To do so, they increased the number of combatants to 32,000 and fought on 80 different fronts (including urban areas). This caused a split in the guerrillas, with different sections having diverging goals and getting involved in drug trafficking (Grupo de Memoria Histórica, 2013). Simultaneously, the government also attempted to suppress dissent by criminalizing revolutionary political activities, but mainly through the support of paramilitaries at the service of the government. These groups did not operate within the law but forcefully displaced peasants from their lands, engaged in drug trafficking, murdered leftists and social leaders, and undertook other activities consistent with their anti-communist ideals (Medina Gallego, 2009). As a result of the prolonged internal armed conflict, which had as the most visible actors the guerrilla groups (with its different branches), paramilitary groups, and the Colombian Army, 220,000 people were killed in Colombia between 1 January 1958 and 31 December 2012 (Goyes, 2015: 82). Of the victims, 81.5 per cent were civilians; the rest were combatants. Additionally, during that period, it is estimated that 5,700,000 people were displaced by force (Grupo de Memoria Histórica, 2013).

Roughly a decade into the conflict between the guerrillas and the state, two new actors entered the scene, ushering a new dynamic. Weak institutions and inequality created fertile soil in Colombia for the growth of drug trafficking. In 1957, the Federal Bureau of Investigation (FBI) and the Colombian police tracked down a coca laboratory in Medellín. Smugglers had heard about the cocaine addiction among U.S. citizens and set in motion a trafficking network; the nephews of two former Colombian presidents ran the business (Aristizábal Uribe, 2018). Medellín contained all the ingredients for the appearance of what Robert Merton would call *innovators*—individuals who break the rules to achieve the socially sanctioned goals of fame, wealth, and power (Merton, 1968).

In addition to Colombia's social turmoil, the unsatisfied needs of the population (Robinson, 2016), and the weakness of a state losing control of territories to the guerrillas and of its sovereignty to the Unites States, Medellín had an entrepreneurial culture that encouraged innovation. The city's population saw work as a 'superior moral value' (Aristizábal Uribe, 2018: 22). Susceptible to the belief in the American dream described by Merton, Medellín's inhabitants also believed that 'anyone could come 'out of poverty and ascend socially. Money was seen to be the means to transcend racial barriers. A "black person"—denoting a poor person—could whiten himself up with money' (ibid.: 23). Love of money ranked above any other value, including Catholic principles: 'philanthropic uses of richness could repay guilt' says Virginia Gutiérrez de Pineda (1975) (quoted in Aristizábal Uribe, 2018: 27). The region had created an identity of creativity and 'ingenious, speculative, audacious usury' (Saffray, 1948, quoted in Aristizábal Uribe, 2018: 25). These factors contributed to the founding of the Medellín cartel in 1976 by Pablo Escobar, the son of a farmer and a teacher.

Yet, Colombian public opinion remained for decades mostly unaware of the potency of drug cartels. Drug smugglers operated without much opposition until the 1980s (Lessing, 2018). Traffickers easily bribed officials and secured the safe delivery of their products to profitable Northern markets. The cartels' influence was most visible through another war actor they helped to finance: the paramilitaries. The paramilitaries represented the aspirations of the nascent cartels and the interests of the elites. Drug cartels needed robust structures to protect their commercial activities and the elites required an organization able to squelch social and political protest and confront the guerrillas. The new armed groups operated illegally, forcefully displacing peasants from their lands, murdering leftists and social leaders, and engaging in drug trafficking (Ballvé, 2012; Grajales, 2013; Leal Buitrago, 2011; Medina Gallego, 2009). The Medellín cartel and the Cali cartel took an active part in founding and maintaining what would come to constitute the strongest paramilitary groups in Colombia (Adams, 2011). The nexus of state–paramilitaries–drug cartels (the dividing lines between which are at times difficult to trace) is therefore a core component of the violence described in this book.

Meanwhile, the United States has been the most visible international actor in the Colombian conflict, mainly through its role in the so-called war on drugs. Between 1985 and 1988, the number of cocaine consumers in the United States doubled exponentially, with an annual expenditure on the white powder estimated between sixty and seventy billion dollars (Boville, 2004). The United States responded through militarized means to combat the trade and by developing a harsh criminal justice policy implemented nationally and internationally. The U.S. government thus approached the spike in the use of cocaine in the United States as 'an external problem, to be resolved by and in other countries with US assistance' (Del Olmo, 1998: 272). The complex, illicit global drug trade became for the U.S. international policy a matter of fighting against an external enemy (Andreas and Nadelmann, 2006). The U.S. government initiated a war on drugs in Colombia, which resulted in aerial fumigations with herbicides that irreparably damaged the ecosystem and deteriorated the health of inhabitants on the ground. The United States also funded local armed forces to fight coca growers, fuelling an already bloody civil war.

The war on drugs was heralded by Richard Nixon's (1969–1974) campaign to restore order in the Americas. Nixon established Task Force One, a Special Presidential Task Force Relating to Narcotics, Marijuana and Dangerous Drugs (Carpenter, 2003). The use of the war metaphor to combat the trade in, and use of, criminalized narcotics signalled—to domestic and international audiences—'a transformation of the means and rationalities by which elites justify and set the desired dimensions of their own governance' (Simon, 2007: 259). In 1973, Task Force One evolved into the Drug Enforcement Administration (DEA), which, during the Carter presidency (1977–1981), was used to impose 'marijuana and opium-poppy crop eradication and interdiction measures in Colombia, Peru, and Bolivia' (Carpenter, 2003: 18). In the 1980s, during the Ronald Reagan presidency (1981–1989), this dynamic expanded even further:

> Washington concentrated on training, equipping, and advising indigenous antinarcotics forces (police or military units), facilitated the creation of special drug eradication paramilitary organisations in those drug-source countries where such units did not yet exist, and injected financial subsidies to support antidrug efforts when local resources were insufficient. The overall goal was to encourage, persuade, bribe or coerce foreign governments into joining the U.S.-led drug war. (Carpenter, 2003: 21)

The rising power and influence of drug cartels provided additional justification for intensifying the efforts and the financial investment in the war on drugs. In 1989, the U.S. Congress 'appropriated $2.2 billion for the Bush administration's five-year program to attack drug production (mostly cocaine manufacture and coca growing) in Bolivia, Colombia and Peru' (Duke and Gross, 1999: 227). The Andean war on drugs was justified on the grounds of providing 'financial assistance and "advise" to law-enforcement officers and the military establishment in the three countries' and promoting '"economic development" that will reduce the countries' dependence on the drug business' (ibid.).

Critical voices in Latin America (including Colombia) condemned the war on drugs for failing to address internal demand in the United States, and instead targeting production in other countries (Goyes and South, 2017). Although half of the cocaine produced in the world was consumed in the United States, this did not mean that the main focus of U.S. agents has been on the internal market (Mejía, 2011). Not only did the U.S. forces confiscate drugs at borders and fund military forces, but they also sought to eradicate crops utilizing a complex combination of toxic chemicals, such as paraquat and glyphosate. 'By that time, it had already been proven that Paraquat causes lung damage and that both Paraquat and Glyphosate are lethal for fauna and sea life' (Goyes and South, 2017: 176). Rosa del Olmo's (1987, 1998) characterized the war on drugs as a transnational crime where the governments of Latin America and its peoples were the victims. The war on drugs, argued del Olmo, was an excuse to neo-colonize Latin America.

The United States attempted to neutralize the critique by labelling Colombia as a *failed state* that had lost control of its territories to various illegal armed groups (Arratia Sandoval, 2022). The U.S. intervention was thus framed '[as] a dynamic in which humanitarian action—thought as altruist action rather than realpolitik—was understood as the correct answer to avoid that state failure [would lead] to massacres and potential genocides' (Tokatlian, 2008: 71; see also Zapata Callejas, 2014). The war on drugs thus continued uninterrupted and gained further momentum with the introduction of 'Plan Colombia': a 10 billion dollar investment to 'train, assist, instruct and equip the army and police of the Andean country' (Arratia Sandoval, 2022). As the borders between army and paramilitary forces became fluid (Goyes and South, 2017), the United States increased its role as a central force behind the drug violence we describe in this book.

Following decades of violent conflict, the first peace agreement in Colombia was signed in 2005, largely through U.S. sponsorship. The paramilitary group United Self-Defences Armies of Colombia agreed on an armistice with former Colombian president Álvaro Uribe Vélez. The Peace and Justice Law implemented in 2005, which granted substantial benefits to the paramilitary combatants who chose to demobilize, was one of the main outcomes of the negotiations (Uprimny Yepes et al., 2006). A decade later, the guerrilla group FARC-EP (Revolutionary Armed Forces of Colombia) and former Colombian president Juan Manuel Santos signed a general agreement to end the conflict and build a stable and long-standing peace.

As mentioned above, five decades of violence between the guerrillas, the paramilitaries, and the Colombian army killed 220,000 people (1958–2012). One in every three violent deaths in the country was directly related to the conflict (Grupo de Memoria Histórica, 2013). However, drug-related violence constituted a considerable part of the remaining two-thirds. This form of violence was not counted in the statistic of casualties of the Colombian war, despite evidence of an existing nexus between drug trafficking and armed conflict. As we shall see in the following chapters, the legislation passed to offer reparations to victims of the conflict did not recognize those who suffered drug-related violence as victims. They were the *wrong kind of victims.*

A war within a war

Pablo Emilio Escobar Gaviria (1949–1993) was born and raised in Medellín. Throughout the 1970s, he smuggled different types of merchandise under relative anonymity. In 1976, however, he became more prominent upon founding the Medellín cartel. From then on, Escobar profited enormously from cocaine trafficking. By the 1980s, he controlled more than 80 per cent of the cocaine shipped to the United States, making him, according to *Time Magazine*, one of the ten richest people in the world (Webley, 2011).

Colombian society, however, was mostly unaware of the Medellín cartels' power until 1981, when the latter entered in conflict with the M-19 guerrilla group. The guerrillas, seeking funds for their land distribution campaigns, kidnapped a member of the Ochoa family, which, together with Pablo Escobar, led the Medellín cartel. The M-19 wanted to extract a significant ransom. The cartel bosses responded by pooling 'money, soldiers, and arms to the collective, which was christened "Muerte a Secuestradores" or MAS ("Death to Kidnappers")' (Lessing, 2018: 130). The kidnapping 'ended up unifying what was until then a group of anonymous actors … it facilitated collective action and broader cooperation' (ibid.). From there on, violence in Medellín greatly exceeded the levels of violence observed in the rest of the country (Maclean, 2015). The power of the drug cartels, fuelled by the rapidly increasing U.S. demand for cocaine, grew out of the state's control.

Escobar and the Medellín cartel used their wealth to establish a 'substantial and enduring power base' in the city, which enabled them to employ 'the disenfranchised youth of Medellín's barrios as *sicarios* [young assassins]' (ibid.: 39–40). Escobar also used his financial resources to acquire electoral votes and political power, which led to an increasingly violent conflict with the country's political elites and state institutions. The violence perpetrated by the Medellín cartel directly challenged the supremacy of the state and included car bombs, assassinations of police officers, judges, and even a presidential candidate. At the peak of the cartel's activity, as we mentioned before, Medellín had 375 homicides per 100,000 inhabitants, which is 'more than 35 times the World Health Organization's definition of epidemic violence' (ibid.: 2). Although other Latin American countries have also been afflicted by violent conflicts between drug cartels and the state, Lessing (2018) observes that only in Colombia have the dynamics of violence been so driven by the actions of a single actor (Pablo Escobar). At the height of his rampage Escobar's conflict with the state overtook the civil war as the nation's primary security threat (Pardo Rueda, 1996, quoted in Lessing, 2018: 38).

The violence was further exacerbated by turf conflicts between the Medellín and Cali cartels related to drug distribution in the United States. On 13 January 1988, at 5:15 a.m., a car bomb exploded in front of Escobar's residence (the Monaco building). The bomb was intended for Escobar, but he escaped unharmed. However, two persons unconnected to drug trafficking died, and Escobar's four-year-old daughter suffered hearing loss, as a result of the explosion. (The fate of the so-called Monaco building is one of the most salient examples of the destruction left in the landscape by a violent clash between the cartel and the state. Although severely damaged during Escobar's lifetime, the building became a fiercely contested landmark of his activities after his death and a site of pilgrimage for Escobar aficionados (see Figure 2.1). As we describe in chapter 7, the building was demolished in 2019 and is now the site of a newly established park dedicated to the memory of victims of the conflict.)

The attack on the Monaco building was, together with the assault on the U.S. embassy described at the beginning of this chapter, one of the first uses of car bombs in the conflict. The technique soon became standard. In a three-month span, between September and December 1991, more than 100 explosive devices went off in Medellín, 22 of which were car bombs (Aristizábal Uribe, 2018; Marcos, 2018). The Medellín cartel waged an open war on the Colombian state, challenging the supremacy of its institutions (Lessing, 2018).

Figure 2.1. The rubble of the Monaco building, demolished on the order of the Medellín's major in 2019.
Source: © David R. Goyes.

The relationship between the state and the cartel was an all-out violent conflict—a war within a war. Although the exact numbers of casualties are difficult to establish, the estimates have prompted journalistic and academic comparisons to describe the conflict as warfare. In addition to causing enormous loss of civilian life, the cartels attacked the foundations of Colombian society and its institutions: judges, journalists, politicians, and the police. Every day, Colombian newspapers filled page after page with descriptions of the incessant violence. The following acts of violence were reported by newspapers.

Attacks on judges

On October 1980, hitmen killed judges Ana Cecilia Cartagena and Jairo Marín Jaramillo. They were the first members of the judicial branch to fall victims to narco-violence. Judge Cartagena, who had written her bachelor's thesis on drug-related crimes, was about to sentence a cartel leader. The U.S. government had offered her a scholarship to expand her knowledge of narcotics. She lost her life days before travelling to the United States (Córdoba Laverde, 1980). Cartagena was sitting in her car in the middle of a traffic jam when a motorbike with two riders pulled up alongside, and one of the men fired two shots. Judge Marín had been killed in front of his house two days before, also by assassins on a motorbike. Marín worked as a criminal judge. He had judged several drug crimes in the past. Days after the murders, eleven more judges received threats. One hundred and eighty-two resigned from their positions in the aftermath of the murders (Hoge, 1981).

Attacks on journalists

On Wednesday, 15 December 1986, *sicarios* on a motorbike gunned down Guillermo Cano Isaza, a journalist and the founder of *El Espectador*, one of the most prominent Colombian newspapers. Cano, a defender of the free press, had implemented a zero-tolerance policy toward drug cartels and denounced the links between cartels and elites (politicians and businesspeople). He received the first death threat after making it publicly known that Pablo Escobar, then a stand-in congressman, had been in prison for drug trafficking. The letter demanded silence about the involvement of Escobar and other 'celebrities' in the drug business. Cano refused to stop reporting on the cartels and declined to use bodyguards. Cano paid for his beliefs with his life. He was sixty-one years old. On the same day, *sicarios* killed Amparo Hurtado, a correspondent for *El Espectador*.

Attacks on politicians

Jaime Pardo Leal dominated the polls for the 1988 presidential election with a 33 per cent favourability (García Hernández, 2017). He represented the Patriotic Union, a left-wing party championing a democratic country. Pardo declared war on corruption and worked for the reduction of inequality. Before running for president, he founded and led the Asonal Judicial, a union for employees of the judicial branch. As a part of the Asonal Judicial, he denounced the murders of judges at the hands of the drug cartels. The Medellín cartel included Pardo on a hitlist along with other politicians, TV personalities, and journalists, who had spoken out against the cartel. On 11 October 1987, Pardo was driving back home from a weekend on his farm, when he stopped his white Toyota truck for what seemed like a road accident, but which was in fact a trap. A blue Renault 9 appeared on the scene. Three *sicarios* emerged from the Renault and shot at Pardo's car, killing him and injuring his wife and son (El Espectador, 1987).

Attacks on the police

On Thursday, 14 June 1990, the Colombian national football team played against Yugoslavia in the FIFA World Cup. Most inhabitants of Medellín watched the match from their homes. One minute into the game, a boom shook the air. 'A smoke cloud arose a few seconds later—another car bomb', reported the *El Colombiano* newspaper the day after (El Colombiano, 1990). Police cars and fire trucks rushed to the scene of the explosion, a police station. Emergency personnel found an incinerated Mazda, the car bomb which had contained 80 kilos of dynamite. They also found shattered windows, cars in flames, and bodies strewn on the ground. Four people were dead, amongst them the police officer inspecting the car seconds before the explosion, and sixty-nine were injured.

The war seen, heard, and felt

The events described above focus mainly on high-profile attacks as reported in newspapers. Newspaper accounts provide us with important historic documentation, but also afford us an 'aerial view' of the world 'as if standing atop a skyscraper or viewing the ground from a blimp' (Clark, 2016: 167). But how did the citizens experience the violence? Herrity, Schmidt, and Warr propose a 'sensory approach' to studies of violence and punishment: 'thinking about sounds, smells, taste, and touch, and utilising these sources of information as a mechanism for understanding' (2021: xxii). A sensory approach to violence means surpassing an 'ocular-centric way of thinking' (ibid.: xxiii) and gaining interest in the bodily experiences of those who lived through the violence. Similarly, in McClanahan and South's (2019) sensory agenda, sounds, smells, tastes, and touch provide deeper information about the violent context than exclusive reliance on the 'aerial' view would. In sum, the body—with all its senses—becomes a source of knowledge about events. A sensorial experience provides rich elements for memory reconstruction. The *senses* and *memory* evoke and amplify each other, with collective sensory memory surpassing the limitations and biases of individual recollection.

Considering the amount of violence that took place in Medellín, it is unsurprising that most interviewees who witnessed it expressed strong feelings of despair accompanied by *sensory memories* of violence. A private guard in his early sixties, Miguel, said, 'those of us who lived during that period remember the past with dread'. For one taxi driver we interviewed, Ivan, this was a dramatic and traumatic time:

> That period left a trauma in me; there was always anxiety, because one was 'just alive', and suddenly, 'boom!'; I experienced that, and had many close friends and relatives who died in those bombings.

Neighbourhoods in Medellín display distinct sensorial textures, depending on their centrality, traffic infrastructure, and class composition; yet, our interviewees connected their memories to their senses regardless of where they lived at the time. Memories were often expressed in visual terms:

> What I remember is the tragedy […], *a city in flames* and constant alarm. A time of not knowing when there would be another attack, another bomb; the sensation of going out in the streets and finding corpses lying there.
>
> (Interview with Daniel, a male schoolteacher, late forties; emphasis added.)

Memories were also connected to sounds: '[T]here was *the noise* of the bombs and the ambulances around the city all the time; there was constant tension', said Rubén, a taxi driver in his early fifties. Smells also played a significant role in the accounts of direct witnesses: 'I remember going to school [. . .] and there were corpses there, *I could smell the blood*, but I had to keep walking, because I did not want to see if it was the body of someone I knew', declared Andrés, an unemployed man in his early forties.[1] Intertwined with memories of suffering were recollections of considerable economic activity: 'a lot of pain, a lot of fear, many murders, but also a lot of money', as Clara, a housewife in her late sixties, expressed it.

Remembering this period, our interviewees described car bomb explosions, executions, homicides, kidnappings, and many other forms of destruction and violence. Most of all, they remembered the pervasive fear that affected all segments of the population, particularly the youth. Luciana said:

> There was not one person who felt completely safe in this city. [. . .] It is that fear when you're going out on a Friday, because you are a teenager and want to hang out with your friends. The parents fear that, at a time where there are no cell phones, there is no way to keep an eye on the young people. We wanted to go out but were afraid we might run into a bomb. The brother of a former boyfriend of mine was killed in the Oporto massacre, so, like it or not, you experience violence through all your friends and family.

Several of our interviewees were children at the time. They remember evacuation drills at school and living with bomb threats and continuous fear. Isabella, the daughter of an influential politician, lived her childhood surrounded by weapons: 'My house had guns everywhere. My babysitters were the bodyguards; my friends were the bodyguards. They held me with one hand and a machine gun in the other. That is what life was like for me.' Daniela, an interviewee who spent her childhood in Cali (another town hard-hit by drug violence) recalled how she could not distinguish between drug violence and war hostilities in the country:

[1] Emphases added.

> It was terrifying to go out. [News] of 'a bomb that is going to fall', so I was afraid of going to the streets because suddenly a bomb can fall. It's like the image in my head, the bomb. I was a child. I have mixed memories because I was also touched here in Cali by the death of Iván Marino Ospina, of the M19,[2] as part of the Colombian war in my neighbourhood in Cali. For me, all those memories are the same; perhaps because I was a child at that time I didn't have the ability to differentiate one thing from another. Everything seemed to me to be Pablo Escobar, that it was the same thing and that we were at war. That's the image of pure war and a guy who planted bombs.

Mariana, a housewife in her sixties widowed by the Medellín Cartel, remembered: 'Airplanes exploding, bombs all over the place. You always felt anxious, thinking, "Am I next?"' Several interviewees remember constantly turning on the radio to get updates about the latest developments. For many people, these events had a lasting impact. One journalist said: 'I still listen to the radio and sleep with it on. The habit stayed with me because the radio was a connection with what one believed to be reality: the bombs, the deaths, and so on.'

The poorer segments of the population felt the violence more intensely. Our respondents living in the communes (i.e., poorer neighbourhoods) described how violence continued to be a defining part of life in their neighbourhoods, even after Escobar's death. Victoria, a fifty-year-old mother of three, recalled:

> They killed one of my cousins up in La Esperanza [a neighbourhood in Medellín] as he was leaving the school. He always visited his bride after school, at around one or two in the afternoon. That day he was on his way to visit his bride, but three different gangs started to shoot. There was an invisible border. One of the bullets hit my cousin. I also saw many times how they killed people in that zone. Women, older people, young people—they shot from the cars. The violence left a mark on the barrio.

[2] Iván Marino Ospina was co-founder of the Colombian revolutionary group M19, or the 19 April Movement.

In most societies, people living in deteriorated neighbourhoods experience crimes against their physical integrity more often compared to those in wealthy areas (for a classical study, see Fishman (1979)). The interviews we conducted left us with the same impression. Martín, who lived near Aldemar, said: 'I was touched by violence. I lost four nephews and a sister [in the neighbourhood]. That happened in the middle of Easter. They [the cartels] arrived and had no compassion for anything. They arrived, and ratatat! They also threw grenades. My sister was right there. Right there.'

In the communes, drug violence was so pervasive that Victoria considered her survival a miracle, a result of divine intervention:

> I was also selling things in the street with a neighbour. I had to sell mangoes, bananas, and zapotes. That was when I was between fourteen and seventeen years old. At that time, in the house, we weren't very well off, so I worked during that time to contribute to my family to get ahead. I had to walk through the middle of the conflict. I don't know; it was something miraculous and God's will that everywhere I passed, they were shooting, and not a single bullet touched me. I was safe wherever I went.

José, an interviewee who also was a teenager at the time, remembered his experience as follows:

> You had a psychosis (it lasted a long time) about going out into the streets. I would often go to the intersection and walk six or seven kilometres—or more—to get to my friends. When a motorcycle came along, it was like, 'Whoa! They're not going to shoot me, are they?' The bike moved on, and phew! You relaxed. If there was a police officer close by, it was terrifying! At that time, they killed police officers. You didn't want a police officer near you; you walked away. A collective psychosis was part of everyone's mentality [...] I mean, at ten o'clock at night, there was a sort of undeclared curfew, which later became official because of all the fighting that would break out. But before that, the curfew had already been declared by the cartels. It was unspoken; you wouldn't give a papaya [make it easy for someone to attack you], as they say around here. It was a time of terrible anxiety.

José's recollection reveals not only the pervasive sense of anxiety and concern for one's self-preservation, but also the feeling that there was a direct threat to state institutions, particularly the police. Salomé, whose uncle was killed by Escobar's cartel, summed it up like this:

> Pablo Escobar brought this country to its knees. And brought this city to its knees. And that man brought civil society to its knees too. He brought us all to our knees. Some let themselves be bought, and the desire to live compelled others. We had brave people like Luis Carlos Galán [a presidential candidate], who knew they were going to kill him, and he was so aware of the role he had chosen, and they did kill him. But the vast majority, what made them bow down? Was it out of fear, ambition, or terror? Whatever. But Pablo Escobar brought this city to its knees and brought this country to its knees.

Many of the interviewees witnessed the attacks on social institutions and their representatives, which we presented above as reported by journalists. Below are vignettes of how the victims' direct experiences.

Attacks on judges

Carlos, a prominent judge at the time and a member of the Asonal Judicial (the judges' union founded by Pardo Leal), pointed out in an interview with us that, in just one year, 'there were ninety-four homicides against members of the judiciary and forty-four threats that led people to leave Medellín'. He recalled an investigation into the links between drug traffickers and state officials where, 'of the fourteen investigators in charge of prosecuting drug traffickers, thirteen were assassinated'. This violent onslaught had a long-lasting impact on the judiciary and its ability to deliver justice in drug trafficking cases.

Attacks on journalists

During the 1980s and 1990s, the daily task of narrating the terrible tales of cartel violence was taken up mainly by local newspapers. They focused on the victims and the events, rather than on the perpetrators, in stark contrast to the global narratives that emerged later. Journalists at that time highlighted the suffering and destruction caused by the attacks. They provided details about the tragic incidents, paying relatively little attention to Escobar himself. Journalists described the time as 'a dire period characterized by blood, destruction and death' (Aristizábal Uribe, 2018: 19). Diana, a journalist we interviewed, reflected on how drug violence deeply influenced the role of the press as a watchdog of power: 'I think that, in this process, many journalists have fallen by the wayside; I feel that the press today is not even the shadow of what it should be, it is beholden to those in power. It is not fulfilling that role.'

Attacks on politicians and the police force

State officials and their relatives were also in the path of the storm. Alberto, the son of a prominent criminal justice official, remembered how people around him started to behave differently after his father had taken office:

> These people really shied away from being with you because that meant putting themselves in danger. So, we lived in isolation for many years. Isolation that, I believe, in many ways affected our lives, our emotional stability, our interpersonal relationships, etc. It was pretty tough; you could say, it was pretty tough.

He also recalled how his family was even threatened abroad. For example, when they emigrated to Switzerland, they received a report from the Swiss authorities about a potential threat: 'So then, our anxiety was permanent, the insecurity, the restlessness of the whole family.'

State officials were not only attacked by the cartels, but also distrusted by the general population, because they worked under threat and because of the cartels' infiltration of the government.[3] José, whom we will meet again in chapter 3, told us about his distrust of the military. José's brother

[3] For a detailed account of drug trafficking permeating the political system, please see chapter 8.

died in a massacre at a night club, and he still feels deep suspicion that there was a collaboration between the police, the army, and the drug traffickers. José is resentful of the silence covering the event:

> At the time of the investigations, there were press releases saying that the soldiers sent from Bogotá to Medellín were very tough. A general in Bogotá also said, 'I was not going to send nuns to fight with the murderers of Medellín; it's time to send very tough people.' These very tough people were the ones who did most damage. These people killed and raped, and I don't understand why no one wants to talk about it.

The trauma of war

The descriptions of everyday life during, and in the aftermath of, cartel violence provided by our interviewees resemble experiences of war. In the early 1990s, the International Committee of the Red Cross commissioned a report on people's war experiences. The consulting firm Greenberg Research interviewed one thousand civilians in fourteen countries plagued by war. Their findings revealed that:

> The consequence of these collective experiences is an extraordinary emotional and physical toll among the civilian populations of the war-torn countries surveyed. Across all these settings, people say that the conflict for them was, above all, 'horrible' (49 per cent). ... After 'horrible', people use the words 'hateful' (30 per cent), 'disruptive' (26 per cent) and 'humiliating' (24 per cent) to describe the conflict. (Greenberg Research, 1999: 2)

Although research on the psychological impact of war on civilian populations reflects cultural and political variations in war-affected societies, it also shows a remarkable level of similarity throughout (Krippner and McIntyre, 2003: 4). The term *war stress* refers to 'the multiple stressors that people are exposed to when they have experienced war, either directly or indirectly' (ibid.: 6). At a collective level, war stress has several long-term health, social, economic, cultural, and political consequences that can be described as *war trauma* (ibid.: 7).

While, at the time of the interviews, many of our participants were still profoundly psychologically scarred by the loss of their loved ones (spouses, parents, and other close family members), they also described more widespread effects of the violence, which easily fit into the category of war trauma. Miguel, a private guard in his early sixties, told us that narco-violence was 'horrendous'. Many of his loved ones fell victims to narco-violence: 'Several of my friends were kidnapped to be trained as hit men; two cousins also died due to that violence.' Luisa Fernanda, a fashion designer in her late fifties, stated how the fear of cartel violence disrupted people's lives:

> I stopped watching the news for a long time because I was traumatized. I experienced terrible headaches, unspeakable pain, and intense fear. I am sure you have heard these words many times: 'We knew we would go out of our homes, but we did not know whether we would come back.'

Others also expressed concerns about the impact of cartel violence on younger generations, i.e., about inter-generational trauma, which is understood as a long-term consequence of war (Downes et al., 2013).

Drug violence left victims, survivors, and the society at large with internalized trauma. However, as we shall see in chapter 8, Colombian lawmakers consider drug related violence to be a crime—rather than a part of war. The similarities between the sensory memories of victims of violence and those described in scholarly literature as war trauma raise questions about this distinction. The question of why the traumatic experiences of victims of drug-related violence were not recognized as war trauma persists. Before we proceed to tackle this question, we will focus for a while longer on the experiences of those directly affected by violence. How have they coped with the consequences of victimization? How has society responded to them?

3

Invisible victims in a commodified world

'We don't talk about it much because it is painful'

Many victims of Medellín's drug war still puzzle over the debris that violence left them. When Ana was still a teenager, her husband fell to the crossfire between drug cartels; violence defaced the landscape she had painted for herself:

> At that time, I was in college studying systems engineering. I had to abandon all the plans I had. I was pushed down on a route I had not imagined. As a widow and raising my son, I had to abandon my studies. My love was in ruins; my heart and my illusions broken. We had had a friendship; we were together from a very young age.

Salomé was pregnant while working as a journalist. In her job, she saw a lot of blood spilt, mourned the murder of her uncle, and, as a mother-to-be, worried throughout her pregnancy about how the stress would affect her baby:

> What hurts me most today is that Escobar is dead, having left many with deep damage. Utterly incurable wounds. For a girl like my daughter: What are the consequences of everything? I was diagnosed with post-traumatic anxiety disorder. The baby in my womb also suffered because of what I thought and felt.

Ana and Salomé, along with most of our interviewees, felt that violence not only destroyed their life goals and aspirations, but also altered who they *were*—a sensation psychologists refer to as *damage to the self*.

Victimhood, Memory, and Consumerism. Katja Franko and David R. Goyes, Oxford University Press.
 DOI: 10.1093/oso/9780192874115.003.0003

The self contains our 'memories, actions, desires, pleasures, and pains'; it gives us an identity; it 'represents the hierarchy of goals that we have built up, bit by bit, over the years' (Csikszentmihalyi, 1990: 34). A traumatic situation may crumble the self by undermining one's actions, desires, and pleasures.

During a traumatic situation, our bodies and minds activate, getting ready to fight, flee, or freeze (APA, 2013; Wilson, 2004): the pulse heightens, adrenaline increases, and attention narrows. Intense activation helps us increase the odds of surviving when we face danger. However, if we are not able to overcome the anxiety and sense of threat when the danger is over, we will remain eternally fighting, fleeing, or freezing (Todd-Kvam and Goyes, 2023). Manuel is an example of remaining frozen after a traumatic situation. Kidnapped by the Medellín Cartel in the early 1990s, he still wakes up in the middle of the night *anxious* about captivity, even three decades after having recovered his freedom: 'I get up at night and wait to see the roof with a piece of gum stuck to it [which he used to see when in captivity], and when I see that the gum is not there, I realize … "I am free, I am home!" '.

When body and mind continue responding as if they were in immediate danger, the person feels alienated: it is as if the self has left and been replaced by an unfamiliar one. The world becomes a dangerous place, uncontrollable and unpredictable, full of treacherous people. Losing the self to trauma provokes a set of internal aches that range from anxiety to fear to rage to a combination of all. These feelings push victims and survivors of violence to redefine their sense of self any way they can. Those who have directly experienced violence try to cope with trauma, to get life to make sense again, to find their self. For example, Salomé renegotiated her identity with herself in an attempt to overcome anxiety. She does not wish to describe herself as a victim and has embraced a new identity, hoping to regain control over a self that violence had turned into chaos:

> To me, the word *victim* is worn out. It refers to a condition, a state of the human being that I do not like. If I am a victim, I am someone who has lost my dignity, my ability to move on, and my ability to *be*. And that image endures. I prefer to think that I am a survivor. I identify with survivors, and I believe that we are all survivors.

Salomé's statement demonstrates not only a need to define oneself as resilient (i.e., a survivor rather than a victim) but also the level of damage made to the plural self of the population.

When trying to find their sense of self, one of the most significant choices victims and survivors of drug violence have had to make is whether to talk about the traumatic events or be silent. *Telling* seems useful to regain control of life's steering wheel by finding a sense of what happened. *Silence* tempts with its promise of taking the unnamed pain away. About half of our interviewees chose to tell their stories, and the other half chose to remain silent.

Telling the story

> On 23 June 1990, a terrible massacre took place at the Oporto nightclub in Envigado. Twenty-six youth died under criminal gunfire opened by a heavily armed group on a night when police and military were posted all around the nightclub. Strange? No, what is strange is that after almost twenty-seven years, the crime still goes unpunished and the case languishes in oblivion.
>
> Blog entry written by José (a pseudonym), brother of a fatal victim of the massacre[1]

Seeking to heal the self, remember their loved ones with dignity, and participate in social memory creation, some victims decided to share their painful memories with society through blog entries and by other means. By writing their narratives, those victims are hoping to reconnect with a sense of self. They are searching for a voice that would allow them to make sense of what happened and honour what they have lost. As a large body of scholarship points out, narratives are important to the construction of the self in interaction with others. Bruner , for example, asks, 'Could it be, then, that what we recognize as Self (in ourselves or in others) is what is convertible into some version of a narrative?' (1996: 161). Similarly,

[1] Even though the documents we quote in this section are publicly available, we refrained from citing them in order to maintain the anonymity of our interviewees. We translated them from Spanish to English. Other sources, such as the *NY Times*, reported nineteen dead, rather than twenty-six.

narrative victimology highlights the centrality of narratives to sense and meaning-making in the aftermath of trauma and grief. Narrativizing is, for some victims, also a way of articulating feelings of justice and injustice (Pemberton, Mulder and Aarten, 2019; see also Presser and Sandberg, 2015).

Victims, however, have unequal access to means of communicating their story to others and to society at large. They might use diverse media, ranging from blogs, to books, to documentaries, to strategic litigation, depending on how much money they have at their disposal and what kind of people they have in their support network. Yet, society assigns more value to books and documentaries than to other forms of narrative, such as blogs or oral storytelling. Hence, the media that victims use, or have access to, to tell their stories allow them more or less visibility and legitimacy.

José, the author of the blog entry we used as an epigraph for this section, has received relatively little attention compared to some other victims. His brother was killed by a group of armed men working for Pablo Escobar, who had decided to take revenge on Medellín's elites by attacking a luxurious night club. Despite José and his brother's frequent visits to the bar, they were both low-income earners. The economic limitations José faced at the time violence hit his life meant that to tell his story, he had to use one of the less prestigious means of communication—a blog. José, unapologetically, states his reasons:

> I have been writing since I was fifteen but have never published. I have never tried, but if someone offers me a contract, I will think about it and then say *yes*. Otherwise, please do not waste my time. I know, I know, I will keep being poor, but I think my mom and my partner will still love me.

Telling (in written form) is José's tool to find a sense of self after the loss of his brother:

> I was seventeen and my brother had just turned twenty. [His death]t had changed my life forever. It strengthened my defiance; and to fight for myself and soothe my desire for revenge, I decided to take out my internal rage by writing. I spent countless nights bent over a blank sheet

of paper, letting out my inner demons in the hour when most people are asleep.

José's blog amasses reflections, poems, music, and videos. New entries have been posted monthly since February 2012. The blog is connected to a Twitter account where José publicizes his story. During the decade it has been running, José's blog has been visited over 70,000 times, which is a considerable number, but remains incommensurate to the more than 400 reflective blog entries. Although the community of its visitors may be limited, the blog has become a meeting site for those who have suffered narco-violence. An anonymous visitor wrote:

> I stumbled across your blog by chance, or maybe because deep down, we are joined by painful bonds. Like you, I also lost a loved one in the massacre of El Bar del Viejo Baúl, months before Oporto, when the same perpetrators were starting their bloody rampage. There have been many years of fighting against pain, loss, and, mainly, indifference.

Silvia, on the other hand, dealt with the trauma of drug violence by writing a memoir—a literary form viewed as a more elevated form of expression, in terms of perceived legitimacy. The subtitle of her book, *Los Días del Dragón* [*The Days of the Dragon*], reads: 'My Correspondence with Pablo Escobar, and Other Ways of Surviving War'.[2] Through her writing, she tried to make sense of how a human being like Escobar could justify to himself causing so much misery. As it was for José, writing became for Salomé a way to deal with the despair caused by the loss she had suffered.

Silvia became a war journalist immediately after finishing her bachelor's studies. She covered more murders than she can remember, and her clothes were often stained with victims' blood. The daily drug war challenged Silvia's understanding of the world:

> The unsettling image of the body of Antonio Roldán [the Governor of Antioquia] charred inside the bombed government car, overrode every

[2] Original subtitle: 'Mi Correspondencia con Pablo Escobar y Otras Maneras de Sobrevivir a la Guerra'.

theory I had recently heard at the university about objective, emotionless reporting, which professors used to insist on—most likely without believing it themselves.

The social conditions in which Silvia exercised her profession can be best described as a war: 'in just one month ... we registered the deaths of over 400 police officers in Colombia, over 250 in Medellín and Antioquia. We were surprised by a dozen car bombs; we lived nights of up to three simultaneous massacres.' Through the years covering drug violence, Silvia accumulated pieces of a puzzle she failed to put together: 'I was dying to ask Pablo Emilio Escobar Gaviria if he really knew the kind of human being my uncle ... was, one of my deaths.' She also wondered: 'How does one talk to one's child about death? What could someone like Pablo Escobar tell his children about death?'

Silvia communicated with Escobar and sought the right moment to ask him the questions that haunted her: 'I felt that it was a way of getting rid of the anger and pain I carried due to all the harm he had caused me; that he had caused us.' She found a way to exchange letters with Escobar and got to learn about his fascination with Stefan Zweig, his interest in journalism, and his protective attitude towards his two children. Nevertheless, the anger and fear in her refused to disappear.

Federico Arellano's way of telling his story has probably achieved the greatest visibility and social approval. He has fought for over a decade to obtain the official status of a victim of the Colombian armed conflict. His father was on the bombed HK-1803 domestic flight from Bogotá to Cali mentioned in the previous chapter. In chapter 8, we analyse further the legal impact of Federico's activism. For now, we can point out that he is one of the few victims who have chosen the avenue of legal redress to achieve recognition and a sense of justice. As we shall see in the next section, many others preferred to remain silent and find personal ways of coping with their loss.

Layers of silence

In addition to trauma, victims have encountered obstacles in their path to finding their self. Mariana, whose husband died in the HK-1803 plane bombing, had to bury him twice, because she was given the wrong corpse the first time. She recalls the chaos that ensued in the aftermath of the bombing and the trauma of having to cope with the practicalities:

> They had to fill out a thousand documents. They did not let me in and I only saw the door when the forensic medicine men entered. I looked inside and he looked very hard.... At that time the National Registry wasn't functioning, and so it did not provide [the victim's] fingerprints. So, if there was someone's hands, that person could not be identified.... And in the middle of all this madness, they began to collect the body parts. Then one team brought together body parts of a man and a woman they had found. Then they said, this leg was a man ... and noted down: 'male of approximately twenty-eight years of age'. On top of all that, the corpses were arriving without clothes. Then it was time to identify them by distinguishing marks on their bodies.

Valentina similarly encountered painful practical obstacles. Orphaned by drug violence, she had to constantly prove that her dad was dead to receive an educational stipend. Neither Mariana nor Valentina received psychological support from the state to cope with their traumas. The way in which society sabotaged their healing process has led many of our interviewees to cover their stories with layers of silence beyond what was necessary.

Carlos became a judge in 1979 and soon joined the Asonal Judicial (judges' union), where he became a leading figure. From the 1980s onwards, Pablo Escobar waged a war against all judges in Colombia, trying to prevent from being extradited to the United States. 'Between 1979 and 1982, only in those three years, there were several murders against the judiciary. Against servants of the judicial branch, above all, the message sent was that Colombian judges continued to be the Cinderella of public power', noted Carlos. The Medellín cartel stepped up the attacks on judges during the late 1980s, and Carlos counted 'ninety-four homicides against members of the judiciary and forty-four threats and forced displacements in Medellín alone'.

In 1988, Carlos acted as a judge in a criminal case against Escobar and confronted him also as a member of the Asonal Judicial: 'I had to leave my home with my daughters when a great judge and close personal friend was killed. The criminal investigators had to leave the country. I was threatened, I had to go into exile to [a European country].' The new judge, who took the criminal case against Escobar, was killed: 'Following an infiltration of the mafia in the Superior Tribunal of Bogotá, the murderers received the information that a decision had been taken against Escobar; ten minutes after leaving the office he [the judge] was murdered in the streets of Bogotá.' Yet, Carlos' convictions brought him back to the country in 1991: '[I]t was not an act of heroism or desire for applause, but a way to express my belief that if we all left the country, then it would get more fucked up than it was.'

For over two decades, Carlos declined to talk about his life in the era of drug violence. Only when he heard about what we were trying to achieve with this project did he agree to speak to us—still with reservations:

> Look, David, I don't like talking about this much, and it's not out of false modesty, but it's simply because of this: when I look back and start making a mental list of all the people who were killed at that time, it is too painful to think that this country stood by and watched as a generation of Colombians were being killed. ... So, when you ask me, I received death threats, I had to go into exile. I don't like to touch on this subject because I am deeply saddened to see that these deaths went unpunished, but also because I am privileged to be alive. As simple as that.

While pain kept Carlos silent, oblivion made Ana forget her words. Ana, her husband, and their baby lived in Cali—a city dominated by the Cali cartel. Ana's husband worked transporting merchandise from Medellín to Cali, enough to become a target for the Medellín cartel, which at the time desired to destroy anything associated with their city of their rivals. The war between the cartels forced the couple to move to Bogotá, which was a promising fresh start for Ana. She was twenty-eight, recently married to the man she loved, and the young mother of a baby boy. Yet, Ana's husband needed to fly to Cali one last time to sign the contract for his new position in the capital. Then tragedy struck. The day her husband travelled to Cali, Ana's father called her to break the news: 'It looks like there was a plane crash. The plane was going to Cali.' It was not an ordinary plane crash: a bomb had been planted by the Medellín cartel on the HK-1803 domestic flight from Bogotá to Cali. This was the same bomb that killed Federico's father. It took the lives of 107 other passengers, including Ana's husband.

Ana did not receive any support from the state to deal with her loss and grief. Instead, she had to channel all her energy toward her son: 'As a dad, [my husband] was the happiest man with him [our son]. Christmas was coming, so I had to pull myself together to soften the blow of my son not having his father and having a sad Christmas.' But violence had left too much of a scar. Ana quit her studies and started working as a secretary. She honoured her husband by devoting all her time to providing for their child. Although she has always been willing to tell her story, she was never asked:

> In the nearly thirty-one years since the attack, during which I have been coping with this issue, nobody has ever cared about us. No one has cared to know who the person [on the plane] was, what was his name, or how much it hurt [to lose him]. No one has ever cared to know what happened to us after the attack. Because, since the attack, a lot of things have happened, all the publicity around Pablo Escobar.... And no one ever asked about us who have been beaten by life, because of what that [Escobar] had done, because of what happened to us. Because you cared, I decided to accept the interview.

Fear joins sadness and oblivion as the third reason why many victims of drug violence have remained silent. For Luis, the violence had a deep impact on his childhood experiences. He recalled how he had once visited the school of Juan Pablo Escobar, the drug lord's son, to play a football match. Juan Pablo, who had already been the centre of attention, had broken his arm. The other kids joked saying that the arm was covered not with plaster but with marble—a reference to Juan Pablo's father's ostentatious wealth. On another occasion, Luis and his friends were wooing a girl, and they forgot the curfew imposed by Escobar. To get back home, they had to sneak behind cars. Although the awareness of violence was strongly present in Luis' jokes and recollections, he fondly remembered his 'school and university years' as 'rather innocent'. However, everything changed when he was seventeen years old. On a Tuesday night he received a call asking him to hurry to the offices of one of the country's largest newspapers, where his father worked. A few meters from the building, he saw a pool of blood in the street; he knew it was his dad's blood.

For Luis, his father's death had not only psychological but also economic and practical consequences. Luis had been accepted to study social work at the University of Antioquia; he had drawn a life plan. But the murder of his father forced him to earn his living: 'I had to abandon my plans of studying and start working. I changed my academic interests. I constantly thought about providing for my mother, my house, and my brother.' Luis found a job as a lawyer's assistant, and eventually ended up studying law himself. He was successful in his profession, and today he works as a lawyer and university professor. He declares that his primary identity is that of 'the father of a family': he shares his life with his wife—another victim of drug violence—and their children. Yet, for thirty-one years (i.e., from the day he lost his father to the day of our interview when he was forty-eight), he had not talked about his victimhood:

> Before talking to you, David, I had somehow unconsciously resisted speaking about what had happened to my dad and my family because I have the same name and surname as my father. So, I think that, unconsciously, I wanted to protect myself. I also wanted to keep that grief inside. But, fortunately, I am expressing myself and have allowed myself to cry, and I have worked through [the tragedy]. My brother has never managed to do it.

Eleven other interviewees told us they had avoided talking about their experiences for almost three decades—until they conceded to our interview. Reasons for their silence ranged between fear, sadness, and oblivion, or a combination of all. Silent victims remain unseen and unheard by the world. The tragic events these victims and survivors experienced have left a strong imprint on them and dramatically changed the course of their lives. Yet, silence prevents society from learning about their pain. While individual particularities play a role in how people respond to trauma, the social arrangements in which people live shape behaviour after trauma (Tekin et al., 2016). Most of the victims of drug violence have not been recognized as official victims of the Colombian conflict; therefore, they have not received psychological support that could have helped them deal with their pain. Silence is also an understandable protection strategy victims adopt, considering that various armed groups, and the powerful people who support them, still operate in Medellín and in Colombia.

Although many of our interviewees felt that the world was not interested in hearing their stories, they lived in a society obsessed with tales of drug violence, particularly those related to Escobar. Victims live in a world where drug violence is hyper-visible, yet its human costs for ordinary people are invisible (for a similar account, see Bredal, 2007). The commodification of violence and trauma means that marketable narratives told by quasi-celebrities receive the most social attention, to the detriment of *ordinary* victims' stories. In the next section, we explain how the business of selling books contributes to the sense of oblivion felt by victims and survivors of drug violence.

Unseen and unheard

In 1989, Uruguayan journalist Eduardo Galeano wrote a poem titled "The Nobodies":

> Those who are not, but could be.
> Who don't speak languages but dialects.
> Who don't have religions but superstitions.
> Who don't create art but handicrafts.
> Who don't have culture but folklore.
> Who are not human beings, but human resources.

Galeano alludes to those who remain unseen, unheard, and unconsidered in society because other forces overshadow them. Just like Galeano's nobodies see their art degraded to handicraft by the authority of aesthetics, most victims of drug violence have seen and continue to see their narratives degraded by the existing rulers of communication. One of those rulers is the *business of books.*

Silvia's book, *The Days of the Dragon*, is a warm, human narrative of a young woman confronted by daily violence, who tries to make sense of life by corresponding with the perpetrator. Silvia's book is a historical document but also a form of therapy. Not all the books about Pablo Escobar have the same characteristics as Silvia's work, though. Many focus mostly on profitability. André Schiffrin 'described the conglomerate takeover of publishing that has transformed the world of words' (2010: vii). International publishing conglomerates monopolizing the world of books want 'returns much closer to those they had gotten from their other media holdings—newspapers, TV networks, and so on' (ibid.). Schiffrin explains that the pressure to increase revenue 'profoundly altered the output of the major publishing houses' (ibid.). The market of ideas is now dominated by the desire to generate profit, which leads to bottom-line-based censorship: 'the new approach—deciding to publish only those books that can be counted on for an immediate profit—automatically eliminates a vast number of important works from catalogues' (ibid.: 104).

While, admittedly, some books are taken on by smaller publishing houses (Silvia's book was published by Semana Libros, a small Colombian publisher), Schiffrin (2000: 105) warns about another problem:

> [T]he playing field is far from levelled. The larger firms, publishing the more commercial books, have vast advertising budgets at their disposal, enormous sales forces, and an extremely efficient network of press contacts, all of which helps ensure that their books get a certain amount of attention. Smaller publishers are unable to compete on an equal footing and have a much harder time finding spaces for their books, both in stores and in review columns.

The books in which Escobar's victims narrate their suffering are promoted in a low-key manner and receive scarce attention. Meanwhile, a flourishing book business has developed around Pablo Escobar's myth. Celebrities (heroes and anti-heroes) have achieved commercial success from their interactions with the drug lord. And publishing houses have used their marketing muscle to position those accounts as international bestsellers. Canongate, the publishing house that has printed the work of the likes of Barak Obama, Julian Assange, Margaret Atwood, Philip Pullman, and Yann Martel, also distributed the book *Loving Pablo, Hating Escobar: The Shocking True Story of the Notorious Drug Lord, from the Woman Who Knew Him Best* (Vallejo, 2018). The author, Victoria Vallejo, a journalist, worked as a news anchor for most of her early career. She proudly declares in her book that when she first met Escobar her boyfriend at the time was the nephew of a former Colombian president. He was 'big, handsome, and free; he [was] loving to the point of exhaustion and generous with his words, his time, and his money, despite the fact that he [was] not a multimillionaire, as all my ex-boyfriends [were]' (ibid.: 17). The book recounts Escobar's and Vallejo's love affair and openly praises the drug lord.

Vallejo recounts that, upon their first encounter, she was more struck by Escobar's personality than his looks. She saw in him 'a certain authority, the air of a respectable older gentleman, the carefully measured words that emerge from his straight, firm mouth. He speaks with a serene voice ... utterly sure that his wishes are commands'. Vallejo, nonetheless, considers that, 'in another setting, [Escobar] would be described as perfectly ordinary, more ugly than beautiful' (ibid.: 26). These accounts focus not only on Escobar's persona, but also his charisma, and thus contribute to his sex appeal. As we discuss in the next chapter, cinematic portrayals of Escobar underwent a process of beautification after media corporations transformed his myth into a brand.

From the very beginning, Vallejo's voice has been louder than that of most victims of violence in Medellín. She was a socialite, a media personality, and now a political asylum resident in the United States. Her alliance with Canongate amplified her voice to influence the social memory of Escobar and the events surrounding his criminal activities. Immediately after the publication of the Spanish version of the book, in 2007, the Colombian Attorney's General Office re-opened the macro-investigation into the links between drug dealing and the Palace of Justice siege of 1985 (Redacción el Tiempo, 2008). Following the siege, members of the M-19 guerrilla group took over the Palace of Justice in Bogotá and held the Supreme Court of Colombia hostage (Carrington et al., 2019). Vallejo's memoir, through the details it revealed, had the power to change the course of one of the most contested investigations in Colombia—a potent example of how the memory of social elites is valued more than the memory of ordinary victims. In 2017, *Loving Pablo, Hating Escobar* became a movie starring Javier Bardem (as Pablo Escobar) and Penélope Cruz (as Victoria Vallejo).

Many of the books about Pablo Escobar have bloody images and morbid titles. The subtitle of one such book advertises, '23 Years and 3 Months in Prison', as a selling point. Its author, Jhon Jairo Velásquez

Vasquez, aka "Popeye," confessed to 'more than 250 murders and participation in three thousand more, as well as the coordination of at least 200 car bombs' (Velásquez Vasquez, 2017: 337). In that book (which sports the title *Surviving Pablo Escobar*), the hitman gives a detailed account of his interactions with the drug lord, up to the moment in which they parted ways, 'Popeye was so close to Pablo Escobar he could feel his breath. ... Clumsily, he [Popeye] reached out to shake the hand of the man who inspired so much respect and admiration, for one last time' (ibid.: 9). The book, filled with morbid details, inspired a TV show, whose first episode was watched by more than 8 million people in Colombia (Publimetro, 2017). The book has been translated into several languages, and the TV show is now streaming on Netflix.

Escobar's brother, Roberto Escobar, produced his own book, titled *Escobar: Drugs. Guns. Money. Power.* The black cover is streaked with blood which outlines Escobar's silhouette. The dedication of the book reads:

> I dedicate this book to God Almighty, as gratitude and to the memory of three extraordinary people: [Mother, Father] and finally my brother, Pablo, a good soul with a vision for the future that turned the impossible to possible, who planted in his heart a place for the poor and unprotected—and whose memory today is part of history. (Escobar, 2010)

Roberto reminds us that his brother Pablo was also a human being, with a difficult childhood: 'I think about him as a young child, lying next to me as we hid beneath our bed while the guerrillas came during the night to kill us all' (ibid.: 4). But he is mainly concerned with mythmaking: 'I know that Pablo was earning so much cash that each year we would simply write off approximately 10 per cent of our money because the rats would eat it or it would be damaged beyond use by water and dampness' (ibid.: 58). The author is unapologetic in his portrayal of his brother: 'I think about the good things he did with that money for so many people. ... And, less often, I think about the terrible things for which he was responsible (ibid.).

Nowhere in the book does Roberto reflect on the immense suffering of the victims; or on the people whose lives were irremediably altered by the violence perpetrated by his and his brother's cartel; or on the trauma that, to this day, overshadows the lives of many. Instead, the book is a celebration of Escobar's 'brilliance' and a panorama of his good deeds: 'Where the poor were involved, Pablo became the man of getting things done. ... Pablo did so much for people. He paid for expenses for those who couldn't afford the medical treatment they needed' (ibid.: 84).

One Amazon user reviews the book by saying that 'Roberto goes to great lengths to present himself and his brother as men more sinned against than sinning—innocent victims of malign external forces'. Yet, most other reviews are positive. A user named Rebecca, under the subject line 'Changed my opinion', writes: 'I remember Pablo Escobar in the headlines as a teenager; he sounded like a horrible monster. We, in the U.S., were never told about the good things he did for his country and his people.' Dylan states: 'This was an amazing book. Pablo was a very inspirational man. ... I learned some things that have helped my business plus personal life.'

The books written by the mother of Escobar's children (Victoria Eugenia Henao) and by Escobar's son (Juan Pablo), fall into a particular category. Victoria Eugenia and Juan Pablo, like most victims we talked to, also saw their worlds demolished by drug violence: '[W]e had to create a life on the ruins of the previous one, our will to stand up and keep going was strong enough to make us succeed', wrote Juan Pablo (Escobar, 2019: 11). Victoria Eugenia Henao uses a tone less concerned with turning her husband into a myth and more preoccupied with conveying the humanity of her situation: 'I tolerated lovers, humiliations, lies, loneliness, death threats ... all for love. ... There were many times I wondered whether I would be able to go on. But I could not leave him, not only because I loved him but also because I was afraid, helpless, and unsafe' (Henao, 2020: 9–10).

Juan Pablo Escobar stated that his intention for writing his book was to honour his father's victims: 'I wish these pages to be my contribution to truth and the symbolic reparation that all victims of Pablo Escobar's crimes have right to demand' (Escobar, 2019: 11). He claimed to be inspired to tell his story by the conviction that documenting history could incite change: 'I was sure I had a story worth telling, a story that should never be repeated' (ibid.: 210). Henao, in turn, was inspired by her son's desire to tell his father's story: 'The bravery my son showed gave me the courage to continue my way, and with his help, I decided that I, too, wanted to tell my story' (Henao, 2020: 11). Henao had two reasons for writing her book: first, she wanted to find herself (ibid.: 12–13).

> Our past is still haunting us, and Pablo's ghost will not leave us in peace. I am merely the widow of Pablo Escobar. I hope to become more than that. In these pages, the reader will encounter a woman who is very different from the one portrayed in the media, movies, and TV shows.

Like her son, Henao also wants to contribute to memory building: 'Pablo Escobar was no role model; he was not the hero shown in movies and TV shows. That false portrayal motivated me to tell the whole story so that history does not repeat itself' (ibid.: 13).

Book publishing, more than ever, are a business driven by a demand to create profit. Marketing strategies for Henao and Juan Pablo Escobar's books tap into peoples' morbid interests and a wish for excitement. Reviewers describe their books as a 'neck-breaking mixture of confession and terrific action'. Amazon, the largest global commercial platform, advertises Juan Pablo's books with the caption: 'The popular series *Narcos* captures only half the truth. Here, at last, the full story.'[3] The author himself shrouds his book in mystery: 'This book reveals stories that are very sensitive, that have never been told, and that uncover many truths about several events with which *he* was directly associated' (Escobar, 2019: 9). The drive to sell the book and make it unique in a sea of competitors is clearly present: 'Little has been told—until now—about the ways and means he used to become as incredibly rich as he did' (ibid.). Book publishers profit from the morbid interest in first-person accounts about Pablo Escobar. The Portuguese cover of Victoria Eugenia's book, contradicting the author's declared purpose, reads: 'Meet the man behind the legend'.[4]

Juan Pablo and Victoria Eugenia have received much more attention than any other victim simply because they are relatives of Pablo Escobar—the object of fascination. The publishing business muzzles

[3] See https://www.amazon.com/Juan-Pablo-Escobar-ebook/dp/B01BSNFS8Q/, accessed on 25 January 2022.

[4] See https://www.amazon.com/gp/product/8542215907/, accessed on 31 January 2022.

the narratives of victims not personally related to the drug lord. The book *My Father* (Escobar, 2016) has been translated into more than thirteen languages. *My life With Pablo* (Henao, 2020) has been translated from Spanish to Portuguese, English, Norwegian, and Italian. Juan Pablo tells about the thousands of messages he daily receives on Facebook and about his encounters with victims across the world: 'I will never forget the face of the first one in the queue [to ask a question], a woman with tears on her face. The first thing she said was, "Juan Pablo, can I give you a hug?" After having hugged for some minutes, she managed to say why she was so overwhelmed: she was a relative of a victim who was on the plane my dad bombed in November 1989' (Escobar, 2019: 213).

Like narco-series described in the following chapter, the top-selling books about Pablo Escobar turn murder and suffering into entertainment and contribute to the mythmaking around the perpetrator. Even the books meant to denounce injustice and the ensuing tragedy are turned into lurid commodities. The few books written by Escobar's victims and survivors of the violence in Medellín are difficult to find and are far from bestsellers. These books, as well as stories published in less prominent outlets, describe lives ripped apart by murder, and work to debunk Escobar's status as a legend. They are the means victims use to find meaning amidst lives filled with pain. However, the commercial best sellers work against these efforts. Alberto, the son of an assassinated criminal justice official, expressed a sense of disillusionment with the situation:

> [Morbid books about Escobar's life] have aroused even more interest in this type of stories, entertainment, and narratives. But there is very little interest in the point of view of the victims ... we have been totally forgotten. People and their sacrifices have been totally forgotten. What I want to say is that, in our country, those who do good for the country are forgotten, and the lives of those who destroy the country are turned into a commercially successful narrative .

Repressed individual and collective traumas

Victims of drug violence struggle to deal with trauma, not only because they lack the financial resources to speak to a therapist but also due to marketing's ability to muzzle their voices. General audiences in Colombia, as elsewhere, worship celebrities and lust for entertainment (Carrabine, 2014). Mundane reports of violence and suffering bore spectators. Julián de Zubiría Samper (2016) documented how war has numbed the Colombian society: 'When an unknown person is murdered, many say "there must have been a reason" or "he surely owed something", showing that life has lost value in our country.' Lust for entertainment and morbid information, added to the privileges granted by economic, social, and intellectual capital, have created a hierarchy of voices. On the top of the hierarchy are Escobar's relatives and close associates who are able, in their books, to disclose personal, morbid details about Escobar and contribute to the building of an urban legend, which nourishes the business of books. Accounts of Escobar's relatives, which are consumed by narco-aficionados because they can reveal intimate details nobody else can, are distributed broadly by commercial publishing houses. In the second tier are the victims who, due to their high position in society before their victimization, have become martyrs of the war against drugs. As Salomé, the journalist we interviewed, observed:

> I do not see there being much interest in the victims unless they're famous, iconic. That is, in people like Guillermo Cano, head of *El Espectador* [a newspaper]; Colonel Valdemar Franklin Quintero; and Antonio Roldan, the Governor of Antioquia. In other words, they have become the visible victims and icons. I think this is harmful, because there is a bias in who we listen to.

The lower layers of the hierarchy are populated by victims who are unrelated to Escobar, and depend on the amount of cultural, social, and economic capital they possess. Capital, in any form, refers to accumulated labour people can exchange for social energy (Bourdieu, 1986; Wacquant, 1995). Cultural capital, as Pierre Bourdieu argues, means the 'long-lasting dispositions of the mind and the body' (for instance, writing skills); 'cultural goods', such as books and pictures; and 'educational qualifications', such as college degrees (Bourdieu, 1986: 17). Social capital 'is the aggregate of the actual or potential resources which are linked to the possession of a durable network of more or less institutionalized relationships of mutual acquaintance and recognition' (ibid.: 21). Silvia used her cultural capital, her writing skills, and other cultural capital she derived from a journalism degree to publish an authoritative, yet commercially unsuccessful, account of her experience. Federico, in addition to investing his cultural capital, used the social capital he had with the organization Colombia con Memoria to initiate a judicial process (see further chapter 8).

Victims with less formal education and fewer economic resources, like José, have to resort to blogs and other outlets which are regarded less highly than a book published by a major publishing house. They therefore have less influence on the construction of cultural and historic memory about the violence that happened in the city. José expressed his awareness of the class differences between victims and their consequences for dealing with trauma: 'The poor victims felt the same fear as the wealthy victims did. Yet, the wealthy victims could leave the country and go see a shrink. We, as poor and middle class, had to move on without any financial means.'

Voiceless victims—those who have for various reasons remained silent—have the least capacity to shape the public memory of the conflict. As we explain in chapter 8, this *hierarchy of victimhood* takes on a whole new dimension when seen at the global level. Although victims may share many similarities, there are also important differences among them in terms of 'distribution of wealth, power, opportunity, or social goods', which are often overlooked in legal discourse and scholarly literature (Fineman, 2010: 253). In the Global North, trauma victims have become culturally and politically increasingly influential, and a large industry of psychiatric and humanitarian help has developed around them (Fassin and Rechtman, 2009). The situation is significantly different in the Global South.

Victims who have aired their experiences, seeking to remember their loved ones with dignity and participate in the social creation of memory, have seen their voices lost amidst actors who speak louder. On the other hand, victims who have remained silent, hoping that time would take the pain away, repressed their trauma and thwarted healing. Society has failed to offer victims support to deal with their trauma. All victims—those who have told their stories *and* those have who remained silent—felt left behind. As María said:

> The memory now being constructed regarding those officially recognized as victims of the internal armed conflict is precarious. Now imagine how it is for the rest of us, the victims of drug trafficking. We live in a limbo.

Psychological research shows that living with repressed trauma has severe consequences for victims (Carter-Visscher et al., 2007; Griffin et al., 2003; Legerski and Bunnell, 2010). Commonly, victims' social networks avoid talking about the traumatic experiences. Some do it out of respect to avoid upsetting the person. Others do it because they feel uncomfortable or helpless. For victims of drug violence, the hierarchy of victims' voices also generates avoidance. Yet, when trauma is silenced and repressed, it leaves victims feeling that their narrative is unbearable, untouchable, and impossible to deal with. The traumatized person is left alone with the burden of carrying the trauma. Csikszentmihalyi (1990: 202) writes that repressed trauma becomes unsurmountable:

> A person may lose the capacity to concentrate on necessary goals. If that happens, the self is no longer in control. If the impairment is severe, consciousness becomes random, and the person 'loses his mind'—the various symptoms of mental disease take over. In less severe cases the threatened self survives, but stops growing; cowering under attack, it retreats behind massive defences and vegetates in a state of continuous suspicion.

Moreover, repressed trauma not only hurts individuals but also entire societies (Goyes et al., 2023). The scars left on the community fail to heal its violent past. The notion of trauma has been critiqued for having Western connotations and for being an individualistic way of addressing pain. At the individual level, trauma is something that victims, with or without support, have to find the strength to deal with in order to become 'survivors' (Sweet, 2021). However, the trauma caused by mass drug violence also has a *collective* dimension. Social trauma 'influences group identity; it shapes individual and collective coping processes as well as transgenerational transmission. The sequelae of violence targeted against whole groups may embrace psychopathological symptoms in both victims and perpetrators' (Hamburger, Hancheva, and Volkan, 2021: v). As it happens with individuals, trauma may leave entire social bodies hypervigilant about potential sources of danger; feeling insecure and misunderstood; envisioning the world as a dangerous place; having little faith in humanity; and avoiding situations that might trigger traumatic memories (Goyes et al., 2023).

Social bodies, just like individuals, have two main ways of dealing with trauma: on the one hand, by constructing cultural trauma 'social groups, national societies, and sometimes even entire civilizations not only cognitively identify the experience and source of human suffering but "take on board" some significant responsibility for it' (Alexander, 2004: 1). The construction of cultural trauma helps remove layers of repressed pain and contributes to reconciliation processes (Brants and Klep, 2013; Karstedt, 2010). On the other hand, when social trauma is repressed, the entire social body is left feeling powerless to overcome a deviant identity (Goyes and Franko, 2021).

The advent of global media companies

In this chapter, we have outlined how commercial processes and varying levels of capital affect victims' visibility and their ability to shape cultural and historic memory. Commercial books published by Escobar's family members and associates have, with their spectacular accounts, effectively side-lined the voices of most victims. Yet even these commercially successful accounts are insignificant compared to the narrative power of the global entertainment industry. In fact, it would be more precise to say that the book publishing business both is nourished by and reinforces the wave of interest created by the popularity of narco-shows, particularly Netflix's *Narcos*. Juan Pablo Escobar, whose books have been among the most successful commercially, acknowledges the overpowering force of these visual products:

I must say I am very uncomfortable with how the shows, with their combination of fiction and reality, send the message that gets the youth to believe that it is cool to be a *narco*. … The impact of the movies and the shows about my dad is so big that I receive messages from youngsters in countries on the African continent, like Kenya and Morocco, and from other places, like the Philippines, Russia, Turkey, Afghanistan, Iran, and Palestine, but also from countries in Latin America like Mexico, Guatemala, Peru, Argentina, Bolivia, Ecuador, Colombia, and Venezuela, in which they tell me, in a nutshell, 'I want to become a narco like in that show. Help me become a *narco*.' (Escobar, 2019: 195–6)

4
Building a global brand

From trauma to entertainment

On Tuesday, 29 May 2012, 79 per cent of TV sets in Colombia displayed the premiere of a new mega-production: *Pablo Escobar: El Patrón del Mal.* The show was the biggest gamble Caracol TV had ever made. The payroll of an all-star national cast and the expenses of shooting on location, represented the daunting challenge of 'being the first attempt to tell the life story of the most powerful and ruthless drug trafficker in the history of the country, on prime time' (Semana, 2012). But the gamble paid off: the pilot was the most seen episode in the history of Colombian television, and *Pablo Escobar: El Patrón del Mal* ended up becoming one of the most watched shows in the history of Colombian television.

El Patrón del Mal was part of a new phenomenon in Colombian broadcasting. Almost three decades after the peak of violence in Medellín, several TV shows, inspired by the lives of the most famous Colombian drug lords, aired on local and national open channels, and became widely consumed entertainment products. This was the beginning of an intense process of commercialization of Medellín's violence and the making of Pablo Escobar into a global icon, as well as a profitable commercial brand. These processes are not limited to Colombia. They have been part of increasingly global-media-driven consumption of violence. The narrative power and visual potency of these violent and excitement-inducing productions have also completely overshadowed the stories of Medellín's inhabitants. The victims' invisibility and inability to make their stories heard thus stands in stark contrast to the global-celebrity status that the entertainment industry has conferred on the perpetrators of violence. This is particularly true of Escobar and his associates.

Victimhood, Memory, and Consumerism. Katja Franko and David R. Goyes, Oxford University Press.
 DOI: 10.1093/oso/9780192874115.003.0004

The birth of narco-telenovelas

The early media productions focusing on drug violence in Medellín were Colombian and followed the script of the telenovela genre. Telenovelas are television series or soap operas produced primarily in Latin America. One of their primary traits is that they foreground emotions and embrace a melodramatic tone (Rowe and Schelling, 1991: 108). They retain the narrative mode of Latin American folktales, such as the 'Brazilian *cordel*, and the chronicle of events in [a] *corrido* and Colombian vallenato songs: these connections have to do with a constantly elongated narrative flow and a porousness to what is going on outside the text' (ibid.: 109). The genre's narrative reliance on neighbourhood solidarity and friendship, explain Rowe and Schelling, reflects the reality of the failing political institutions on the continent where they first appeared: Latin America. Another expert on telenovelas, Carlos Monsiváis, suggests that the appeal of telenovelas lies in the political disempowerment of the lower classes:

> Collectives without political power or social representation ... sexualize melodrama, extract satirical threads from black humour, enjoy themselves and are moved emotionally without changing ideologically ... the subaltern classes accept, because they have no alternative, a vulgar and pedestrian industry, and indisputably transform it into self-indulgence and degradation, but also into joyful and combative identity. (ibid.)

The power of telenovelas lies in their ability to turn life's challenges into an entertaining plot that keeps the community of spectators at the edge of their seats. By combining popular aesthetics, democratic emotions, and references to shared memories, telenovelas individualize social problems and their solutions. They offer an escape, allowing us to forget our own problems even as we relate to the characters and find solace in the knowledge that they, and others around us, deal with similar issues. Audiences gather around telenovelas, relishing in the familiar while enjoying the safe distance from the problems on the screen with their own lives. Yet, telenovelas also receive criticisms for their 'simplistic analysis of the problem which is posited on the character of certain individuals and not the socio-economic reality of the country which is the real issue' (Bibliowicz, 1980: 482 cited in Rowe and Schelling, 1991: 108).

While few expected that telenovelas could transform the fear of the 1990s' drug violence into entertainment, the first narco-telenovela, *Sin tetas no hay paraíso* [*No Tits, No Paradise*, 2006] became an immediate hit. It drew inspiration from Gustavo Bolívar's (2006) eponymous book. The author wished to 'bring attention to the problem of young women in Colombia using prostitution to pay for plastic surgery' (interview with Gustavo Bolivar by *El Tiempo* newspaper, quoted in Morello, 2015: 1). According to Alejandro Herrero-Olaizola (2022) the book represents an early example of the cultural commodification of violence and has been criticized for allegedly 'riding the wave of narcoculture' and its cultural and financial 'juggernaut' (Morello, 2015: 2).

Sin tetas no hay paraíso 'revolves around the figure of a teenage girl from a poor family who seeks to improve her social status by augmenting her breasts with silicone implants so that she can become an escort for important local drug traffickers' (Cabañas, 2012: 75). The telenovela has been described as 'the mother of all narco-telenovelas because it was the first one and opened the door for the national and international success of this type of shows' (Las2Orillas, 2020). It signalled the profitability of allowing global audiences to enter 'the secret world of drug traffickers and their women' (Cabañas, 2012: 75).

The profitability of *Sin tetas no hay Paraíso* motivated broadcasters to produce similar shows. Telenovela after telenovela ran in prime time. *El Cartel de los Sapos* [*The Snitchers' Cartel*] aired in 2009. It is based on a book by a former drug dealer Andrés López. The author spent years in prison for drug trafficking and was released after an agreement with the Drug Enforcement Administration (DEA). In his book, Lopez gives insights into the *mythical* Pablo Escobar and 'exposes the conflict between Escobar Gaviria and the military and police forces over proposed legislation to allow the extradition' of cartel members (Duarte, 2014: 149). Caracol TV, the largest media channel in Colombia and producer of *Sin tetas no hay Paraíso*, purchased the rights to López's book. Colombian critics aired their concerns about the damaging consequences of such productions, 'the centrality of the scenes laden with the frivolous abundance', and their power to captivate 'audiences interested in seeing the minute details of the operation of a drug cartel from the inside' (ibid.: 149–50).

Caracol TV also released *Las muñecas de la mafia* [*The Mafia Dolls*] in 2009. The show follows Lucrecia, a drug lord's 'submissive but cunning' wife, who yields to the whims of her husband as a way to achieve power, beauty, and a life of excesses (Armenta, 2017: 123).

The same year, RCN, the second biggest Colombian TV broadcaster, launched *El Capo*. The production's hero is a drug cartel boss. The show follows the protagonist's journey from rags to riches, by way of his illegal drug business. The plot describes the pains of a childhood in poverty, the manoeuvres that led the hero to engage with drug dealing, the risks he undertook, and his rise. Although the show is fictional, 'it pretends to re-create a Pablo Escobar with its many details and resemblances' (Ordoñez, 2012: 50). Escobar's transformation from infamy, to notoriety, to a brand began with *El Capo*.

Between 2006, when the first narco-telenovela aired, and 2015, when Netflix released its major hit *Narcos*, Colombian TV broadcasted several soap operas about the narco-lifestyle, including *Sin tetas no hay paraíso El Capo*, *El cartel de los Sapos* and *Las muñecas de la mafia*. A commentator for *El Tiempo*, one of the two largest Colombian newspapers, reported that 'it is an indisputable truth that, over the past ten years, national television has been inundated with this type of content [i.e. narco-telenovelas] and this is, somehow, accepted by the audience' (El Tiempo, 2019).[1]

What attracts the Colombian audience to consume such productions? Benavides argues that narco-telenovelas 'manage to disaffect the elite, a small part of the population, while entertaining the rest' (2008: 121). Narco-telenovelas tap into fundamental psychological mechanisms to attract viewers: 'The violence, which is so explicit and central in narco dramas, responds to both North American and Mexican (and Latin

[1] A noncomprehensive list of Colombian narco-telenovelas includes:

3 Milagros [*3 Miracles*] (2011–2012), a show about the involvement of women in drug trafficking;

Alias El Mexicano (2013–2014), which narrates the life of Gonzalo Rodríguez Gacha, one of the heads of the Medellín cartel;

Tres Caínes [*The 3 Cains*] (2013) about the paramilitary army financed by drug traffickers;

El señor de los cielos [*Lord of the Skies*] (2013–2023) about a Mexican drug dealer;

La Viuda Negra [*The Black Widow*] (2014–2016) about Griselda Blanco, lover of Pablo Escobar; and

Alias J.J. [*Surviving Escobar: Alias J.J.*] (2017), released after *Narcos* was streamed on Netflix, it narrates the life of John Jairo Velásquez, Escobar's main hitman.

American) forms of aggression that the narco-drama synthesizes to express a survivor mentality' (ibid.: 135). Similarly, Pobutsky (2010) explains that the success of narco-telenovelas has to do not only with 'the physical exuberance of the protagonists and their deep cleavages' but also 'the irreverent humour and the narrative mirroring that allows the audience to relate with the production and see their own realities in the adventures of the protagonists'. For Pobutsky, narco-telenovelas resonate with the culture already established in the country: 'the vain youngsters, the new rich, and the corny aesthetics of the dominating narco culture'. Unlike traditional crime drama, which celebrate the re-establishment of social order when the 'good guys' defeat the 'bad guys', narco-telenovelas celebrate non-elite aesthetics and are marked by an acceptance of an implosion of law and order.

A notable omission from the list of narco-telenovelas mentioned above was *Pablo Escobar: El Patrón del Mal* [*Pablo Escobar: The Drug Lord*] (2012), a landmark in the genre whose impact we described at the outset of this chapter. The show contains all the elements that Benavides (2008) and Pobutsky (2010) argue attract the masses: a distinctly local flavour combined with U.S. crime drama scripts and the structure of South American telenovelas. More importantly, *El Patrón del Mal* showed global corporations that it is possible to profit from Pablo Escobar, the brand.

Beautifying Escobar

El Patrón del Mal reveals how narco-shows, as a genre, are a hybrid of exogenous and endogenous influences, an interplay between national and international styles. The U.S. set the example for making heroes out of mafia bosses (up until then an unusual move in Colombian productions). A scriptwriter for *El Patrón del Mal* we spoke to explained:

> The United States has always been at the forefront of this trend, with *The Godfather* or *The Sopranos*. This was a great inspiration, because having seen *The Sopranos* and having them in the back of my mind was always the most significant influence I had when writing this kind of product.

Following the lead of U.S. dramas, which centre on mafia bosses and their personalities, Colombian narco-telenovelas combined 'the other-worldliness of the gangster lifestyle' with familiar Latin American tropes such as work, family dynamics, stress, and personal demons (Vincent, 2008: 5), seemingly without passing judgement on the violent actions of their protagonists. (As discussed below, several of Escobar's victims saw this as deeply problematic.) Like U.S. mafia shows, narco-telenovelas harnessed the appeal of wrapping the unusual in a usual frame. Narco-telenovelas placed Escobar's moral ambiguity and horrendous acts into a scenery of everyday life, relatable events, and feelings. They also tone down Escobar's radicalism by presenting his beliefs and ideas in ways that are less shocking and more appealing to mainstream audiences (see Grant, 2017).

According to Brenton Malin productions like *The Godfather* (1972) and *The Sopranos* (1999–2007) set the tone for narco-telenovelas by 'humanizing the Mafioso and blurring American television's typical line between good and evil characters' (2010: 377). In mafia shows, the audience identifies with a hero that lives 'an upper-class lifestyle [but] regularly celebrates working-class values' (ibid.). Mafia shows have also been praised for their authenticity; for putting forward 'a realistic view of the world'. Audiences identify with the Western anxieties of Tony Soprano, 'a suburban middle manager dealing with the stress of surviving the American Dream' (Toscano, 2014: 452). By reflecting Western existentialism and moral uncertainty, the Sopranos captivate their audience. To Hollywood's framing of the Mafioso, narco-telenovelas added the background of Latin American realities marked by state weakness, colourful biodiversity, and violent conflict.

Despite the intricate global–local interconnections that may have allowed its creators to take considerable creative liberties, *El Patrón del Mal* aimed for historical accuracy and a victim's vantage point. One of the show's producers, whose parents were murdered by Escobar's cartel, told us that they wished to 'show the points of view of widows, politicians, and children'. The producers also sought an actor who physically resembled Pablo Escobar. They were not far off (see Figures 4.1 and 4.2). Like in real life, Escobar's colourful character overshadowed the victims in the show. Diana, who was involved in the production, told us about her ambivalence regarding the show. She felt deeply affected by the victims' stories in

Figure 4.1. Pablo Escobar.
Source: Reproduced under the Creative Commons CC BY-SA 4.0 license.

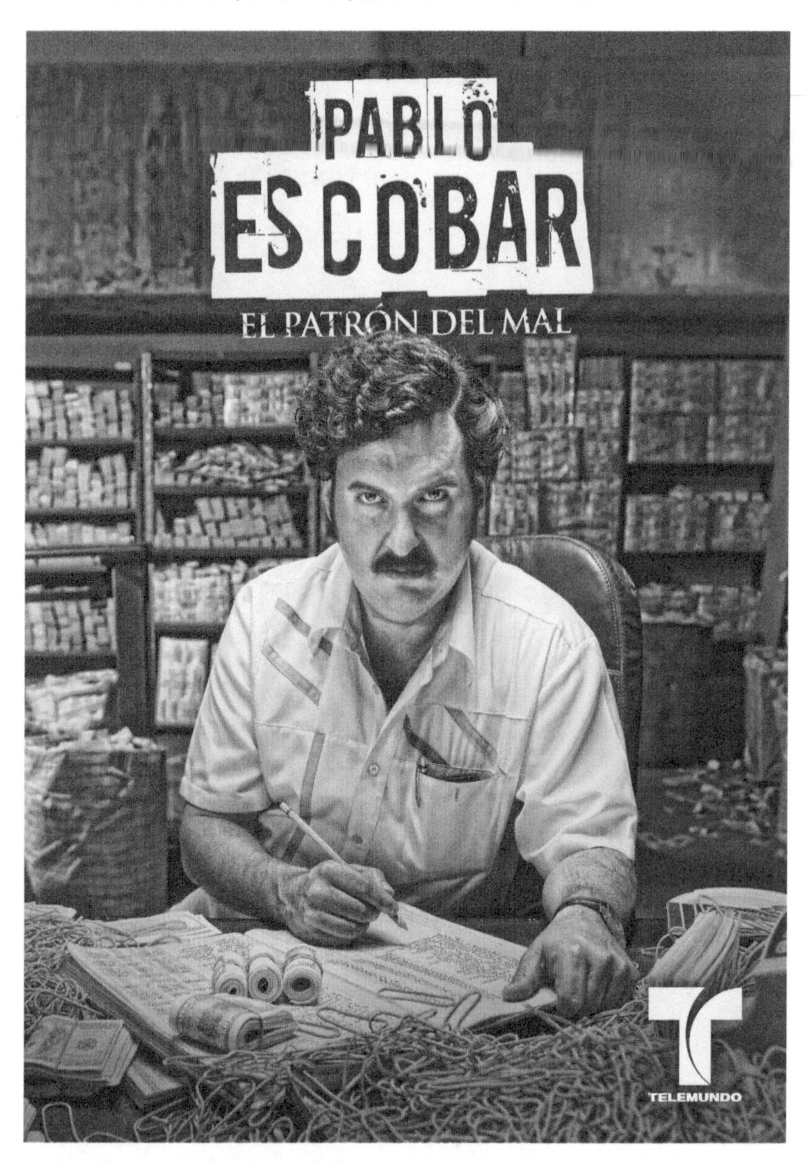

Figure 4.2. Andrés Parra in his role as Pablo Escobar in *El Patrón del Mal.*
Source: Photo 12/Alamy Stock Photo.

the show yet considered the series garnered more attention and commercial success as a show than a memorial, partly due to how Escobar was portrayed and played:

> Andrés' [the actor playing Escobar] performance, in my opinion, was so strong that it went a little beyond what we wanted, which was to forefront the victims. So, we didn't want it that way. Many people who saw the series identified with Andrés' role, that is, with Pablo Escobar. Many people saw him as an icon, like: 'Wow, this man is an icon, an idol, who knows what.' That was exactly what we wanted to avoid from the beginning, but his performance was so impeccable that it was inevitable.

The role of Escobar brought fame to the Colombian actor. However, despite the declared intentions of its producers, the show became a source of entertainment rather than placing victims' narratives at the forefront. In the list of the 'seven narco-telenovelas that have harmed Colombia the most', a local magazine declared that 'despite the excellent production and performance by the actors' *Pablo Escobar: El Patrón del Mal* 'contributed to impress millions of foreigners with the image of a person who deeply harmed Colombia' (Las2Orillas, 2020). *The Sopranos*-inspired framing of the narrative was part of broader displacement that increasingly focused on Escobar the persona rather than the tragic destruction which Escobar the person had set in motion.

Yet, narco-telenovelas were only the beginning. The commercial success of narco-telenovelas—specifically those revolving around Escobar—led to a rapid globalization of the genre, and Escobar became a *brand*. A brand can be defined as:

> a type of product made by a particular company and sold under a particular name; the set of qualities that people connect with a particular product or organization; the set of qualities that people connect with a particular person, or the idea of themselves that the person tries to present to others.[2]

[2] See 'brand', noun, *Cambridge Dictionary*, https://dictionary.cambridge.org/dictionary/english/brand, accessed on 15 February 2023.

Figure 4.3. Wagner Moura as Pablo Escobar and Paulina Gaitán (middle) as Escobar's wife in Narcos.
Source: Daniel Daza/©Netflix/courtesy Everett Collection/NTB.

U.S. media companies, such as Netflix, co-opted the story of Escobar and of Medellín's violent past.

Two changes occurred when Pablo Escobar became a global brand: first, his image was beautified (to comply with Western standards). Compare Figures 4.1 (Pablo Escobar), 4.2 (Colombian Andrés Parra in *El Patrón del Mal*), 4.3 (Wagner Moura in *Narcos*), and 4.4 (Javier Bardem in *Loving Pablo*). The beautification of the main character reveals the interest in making Escobar more attractive to the international masses. As one reviewer of *Narcos* observed:

> Moura [the actor portraying Escobar], with his soft, brown-eyed gaze and youthful face (much better-looking than the real man), makes Escobar so appealing in his self-confidence that it is difficult not to root for him, even as he subtly threatens the children of an army official who initially dares not to be paid off, even as he poses with corpses. (McNamara, 2015)

Figure 4.4. Javier Bardem as Pablo Escobar and Penelope Cruz as Virginia Vallejo in *Loving Pablo* (2017).
Source: Raul Soto Escobar Films/Kobal/REX/NTB.

Second, the branding of Escobar reflects the constant displacements that take place in processes of memory creation, particularly in the Global South. *El Patrón del Mal* aimed to show the victims' perspective (although, as we saw in chapter 3, it was really the perspective of a small group of privileged victims). When Escobar, the brand, was globalized, the story was told from Northern media companies' perspective. According to Aldona Pobutsky, Escobar became a global brand because *it* contains all the elements of a good story:

> From elements as basic as his moustache and floppy hairdo to aspects of human nature as complex as desire and transgression. The cultural wealth of Escobar-themed products project the zeitgeist of the narco universe: high on adrenaline, consumer oriented, capitalist, amoral, and hedonistic. (Pobutsky, 2020: 230)

However, the branding of Escobar stripped history of its complexity. Netflix adapted the Colombian productions for Western consumption by fitting them into a familiar narrative in which heroic U.S. Drug Enforcement Agency (DEA) agents save the world from exotic foreign threats (Rincón, 2018), a narrative archetype that can be traced as far back as Kipling's 1899 *The White Man's Burden*. Paying homage to Hollywood movies such as *Good Fellas*, *Narcos* also frames its story as a classic gangster movie (Britto, 2016). As Nochimson points out, one of the main characteristics of the gangster genre is that 'the protagonists with whom we empathize reverse our usual patterns of identification by engaging us and our feelings with career criminals, often to the exclusion of empathy with law-abiding citizens' (2002: 3).

Netflix: The business of entertainment

So, what's the role of Netflix in all of this? Netflix portrays its rise as a company as an unlikely success story—a tale of two entrepreneurs who started from scratch and overcame big challenges. A closer look at Netflix's origin, policies, and practices reveals the company is a ruthless capitalist business, intensely focused on profit. Marc Randolph, co-founder and Netflix's first CEO, says in his 2019 autobiography that Netflix is 'the amazing life of an idea . . . that [people said] will never work' (Randolph, 2019). While, today, Netflix is one central force in the global market for streamed entertainment, the corporation began as a traditional video rental business. After months of playing with ideas for a start-up, Randolph and his colleagues zeroed in on an online VHS tape rental. The plan was to have a massive collection of movies to rent, set up an online catalogue, and use the postal service to deliver the cassettes to the customers' doors. However, DVDs entered the market just as Randolph was about to invest in VHS tapes. That changed Netflix's course.

Randolph's start-up received a US$2 million investment from Reed Hastings, an American billionaire businessman. On 14 April 1998, Netflix launched its platform with a rental offer of 800 DVD titles. From there on, the company grew fast. In 2002, Netflix went public, valued on the stock market at US$50 million (Hastings and Meyer, 2020). In 2007, the Internet infrastructure allowed Netflix to stream some of its content directly to its users' computers, thereby capturing new subscribers. By 2016, the number of paying customers (not including those who share accounts or passwords) totalled 'nearly eighty-seven million' (Barker and Wiatrowski, 2017: 1). In 2021, Netflix's net worth was estimated to be approximately US$19.08 billion (Uhlig, 2022). How did Netflix achieve such amazing growth?

In an autobiographical book, Reed Hastings argues that the secret lies in creating a culture of freedom and responsibility. A culture where employees have 'control over their own projects' (Hastings and Meyer, 2020: 133). A culture of few rules. Hastings' book bears the revealing title *No Rules Rules*, and uses the case of *Narcos* to exemplify the approach:

> Paolo was hired at Netflix to promote shows to Italians. The popular Netflix original *Narcos* was one series he was sure would be a big hit. It's the story of the Colombian drug lord Pablo Escobar. Pablo is handsome, with 1980s coiffed hair and a bushy moustache. "Despite all the deplorable things he does you find yourself rooting for him", explains Paolo. 'Italians—who love Mafia shows—were going to love it'. ... But Paolo wonders if his new boss, vice president of marketing Jerret West, an American living in Singapore, would agree with his idea.
>
> Paolo couldn't believe Jerret's response: "Did you have elements you wanted to discuss? It's your decision, Paolo. Is there something I can do to help? (ibid.: 132–3)

Netflix cared for results and far less about how they were achieved. 'When I started at Netflix', declares one employee quoted by Hastings, 'Jack [the employee's supervisor] explained to me that I should consider I'd been handed a stack of chips. I could place them on whatever bets I believed in' (ibid.: 139).

Communication researchers Cory Barker and Myc Wiatrowski link Netflix's success with a strategy of buying, developing, and distributing 'as many types of content to as many microtargeted audience groups as possible [and] introducing more non-English language series' (2017: 1). They also highlight how Netflix's 'role in the popularisation of streaming video fundamentally altered the ways in which we watch, discuss, and generally consume media' (ibid.: 2). In sum, 'Netflix is the central force in the contemporary experience of media consumption' (ibid.).

Narcos was one of the main rungs in ladder of Netflix's commercial success. In 2016, the year of the series' release, 12 million new users signed up to the streaming service, and the corporation, for the first time exceeded US$2 billion in quarterly streaming revenue (Heathman, 2016). *Narcos* reflects Netflix's philosophy and policies. The series was thus an important building block in making the corporation profitable and internationally known. Pedro (also a pseudonym), one of the producers behind *Narcos*, provides an example that illustrates well Netflix's reputation before and after the production: '[S]omeone contacted Javier Bardem and suggested he play Escobar; but at that moment Netflix was unknown, and Javier declined. The show went on without Bardem.... Pablo Escobar opened new doors for Netflix.'

The person in charge of bringing Escobar's story to Netflix audiences was José Padilha, a Brazilian director who had his first international success with *Tropa de Elite* [*Elite Squad*, 2007]. The movie looked at 'the day-to-day operation of the police forces and their interaction with crime, drugs and violence in Rio's favelas' (Gutiérrez-Rexach, 2012: 136). *Elite Squad* follows a police officer, played by Wagner Moura, who directs the operations of the Special Police Operation Battalion. The battalion 'is charged with cleaning the favelas from drug traffickers and violent elements' (ibid.). In *Elite Squad*, Padilha used narrative and stylistic devices he also used in *Narcos*: fragmented stories that converge at a violent point, the constant use of a narrator's voice-over, and a semi-documentary narrative style. 'Padilha wrote the film in cooperation with Rodrigo Pimental—a former BOPE captain' (ibid.: 137).[3] As in other popular series, such as *The Wire*, getting law enforcement agents involved in the process of production is done to achieve authenticity. *Elite Squad* sold several million copies in Brazil (including pirated versions).

When working on *Narcos*, as he did in *Elite Squad*, Padilha drew inspiration from police officers to build his narrative. 'In working on *Narcos*, Padilha interviewed everybody from the American DEA agents who worked in the field—the show is told from the point of view of Steve Murphy, the real-life agent assigned to take down Escobar', writes *The Guardian* journalist Chris Campion (2015) in an interview with

[3] BOPE (Batalhão de Operações Policiais Especiais, Special Police Operations Batallion) is a police tactical unit of the Military Police of the State of Rio de Janeiro.

the director. Padilha stuck to the (commercially successful) formula of narrating the story of the war on drugs from the perspective of the police.

Padilha's skills at creating semi-documentary shows shaped *Narcos* to the point that Netflix promoted the show as: 'the true story of Colombia's infamously violent and powerful drug cartels' (ibid.). Yet, Padilha confesses feeling ambivalent about telling a story that is truthful and historically accurate: 'I guess I'm sceptical when it comes to social processes and I feel like we know less than we think we do'—said Padilha in an interview with *The Guardian* (ibid.). Not surprisingly, in *Narcos*, he deliberately blurred the lines between heroes and villains. His interviewer described Padilha as 'an anarch-stylist, Brazil's answer to Martin Scorsese, tackling difficult subjects and turning them into gritty, uncompromising entertainment' (ibid.).

In conversations with us, other members of the production team confirmed Padilha's reservations about portraying with historical accuracy the violence that transpired in Medellín in the 1980s and 1990s. The production team confirmed that Padilha set out to create 'uncompromising entertainment'. Ignacio, a European who assisted in the production of *Narcos*, declared that the show had the sole goal of entertaining. 'If you want to learn about history, go elsewhere', he told us. And then added, 'there was no interest in being rigorous with the content; the goal was to entertain and make a profit'. According to Ignacio:

> Netflix chose the story [of Pablo] because it had sex appeal, so to speak. It is a story that stays with you. That is why we told the story of Pablo, because of its sex appeal, disregarding the social connotation. The difference between European and U.S. [productions] is that the U.S. does not care about good and evil. Neither stance is relevant.

Hector, another producer, said: 'Whether it is *Narcos* or any other series, making shows is a business. Our industry is a business, always. When we tell a story, we make it entertaining.' Similarly, Susana, a scriptwriter for the show, said the producers 'lacked interest in exploring the complexity of the conflict. They were committed to glorifying violence and creating something cool.' While Susana expressed genuine concern about the lack of nuance and depth, Hector, the producer, denied responsibility for the social consequences: '[T]o us who did not live through it [the violence], we are only making just another entertainment product.'

We also inquired about the research process behind the production. Several Latin American participants in the production were critical of the narrative power given to U.S. actors and North American perspectives. Pedro, who worked as a top producer on *Narcos*, told us that the series set out 'to show the perspective of the DEA with a very North American point of view'. He continued:

> North Americans wrote *Narcos*; there was not one Latin American among the scriptwriters. The show got a very particular perspective. The director is an oligarch, the son of oligarchs, with a frivolous outlook typical of the oligarchy. I disagreed with the show's contents and had many discussions with the scriptwriters, because they entirely ignored what Latin America is. The show has exclusively a North American slant. The show lies.

Hector, the producer, also declared, 'the consultants for the show were the two police officers [who were] part of the forces deployed against Escobar. They narrated Escobar's story'. Likewise, Susana, the only Latin American scriptwriter, told us that she was instructed that:

> [T]he story's heroes should be *gringos*, the DEA. We knew that, in reality, the DEA and the CIA fuelled, and profited from, drug trafficking. There were many interesting things that could be told that the audience is unaware of. But the producers wanted to have the *gringo* point of view. Meanwhile, the victims were neglected.

Susana characterized the creation of the script as 'moving the characters as if they were chess pieces', based on mere convenience rather than historical accuracy. Ignacio concurred: '[T]he dialogues do not come from history, we create them to fit our story. … [A]s a piece of fiction, *Narcos* works pretty well.' Pedro, who oversaw the production, explained:

> [The scriptwriters] first create the characters, the DEA agents, their environment, where they live, what they do, where they are. Based on that, they invent where Escobar was at that moment and the interactions he

had. This is a technique far removed from reality and only concerned with building a coherent script.

Other voices were also critical of Netflix's lack of interest in securing historical accuracy in the series. Escobar's son, Juan Pablo, writes:

> After a meeting with representatives from Netflix, during which we offered unrestricted access to the large family archive, which paints a clear picture of my father's life, we received a clear reply: 'We are not interested in the offer, we already know the story, we have bought it from Javier Peña, the agent who worked for DEA in Escobar's time, and we do not want to cooperate with Escobar's family.' (Escobar, 2019: 197)

While Escobar's family may be interested in advancing their agenda and telling their truth, Juan Pablo's denouncement shows Netflix's disinterest in seeing the story from various perspectives. Susana, the screenwriter, was sensitive to the lack of cultural knowledge among the crew. Describing her boss, she said: 'His parents were immigrants, but he had never visited Colombia or Mexico; he did not speak Spanish; he had never visited Latin America. He had never left the country. He was very American, and his point of view was very *gringo*.' Despite her best efforts, she thought that 'ignorance of the culture was such that it would be tough to make [the show] authentic or profound in many ways'.

It will not, therefore, come as a surprise that there are blatant historic inaccuracies in the show. For example, Agent Steve Murphy—depicted as the DEA agent who takes down Escobar—arrived in Colombia in 1988, at the height of drug violence. In reality, Murphy arrived only in 1991—when the conflict with the drug lord was nearing its end. Most importantly, the show misrepresents central social dynamics in Colombia's war on drugs. It individualizes the responsibility for violence and neglects the historical and structural dynamics that have led to the emergence of drug cartels in Medellín in the first place (see chapter 2). Pedro, a producer, expressed concern with *Narcos*' shallowness and lack of a political perspective: '[The conflict in Medellín] was not a police issue; it was a political issue. Netflix did not want to meddle. *Narcos* is a shallow story about a smuggler. It misses all the political history of Colombia.'

Narcos portrays Escobar's life as glamorous. A romantic bolero that serves as the show's musical theme, and the intro featuring seductive women, set the tone of light-hearted nostalgia and sophistication. Simultaneously, the show trivializes the horrors of violence. The juxtaposition of massacres (police officers entering a bar and shooting everyone on the dance floor) and revelry, to the sound of upbeat music, attenuates the emotional impact and the moral gravity of the atrocities perpetrated during the 1980s and 1990s. Such narrative framing stands in stark contrast to the intense sensory memories of those who directly experienced the violence: the smell of corpses on the streets, the oppressive sounds of car bombs and sirens, and the daily fear of death and destruction. While critics of the show, including members of the production team, point out its failure to live up to its claims of historical accuracy, attention should also be paid to the sensory aspects of its narrative.

Released on 28 August 2015, *Narcos* had become, by 2018, the most watched show on Netflix's platform. It was renewed for three seasons and was also made into a popular spin-off series set in Mexico (*Narcos: Mexico* (2018–2021); Vicedo, 2018). The show effectively imprinted its vision of Medellín's violent past in the minds of audiences worldwide. Yet, the victims of Escobar played no role in the reconstruction of this history. Their perspective made no mark on the show. When we asked Ignacio, the European co-producer of the show, whether victims of the violence were consulted during production, he succinctly responded: 'No, they had no voice.' Instead, violent death is often used as a source of comic relief and entertainment.

As will be discussed in the following chapters, the feelings of disrespect for their pain and a sense of glorification of violence were the primary concerns that the victims and survivors expressed about *Narcos* in our conversations. Yet, these developments have not only been driven by the specific dynamics motivating the production of the show, but also by the seemingly insatiable demand for entertainment among global audiences.

Why do we consume violence?

We learned from conversations with producers, scriptwriters, and assistants that Netflix is first and foremost a business interested in selling entertainment. But why do we buy their products? Why are audiences fascinated by violence? Why do we consume so much violent entertainment? Why did *Narcos* become one of the most watched shows on Netflix? According to Simon McCarthy-Jones (2021), there are four existent hypotheses in scholarly literature that try to explain our consumption of violence. The cathartic theory indicates that we drain out our excess aggression by watching violence on TV (this theory, however, has been broadly discredited for lack of evidence). The adrenaline hypothesis indicates that viewers get a rush from watching others suffer. The eudemonic thesis signals that violence attracts due to its learning potential (see more below). Finally, the hybrid theory indicates that viewers are both entertained—as in the adrenaline hypothesis—and educated—as in the eudemonic thesis.

Communication scholars Anne Bartsch and Louise Mares (2014) added evidence to the hybrid theory. They conducted an experiment to test the reason why violence appeals to audiences. The researchers selected 482 participants in Germany and the United States. After watching trailers with varying levels of violence, the participants rated from 1 to 7 on the perceived level of violence, the meaningfulness of the production, and how attracted they were to watch the entire movie. The researchers found that viewers watch violent movies for two reasons: entertaining suspense (a hedonist reason in line with the adrenaline hypothesis) and assistance with life meaning making (a eudemonic reason). Regarding the eudemonic function, the authors explain: 'participants who thought that the depiction of violence in the movie would be meaningful, moving, and thought-provoking expressed high likelihood of viewing, regardless of the anticipated amount of gore' (Bartsch and Mares, 2014: 970). Violence on the screen appeals to some audiences because it offers the feeling of a just world in which the good guys win and logic prevails. For instance, Ethan Stoneman and Joseph Packer argue that true-crime documentaries satisfy the audience's lust for retributive justice:

> The films elicit and co-create an affective economy centred around an emotional complex perhaps best described as voyeuristic vengeance (or vengeful voyeurism), an economy that solidifies the community of true-crime aficionados as a self-identifying force for social justice while

implicitly framing systemic problems as discrete errors or evils that are solvable by the actions of individual actors. (2020: 406)

This vengeful voyeurism has also been discussed in different ways. Guy Debord (2002: 7) coined the concept of *the society of the spectacle* to refer to those societies in which 'life is presented as an immense accumulation of spectacles. Everything that was directly lived is now merely represented in the distance'. In the society of the spectacle, real life becomes a commodity, and 'the real world is replaced by a selection of images which are projected above it, yet, which at the same time succeed in making themselves regarded as the epitome of reality' (ibid.: 12). Supporting Debord's thesis, Michelle Brown notes that 'American citizens access punishment removed from formal institutions like prisons' (2009: 4)—i.e., through the mediated spectacle. And, quoting an art exhibit, she continues: 'Most of what the average person knows about prison life comes from pop culture: literature, history, news and most importantly television and film ... but where do the memories come from?' (ibid.: 55).

Brown's analysis of mediated violent practices coincides with Bartsch and Mares' thesis: we try to find meaning in the incomprehensibleness of violence by consuming the simplified version of reality offered by the media. Mediated access to violence allows audiences to grasp control over the untamed and chaotic human life. In Brown's words: 'This manner of cultural engagement perhaps occurs because it is simply easier, convenient, and more accessible, but it also marks a choice. Americans choose when and under what conditions they would prefer to see' (2009: 4).

Audiences consume all kinds of violence: contemporary, fictional, and historical. Consuming historical violence links three sociological phenomena: mediated representations of society, processes of collective memory creation, and consumerism. The intersection of the first two gives rise to *media memory*: collective pasts are essentially narrated by the media. Neiger Meyers, and Zandberg (2011: 1) point out that media memory is increasingly influenced by 'the intertwined globalization and localization of the media, the numerous technological developments, and audiences' ever-widening access to media' (ibid.: 2–3). With the eruption of broadcasting technologies, smaller computing devices, and robust internet connections, media plays an ever-expanding role in the construction of memory:

> Television is the principal means by which most people learn about history today. . . . Just as television has profoundly affected and altered every aspect of contemporary life—from the family to education, government, business and religion—the medium's nonfictional and fictional portrayals have similarly transformed the way tens of millions of viewers think about historical figures. (Edgerton, 2000: 7, quoted in Neiger, Meyers, and Zandberg, 2011: 3)

However, media is not a democratic medium or one concerned with contributing to healthy social dynamics. Their commercial profits are tied to the viewers' hedonistic and eudaemonic voyeurism. As Carrabine points out, 'dynamics of celebrity, criminality, desire, fame, trauma and voyeurism' play a significant role in the production, consumption, and interpretation of mediated accounts of violence (2014: 134–5).

Violence in the media entertains, brings a sense of order and justice to life, and offers an escape from *ontological insecurity*. Individuals increasingly doubt the existence of stable self-identities due to unstable work conditions, weak welfare institutions, and individualized societies. People also fear redundancy and fail to see a safety net that can protect them. As Anthony Giddens explains, the sum of those conditions exacerbates ontological insecurity, a lack of 'confidence that most human beings have in their self-identity and the constancy of the surrounding social and material environments of action' (Giddens, 1990: 92). The sense of reality provided by violence on the screen gives viewers the feeling there is an order to society they can hold onto while everything else crumbles.

The entertaining simplicity of mediated violence offers consumers the opportunity to experience *reality*, and its many discomforts, from the position of spectators—as 'innocent outsiders, mere observers whose actions are believed to have no effect on what they see' (Sturken, 2007: 10). Violent shows provide a safe place to experience history without the burden of 'trying to understand the contexts of volatile world politics that produced the attacks' (ibid.). Narco-shows allow spectators to make a sense of the world and experience fiction as if it was reality, while allowing viewers keep a safe distance from the violence, such as to limit, or entirely deny, any moral responsibility for the suffering.

However, the rise of Netflix and other streaming platforms has introduced an additional dynamic into the practices of violence consumption, making it more embedded within people's everyday lives (Turner, 2019). Opening for possibilities of on demand binge watching, streaming platforms like Netflix bring hedonism to a new level and offer complete immersion into their products. They offer instant gratification which is in line with the values of contemporary consumerist societies.

> Consumerism appears to have become part and parcel of the very fabric of modern life. Arenas of social life that were previously free of the demands of the marketplace, including religion, have had to adapt to a world where the needs and desires of the consumer are apparently paramount. (Miles, 1998: 3)

A consumerist society creates collective and individual identities based on the commodities consumed. As (Miles, 1998) points out, consumerism is the religion of the twenty-first century: it is omnipresent and the most often used response to the troubling realities of our mundane life.

With the digitalization of many aspects of life in the twenty-first century, society has advanced into *meta-consumerism*. As *Forbes* reporter Steven Dudash (2021) points out: '[Today] you don't actually buy movies or songs anymore—you don't even have ownership. Instead, you have a subscription'. Meta-consumerism, like any other form of consumerism, is about 'posturing for your peers' (ibid.). Yet, in entertainment meta-consumerism, spectators lower their shields and are less critical of what they consume. The expression 'Netflix and chill' (besides being a slang euphemism for sex) refers to 'a routinized form of relaxation while binge-viewing Netflix' that produces a bodily and mental disconnect from the source of entertainment (Pilipets, 2019: 4).

Consumerism shapes 'who we are and how we construct our social lives, in terms of how we use such goods and services and how we relate to other people *through* such goods and services' (Miles, 1998: 3). Escobar's 'resurrection' and 'haunting' of Medellín—more than a decade after his death—has been to a large extent fuelled by the global popularity of *Narcos*. And as we saw in chapter 3, the popularity and omnipresence of narco-shows hinders many victims and survivors of drug violence from overcoming their traumas and moving on with their lives. The endless possibilities of binge watching and instant consumption make sure that the story never goes away and that wounds never heal.

How violence as a spectacle hinders trauma healing

There is only one instance in the first season of *Narcos* which (however briefly) tries to capture the victims' perspective. Gustavo Bolivar, Pablo's cousin, dies at the hands of revengeful men—the scene presents victims as violent and hungry for vengeance. This portrayal is in line with the spirit of the show: action and entertainment with questionable sociological accuracy. Yet, as noted by Uprimny Yepes and colleagues (2006), most victims and survivors crave truth, justice, reparation, and non-repetition rather than vengeance. Not one of the victims and survivors of violence in Medellín that we talked to expressed a wish for vengeance. Although the sense of impunity was difficult to accept for many, as we shall see in chapters 6 and 7, victims and survivors were mostly concerned with issues of collective memory and recognition.

For inhabitants of Medellín—including local authorities, witnesses, and victims of violence—the commodification of the city's violent past represents an affront to their attempts to deal with trauma. Global capitalism challenges the local construction of collective memory by eclipsing official history and victims' voices, and imposing its own narrative on the city. Several of our interviewees, who had lost family members to the violence, refused point-blank to watch narco-shows. They considered the consumption of such entertainment painful and disrespectful to the victims. They resented friends and acquaintances, in Colombia and elsewhere, who were fascinated by the shows. A man who had lost his wife told us:

> I don't agree with these [TV] series. And even less do I like the fact that, here in Colombia, they have used suffering as something to exploit, profit from, and export worldwide. To me, that is like a lack of respect for everyone who died because of all these situations.

Our interviewees were critical of *Narcos* not only for commodifying violence but also for idealizing Escobar, glossing over violence more generally, creating significant historical inaccuracies, and neglecting victims' perspectives. Emiliano, who lost his father to the violence, said:

> I confess that I am not a follower of those [TV] series because I do not wish to excuse crime. What I am looking for is the opposite. We want that story told from the victims' perspective—not exalting the criminal—by showing [for example] how good life could have been for these four magistrates who fought against drug trafficking.

The global productions, therefore, do not simply profit from tragic events but, in the process, change the very meaning of traumatic experiences by turning tragedy into entertainment and making light of violence. The commodification of suffering is, according to our interviewees, the biggest hindrance to healing trauma. Carlos, a judge at the time, said he did not follow the series 'for mental-health reasons'. He sensed that they were building a 'sugared story about these characters [drug lords]'. His statement points to the displacement that happens when the tragic story of the city is told by the entertainment industry: the seriousness of victims' suffering is undermined because the focus is on the perpetrators' violent but glamorous figures.

When Netflix launched *Narcos*, it orchestrated a marketing campaign which included TV and internet ads and billboards (see Figure 4.5). As a powerful example of haunting, the face of the actor portraying Escobar was splashed across billboards in numerous cities around the world. Colombian authorities reacted, among other things, by asking Madrid's city hall and Netflix to remove the poster. Former Colombian President Juan Manuel Santos said that, although he considered *Narcos* a 'very good' show, 'Pablo Escobar was a murderer who doesn't deserve to be praised as a hero under any circumstance'. He added: 'We, as Colombians, lived through the Pablo Escobar tragedy and suffer from the memories of a man who had thousands killed'. Madrid city authorities declined the request (The Local, 2016).

Netflix's campaign created a broad market for Escobar's collectibles beyond what the company's gift offered (see more in chapter 6). Luis, a close

Figure 4.5. A billboard for *Narcos* in Madrid, Spain.
Source: Photo by Senhan Bolelli/Anadolu Agency/Getty Images.

relative of one of Escobar's victims, explained how upsetting these commercial activities were to him:

> Something that affects me is seeing T-shirts with his mug shot. And stickers on the taxi cabs in the *comunas* [shanty towns]. I find that really offensive. That does hurt. The guy was a criminal, completely brutal—having him defended, celebrated, and admired, taken as a role model, offends me.

While contemporary social sciences lack the tools to understand the meaning of 'haunting' (Klima, 2019), our interviewees reveal the emotional impacts of experiencing Escobar's 'resurrection'.

Debriefing immediately after a traumatic event can aggravate post-traumatic stress disorder, depression, and anxiety. Instead, 'catharsis seems to work best once a certain period of time has passed', explains psychologist Adam Grant (2017: 240). He continues: 'expressing our thoughts and feelings about a stressful or traumatic event is most salutary after we've had some time to process the event, when we're not blinded by anger or consumed by distress' (ibid.). When victims of narco-violence started to come out with their narratives, *Narcos* came and took away their possibility of *telling* their stories. As *Narcos* became the global reference to learn about Medellín and its violent past, victims saw the empathy with which the world could receive their grief reduced.

Narco shows hinder trauma healing by silencing the victims *and* through their explicit celebration of Escobar. Re-traumatization refers to the reactivation of trauma symptoms via thoughts, memories, or feelings related to the past traumatic experience (Schippert, Grov, and Bjørnnes, 2021). Constant exposure to *trauma triggers*—the internal or external cues that symbolize or resemble aspects of the traumatic event (Todd-Kvam and Goyes, 2023)—re-traumatizes. Even *discriminatory gestures*—' "minor", interpersonal incidents [which] can seem slight on the surface, yet [have great] emotional toll' (Hart, 2019: 6)—can trigger post-traumatic stress responses and have an 'annihilating power' (ibid.).

Movies about violence are not necessarily harmful to the victims who had suffered it in real life. Films that portray victims being hurt and vilified, but which also show their struggle and eventual survival, offer the survivors a model for hope in which they can see themselves reflected and gain inspiration from (Podraza, 2021). Even representing the effects of trauma can help those in the audience who have experienced psychological trauma to understand the changes their *self* might be undergoing (Spallacci, 2019). The problem lies in the productions that deal with traumatic events without reflecting on the product's potential consequences for the victims. Psychologist Tiarra McKinney (2020) asserts that 're-traumatization by film and entertainment media can occur when watching depictions of violence, abuse, or neglect, especially if these traumas have been experienced'.

Narcos' emphasis on the actions of perpetrators and supposed heroes diverts the voice and focus away from the victims. The show's interest in entertaining through action-filled scenes leaves no space for critical reflection about the aftermath of narco-victimization. *Narcos*' global popularity diminishes victims' possibility of being heard when telling their stories. The show actively hinders trauma-healing processes by flooding society with trauma triggers.

The negative impact of the show goes beyond how it might affect the victims and audiences. As we show in the next chapter, the production team itself suffered as a result of the re-enactment of the sexism and racism informing the series.

5

'There are many uncomfortable dynamics in a production'

Toxic masculinity and violence

The term 'toxic masculinity' has been trending in pop culture from 2017 onwards and has spearheaded a new feminist moment reinvigorated by Beyoncé and other major cultural figures (Harrington, 20: 346). *Narcos* has not escaped scrutiny, with critics accusing the show of 'uplifting toxic masculinity'.[1] Although Escobar's masculinity—in real life and as portrayed in *Narcos*—is undoubtedly toxic, the notion of toxic masculinity builds on an individualizing toxic/healthy binary that serves to reproduce existing gender hierarchies (ibid.: 346–7). 'Toxic masculinity', as an analytical category, fails to take into account broader cultural forces and structural arrangements that support the harmful genderization of society. In other words, Escobar's gender identity is not an exclusive product of his individual flaws, but rather, it can be said that his real-life and on-screen personas incarnate widespread social views and cultural ideals about gender that have a long and troubled history. In this chapter, we trace the lines of continuity between Escobar's real-life gender practices to their cinematic representations, and, furthermore, show how unhealthy gender roles even shaped the working dynamics during the production of *Narcos*. Our main aim in this chapter is to document how narco-shows' commodification of trauma and branding of Escobar not only re-victimizes the survivors and hinders individual and collective healing through the glorification of the perpetrator, but also perpetuates gender and racial stereotypes.

[1] For further information, see comment in Luis García, 'Pop Culture Critique: *Narcos*', *Bartleby* (2017), https://www.bartleby.com/essay/Midterm-Pop-Culture-Critique-Narcos-PKGBC3BYS4FP, accessed on 15 February 2023.

Victimhood, Memory, and Consumerism. Katja Franko and David R. Goyes, Oxford University Press.
 DOI: 10.1093/oso/9780192874115.003.0005

Living the Al Capone and James Bond life

The Escobar Family Museum we visited during our fieldwork bears witness to the centrality of gender to the understanding of Pablo Escobar and the 'Escobar brand'. Escobar idolized Al Capone and James Bond, and spent part of his wealth acquiring objects belonging to these 'action heroes'. Several types of vehicles—cars, motorcycles, planes, and even a wetbike—populate the museum. Escobar aimed to shape his persona following the examples of the action heroes whose vehicles he collected.

Al Capone, a mafia boss who ruled Chicago's underworld in the 1920s, stands in our culture as the paradigmatic gangster. Al Capone's identity, according to journalist William Helmer (2011), spun around violent masculinity. The biography's title—*Al Capone and His American Boys*—signals the importance of a macho persona for Al Capone and the binary world he lived in: girls entertained at the club; boys carried out special (violent) assignments. However, the mafia boss, as a macho persona, pre-existed Al Capone. 'Al Capone is said to have crafted his persona ... after the characters in one of the earliest cinematic forays in the [mafia] genre: D.W. Griffith's *The Musketeers of Pig Alley*', writes media analyst Michael Posner (2016: 185).

The exhibits in the family museum also reveal Escobar's yearning to live like Ian Fleming's character, James Bond (see Figure 5.1). Bond has been described as a 'suave, sophisticated super spy' (Gerrard, 2020: 1). He is a secret agent working for the British crown, who stops enemies of the empire from achieving world domination. In all the different forms in which his story is told, ranging from books to movies to comics, Bond takes on an 'emphatic version of the promiscuous playboy' that lives in a world where 'sex, snobbery and sadism' mark male-female relationships (Shail, 2020: 50–1). Although these expressions of masculinity, like Al Capone's, rely on 'violence and power to exert dominance' (ibid.), Bond's character also embodies perceptions of effortless elegance. As O'Brien observes, Bond's gender identity is best captured by the concept of *suave machismo*: 'a sharp-dressed man who spins, makes his jacket twirl, carries a gun, and shots directly at the camera' (2020: 104). Women, in the Bond franchise, are to be 'seduced, subdued and converted ... or failing that, destroyed' (Bassil-Morozow,

Figure 5.1. A replica of James Bond's jet ski at the Escobar Museum in Medellín.
Source: © rocharibeiro/Shutterstock.

2020: 101). These female characters that fall for Bond have contradictory qualities: 'tough, strong, intellectual, successful and dangerous yet also feminine, sexual, beautiful and exotic' (ibid.: 92). Women's bodies in the franchise are provocative 'silhouetted, naked or semi-naked bodies' (O'Brien, 2020: 101). In the Bond universe, women spin around the male hero's world.

Performing like the ideal suave macho, Escobar reified women around him, he objectified them. He also left a society impregnated with the idea that men are violent, and women are voluptuous. Escobar had a system in place to receive 'a steady supply of adolescent virgins'; predominantly 'high school students, volleyball players, and models, with the common denominator of youth and sexual innocence' (Pobutsky, 2020: 166). 'Pablo would tell the *muchachos* what he wanted—the most beautiful girls from the colleges of Medellín, and how many' (Castro Caycedo, 2012: 41 quoted in Pobutsky, 2020: 167). Aldona Pobutsky explains the role of women in narco culture:

> Escobar and his entourage had the buying power to pick and choose virtually any girl they wanted. In the code of consumer values, narco wealth represented distinction and social status, thereby prompting the underprivileged (but not only the underprivileged) to sell themselves to the highest bidder regardless of the consequences. On various occasions Popeye [Escobar's hitman] commented on how woman's physical attractiveness was directly proportional to the narco cachet and how perfectly sculpted mafia dolls were their sought-after partners: 'Women always were the warrior's trophy' and 'the more guerrero, the hotter the woman'. (ibid.: 167)

Soon, 'the narco taste for excess and artificial enhancement spilt over to society as a whole' (ibid.: 168), becoming the gender element of what Oscar Mejía termed the *narco culture*: 'exhibition, of luxury, of "plastic" women, of easy money' (Mejía Quintana, 2018: 27).

Although the notion of 'narco culture' may indicate a set of male-centred values pertaining to Medellín's drug cartels, its inspirations and cultural roots go deeper and farther away. Al Capone and James Bond inspired Pablo Escobar; D.W. Griffith inspired Al Capone; Dashiell Hammett inspired Ian Fleming's fictional hero. We could keep excavating the cultural references through which men have inspired men to treat women as objects of domination. Toxic masculinity is not—as the concept indicates—the matter of a few men 'going wrong', but a widespread ideology. Escobar's efforts to appropriate objects belonging to Western cultural icons, such as Al Capone and Bond, indicate his wish to emulate a hegemonic male role model, frequently reproduced and incarnated in our culture.

To capture these deep-seated cultural perceptions, sociologist Raewyn Connell (1995) coined the term *hegemonic masculinity*. Unlike toxic masculinity, which conceptualizes toxicity as an exception, hegemonic masculinity captures the widespread harm of dominant gender roles. 'Masculinity that occupies the hegemonic position in a given pattern of gendered relations, a position always contestable' (ibid.: 76), explains Connell, and adds that the concept of *masculinity* exists in opposition to *femininity*. With roots in the North Atlantic region around the sixteenth century, hegemonic masculinity was developed and reinforced during the Renaissance secular culture, the Protestant

Reformation, the colonial creation of overseas empires, the establishment and consolidation and growth of capitalism, and 'the onset of large-scale European civil war' (ibid.: 188). Inspiring a burgeoning field of contemporary gender studies, Connell's analysis reveals how gender roles formed in the modern North Atlantic are a product of longstanding social developments.

The construction of masculinity, in opposition to femininity, became a normative constraint dictating 'what men ought to be' (ibid.: 70). Beyond becoming prisons for individuals captured in oppressive gender roles, this gender order significantly impacts society, shaping power, production, and emotional relations. It implies 'the overall subordination of women and dominance of men' (ibid.: 74); the differential 'allocation of tasks, sometimes reaching extraordinary fine detail'; and, in emotional realms, manhood is connected to sexual desire, while femininity to submission. Hegemonic masculinity rewards heterosexuality, violence, cynical rationality, and power. The gangster persona of Al Capone, the suave machismo of James Bond, and the conquistador masculinity of Escobar give continuity to a harmful identity that the hegemonic gender order ascribes to manhood.

Crime films have, since the inception of cinema, as Yvonne Jewkes (2015: 197) points out, 'presented an archetype of individualistic masculinity set against larger forces.' This is not to say that all portrayals of male heroes in the movies are the same. Yet, the gangster's hyper-violence is not simply an individual shortcoming, as the notion of toxic masculinity might suggest, but points to pervasive historic and cultural influences. In *Narcos*, Pablo Escobar (portrayed by Wagner Moura) physically and emotionally 'dominates' his lovers, thereby enacting the binary dominant/submissive gender stereotype perpetuated by the entertainment industry and embedded in institutional practices and popular culture (see Figure 5.2).

Branding the macho conquistador

Well before the release of *Narcos* by Netflix, commentators critiqued the narco-genre for its problematic gender performativity. Giraldo (2015: 79) found that narco-telenovelas 'reinforce a male subject as the "alpha"

Figure 5.2. Wagner Moura (as Pablo Escobar) 'dominating' Stephanie Sigman (as Valeria Velez) in *Narcos*, season 1, episode 3.
Source: Netflix Studios, LLC.

individual whose value is highly dependent on his power—symbolic and material—over other masculine subjects and over *all* female subjects'. Following the hegemonic gender order, women stand in opposition to men and are 'frequently seduced by the symbolic and material power of the hyper-masculine drug lords' (ibid.). Giraldo analysed the Colombian telenovelas *El Cartel* (2008) and *El Capo* (2009) (see chapter 4), but her findings are likely to apply to most other narco-shows. Miller, Barrios, and Arroyave analysed 532 programs screened on national Colombian television networks to examine gender portrayals in the country's narco-telenovelas. They found that:

> There were more male than female characters per program across all genres. This finding holds true for protagonists, antagonists, and secondary characters, on both national and regional channels. Such figures follow a well-established narco-telenovela formula: an immensely wealthy capo, an adolescent assassin, a young beautiful sex worker, an ambitious police officer, a corrupt politician, and bloody paramilitary .... Not only are women unequally unrepresented on and off screen, but when they *do* appear, they are represented negatively. For instance, there is a strong tendency to portray women as

victims or weak and in need of help, support, or succour of men. (2019: 355)

The analyses conducted by Giraldo (2015) and Miller and colleagues (2019) of Colombian narco-telenovelas also apply to international productions, including *Narcos* and the Escobar-themed movies.

Here is a list of the women who appear in season one of *Narcos*:

- Pablo's wife;
- Pablo's mother;
- the DEA agent's wife;
- a journalist (who becomes Escobar's lover);
- an M-19 revolutionary (who was the lover of a guerrilla leader and then of a DEA agent);
- the sister of the Cali Cartel leaders (who becomes the lover of Gustavo Gaviria);
- prostitutes;
- drug smugglers; and
- Diana Turbay, a journalist who displays some signs of intelligence (and who is swiftly killed off in the show).

In *Narcos*, men are heterosexual, violent, strategists, and powerful. Women are men's appendages: their wives, mothers, or sexual partners. In their analysis of *Narcos*, Lacalle and Solá (2018: 185) found that the show 'creates a narrative constellation structured around some masculine characters (Pablo Escobar, Murphy, Peña . . .) where some secondary female characters emerge in relation to the former'.

Lacalle and Solá identify two main types of women in the show (also reflected in the list above): (1) lovers, who 'are narratively constructed around their aesthetic contribution to the male trafficker; they represent a tribute to the power and wealth of the narco-bosses' (ibid.: 187); and (2) wives/mothers/daughters, who 'belong to the archetype of women that are the private property of the husband' (ibid.: 188). Similarly, Marina Soler Jorge (2021: 6) suggested that, in *Narcos*, the male drug lords 'largely assume this ideal of the self-made man, because they are constructed as successful men who are never satisfied with what they have achieved', and so 'aggressivity and success in the market combine in *Narcos* in the construction of male characters identified above all with hegemonic masculinity'. Meanwhile, 'the female characters of *Narcos* are largely submissive towards men, whether as well-behaved and understanding lovers, wives or mothers'. This effectively involves a symbolic universe in which male domination is nearly unbreakable, indicates Jorge (ibid.: 10).

These critical observations were supported by the insights of the show's creators we interviewed. Susana, a scriptwriter for *Narcos* said:

> The view of the women in the show is either as caretakers or prostitutes. I mean, you are either the wife of Pablo (she was a saint) or you are the character of the journalist (who is a prostitute). Or you are the character of Adri Arjona, who was literally a prostitute. And [the male producers] wrote the scripts ... for example, there was a time when my boss wrote in the first episode 'there are a bunch of prostitutes', and all the Latin American characters were called 'prostitute, police, etc.'. Nobody was human.

The perpetuation of the gender hierarchy happens, partly, by way of glorifying male violence. Many of our interviewees were deeply upset about this and thought the series glorified violence. Isabella, the daughter of an influential politician in Medellín, lived her childhood surrounded by bodyguards. On many occasions, she witnessed attacks on her own life and her family's—on more than one occasion, her body was covered in someone else's blood. In an interview, she told: '[I]t seems to me that [*Narcos*] portrays as heroes those who should not be portrayed that way. It glorifies those whom we must not glorify. We create violent masculine role models.'

Not only the *content* of the show perpetuates Escobar's macho masculinity, but the conditions on the set also reflected a patriarchal order. Sexism dominated the production. Valeria, a Colombian set assistant, confirmed the gendered task distribution during the production of *Narcos:*

> There are many female audio-visual producers in Colombia. But those in charge—those who have the financial muscle, those who earn good money, and those who decide—were invariably men. I wish, at some

> point, we redress the legacy of toxic masculinity that *Narcos* left. We need more female characters and above all more workplaces that value the contribution of women.

Similarly, in their analysis of Colombian telenovelas, Miller and colleagues (2019: 354) found that 'stories are told from masculinist perspectives. Men directed four out of five telenovelas at regional and national levels, and provided three-quarters of the scripts.'

Our interviewees also bore witness to the discrimination and degradation of women on the set. Susana continued: 'I would even say that they treated us, women, in the same way [as narcos treated women in the show].' While we omit further details Susana shared with us, seeking to protect her anonymity, Valeria told us in detail what transpired on the set:

> It was very uncomfortable. Many times I felt threatened. There are reasons why I don't want to work again on something like that. [The men on the set] sexualized us a lot. I did not even feel comfortable working in jeans; I wanted to use a pair of baggy overalls. I tried to establish boundaries, but there are many uncomfortable dynamics in production. I try to deny that that happens.

These experiences resonate with the issues raised by the #MeToo campaign protesting the working conditions of women in the film industry. In the wake of allegations of sexual harassment and assault levelled against the Hollywood producer Harvey Weinstein in 2017, actress Alyssa Milano invited 'women to share their own experiences of sexual violence using #MeToo' on Twitter (Fileborn and Loney-Howes, 2019: 3). The campaign took off, intending to challenge the assumption that 'rape, sexual assault and sexual harassment are the products of the random acts of individual men who are regarded as "sick" or "social deviants" and unknown to their victims' (ibid.: 1), but rather a cultural problem. The movement was not only 'a welcome contemporary addition to the long struggle to end sexual harassment against women' (Nakashima Brock and Brooks Thistlethwaite, 2020: 205), but also challenged broader power inequalities between men and women in the film industry.

Hegemonic masculinity in the South

Gender relations, however, acquire an additional dimension in the Global South: masculinities and femininities become more exotic. As Connell explains:

> Because gender is a way of structuring social practices in general, not a special type of practice, it is unavoidably involved with other social structures. It is now common to say that gender 'intersects'—better, interacts—with race and class. We might add that it constantly interacts with nationality or position in the world order. This fact also has strong implications for the analysis of masculinity. White men's masculinities, for instance, are constructed not only in relation to white women but also in relation to black men. (1995: 75)

A vibrant body of feminist scholarship has in the past decades critically examined the position of women of colour and the social inequalities produced by the intersections of race, gender, and class (Carbado et al., 2013). Although initially focused on the legal structures supporting marginalization and inequality, particularly in the context of domestic violence, this influential body of work has pointed out the importance of paying attention not only to gendered but also to racialized scripts.

Some of our interviewees were deeply aware of this and were critical not only of gender dynamics in the show, but also of racial stereotypes in the productions. Valeria, the Colombian set assistant, told us that what she saw in the production of *Narcos* reminded her of the stereotypical portrayal of Colombians in Hollywood:

> [In the 2000 movie *Bedazzled*—see Figure 5.3] Elizabeth Hurley grants the main character seven wishes. He replies, 'I want to be rich to conquer the woman I love.' She says, '[G]ranted, you can be a millionaire'—but she played the devil and trickster, so she added—'but you will be Pablo Escobar'. Then the character is transformed into Pablo Escobar, living in Colombia, in the middle of the jungle, snorting cocaine. I watched that movie ten years ago. That is how Colombia was represented then. I keep watching it. Hollywood has always exoticized Colombia. They

Figure 5.3. Brendan Fraser playing Pablo Escobar in the movie *Bedazzled* (2000).
Source: © 20th Century Fox Film Corp./Courtesy Everett Collection/NTB.

> misrepresent Colombia as much as they represent Africa and Asia. These are very offensive representations. It is sad.

Wearing a tight red jumpsuit with a plunging neckline, Elizabeth Hurley plays an exaggerated stereotype of a sexualized woman. Fraser, her male counterpart, is a similarly inflated parody of a Colombian drug lord. Valeria's mention of *Bedazzled* in connection with *Narcos* indicates her unease, not only with the gendered dynamics on the set, but also with Hollywood's portrayal of Colombians as the drug addicted, unruly other.

Hollywood is not only marked by power inequalities between men and women, but also by global inequalities. Its economic clout promotes a narrative that defines other, poorer, parts of the world. Almost two decades after her exploration of hegemonic masculinity, Connell (2014a: 217) highlighted that 'discussions of globalisation and masculinity need[ed] to be reconsidered through a critical examination of the global economy of knowledge' as one of the social structures with which gender intersects. With that, Connell recognized that much of the conceptualization of hegemonic masculinity was scripted by the Global North. Connell explained that because, overwhelmingly, social theory is produced in the Global North, scholars are socialized into what Connell terms 'reading from the centre' (Connell, 2006: 237) also when it comes to gender studies.

Connell's analysis points to the central role of unequal economic relations in perpetuating unequal gender relations: 'It is transnational corporate businessmen rather than local patriarchs who are now the most powerful group in the world' (2014b: 522). Globalization has spread Western hegemonic gender hierarchies to all corners of the world, partly through the global corporate economy: 'some recent studies have traced the gendered character of markets themselves as social institutions. An aggressive, misogynist occupational culture appears in arenas such as commodity and currency trading' (Connell, 2016: 312).

The global hegemonic masculinity project works on two levels. The normative level marks what men should aspire to be. The descriptive level assigns gender roles to people across the world. Western ideals determine the normative level; racialized stereotypes shape the descriptive level. Both follow the tracks of colonialism and coloniality. As Bhabha (2004 [1994]: 96) explains, 'the construction of the colonial subject in discourse, and the exercise of colonial power through discourse, demands an articulation of forms of difference—racial and sexual'. Coloniality of power allowed the imposition of a global gender system, and the existence of a global gender system secures the perpetuation of the coloniality of power (Lugones, 2007, 2014). Economic profit is also involved in the colonial conceptualization of gender (Quijano, 2000, 2007). Gender, in the colonial system, followed an economical script, 'the reduction of gender to the private, to control over sex and its resources' (Lugones, 2007: 202). Colonized humans 'were understood as animals in the deep sense of "without gender"' (ibid.): sexually marked but without more sophisticated traits of gender. Gender, in colonial locations, equates to assigned enlarged sexualized traits, part of a mass identity (Lugones, 2014). The gender order in the Global South entails the exoticizing and othering of hegemonic masculinities and femininities. In the hegemonic global gender order, Western standards are the *normal* and everything outside is exotic.

Exoticizing the post-colonial Other

North America dominates the statistics of investment in motion pictures with US$149.3 billion in 2020, followed by Europe with US$32.6b, and Asia with US$27.7 billion; Latin America (US$5.2b), Africa (US$2.8b), and Oceania (US$0.9b) trail behind (Purely Streanomics, 2021). Our interviewees from the entertainment industry were acutely aware of the economic supremacy of the North, which they saw played out in the production through the unequal power relations between the local and international members. There was a clear divide in the decision-making on the set of *Narcos* between foreign staff and the locals: bosses came from the Global North, assistants from the Global South.

A European producer, Ignacio, told us that 'all the bosses on *Narcos* came from abroad. The director of photography was Brazilian, the director of special effects was Mexican, and the coordinator was Spanish. In general, for the big productions, the leaders come from abroad.' Hector, in charge of the budget and administration, declared that 'the heads of almost all departments were foreigners: the customs director was Spanish, Ignacio was European, and he brought his team … and then those below were Colombians.' When we interviewed them, we also asked about the scriptwriters. 'All were [North] American,' replied Hector. There was, of course, one exception—Susana, who explained that she was the only local scriptwriter among the decision-makers. Valeria, a local assistant, told us that while the heads were foreigners, the workforce was Colombian: 'the audiovisual producer was Colombian. The contractor doing the hard work in Colombia was Colombian.'

According to Gokul (2019), 'the penetration of foreign capital into the hinterlands' also leads to a cultural dominance of Northern scripts akin to an internal 'cultural co-option.' The North influences the tone of Southern productions. Several of our interviewees felt that the unequal division of labour in the production had an impact on the narrative framing of the story. Colombians are portrayed as exotic, violent and uncivilized others as seen through 'civilized eyes.' The story of *Narcos* is, as we have seen, told through the voices of two U.S. law enforcement agents.

The opening line in the show says: 'Imagine you were born in a poor family, in a poor city, in a poor country, and by the time you were twenty-eight years old you have so much money you can't even count it.'[2] The narrator invites viewers to imagine they live in a country that resembles their vision of Colombia—a scene that is exemplary of the permanent othering happening in *Narcos*. The opening line uses the word *imagine*, implying that most global viewers of the series live in high-income countries and have to stretch their imagination to grasp what being poor is like. The narrator then continues: 'What do you do? You make your dreams come true. Problem is, nobody can control the dreams they have. Especially if you were Pablo Escobar. Especially if you grew up in Colombia.' The reference to (a lack of) *control* taps into a longstanding cultural imaginary of inhabitants of the Global South as unruly. Indeed, Latin America is often represented in popular culture as epitomizing 'poverty, a rural environment, shantytowns, exotic indigenous, economic and technological backwardness, the Catholic religion's governance of every aspect of life, personality cult, dictatorship, authoritarianism, corruption and disorganization, machismo, violence in the streets, drug trafficking, and revolutionary movements' (Alarcón, 2014: 71).

Media play a central role in maintaining the existing stereotypes, which continue to dominate global imagination and are strongly present in the framing of *Narcos*. In a vast study conducted by the National Hispanic Media Coalition (2012), in which 900 non-Latin North Americans filled out a questionnaire and 3000 non-Latin North Americans registered opinions about Latinos in open-ended responses, researchers found that media contribute to seeing Latinos as disorganized in all areas of life. The most common tags associated with Latin Americans were '[they] don't keep up their homes', 'have too many children', are 'less educated' (ibid.: 4). Media have successfully naturalized the view of the West as normal and the periphery as exotic. 'Access to a multitude of images and texts' that give inhabitants of the Global South 'a vivid sense of their own locale as "Other" to the North' means, arguably, that even inhabitants of the periphery embrace the equation West = normal, periphery = exotic (Nimis, 2014: 1).

[2] 'The Men of Always', *Narcos*, season 1, episode 3, 28 August 2015, *Netflix*, https://www.netflix.com/watch/80025315?trackId=14277281&tctx=-97%2C-97%2C%2C%2C%2C%2C%2C%2C%2CVideo%3A80025172%2CdetailsPagePlayButton.

Observers point out that in neo-colonial locations—including Latin America—cultural, racial, and gender stereotypes are drawn together in ways that connect violence with cultural identity (Evans, 2020; Hastie, 2020). As Berg (2002: 68) observes, in Western movies and TV shows, Latinos are often assigned roles of *bandidos*:

> [D]irty and unkempt, usually displaying an unshaven face, missing teeth, and dishevelled, oily hair. . . . Behaviourally, vicious, cruel, treacherous, shifty, and dishonest; psychologically irrational, overly emotional, and quick to resort to violence.

Media thus play a central role in maintaining the existing stereotypes of the West as 'normal' and the periphery as unruly, sexually promiscuous, and exotic. Such an approach, which builds on cultural essentialism, locates the source of the problem in historically established patterns of behaviour and 'lets politics and politicians off the hook' (Scott, 1997: 142 quoted in Evans, 2020: 57).

Narcos, like most other Hollywood productions, offers little critical reflection on the role of the U.S.-sponsored war on drugs in the escalation of violence in Medellín, while framing the story as a case of Colombian magical realism[3] (as stated in its title sequence). Clara López Alcaide and colleagues (2018) found that 40 per cent of people who watch *Narcos* consider narco-violence as a natural, constitutive part of Colombia. And, according to Sallenave (2018: 140), *Narcos* legitimizes the construction of the *other* as the enemy(s) who endangers the unquestionable nature of the good. The series thus promotes U.S. foreign policy values, while putting in place negative portrayals of Latinos as the perceived exotic Other (Hachenberger, 2019). In the process, Medellín and its inhabitants are transformed from victims into collective culprits. By equating the city with a culture of violent Latino criminality, the violence experienced by its inhabitants becomes a sign of their exotic otherness. As we shall see in chapter 7, the city authorities have made great efforts to obtain international solidarity for the loss of life that has taken place in the city, albeit

[3] The term magical realism is a reference to the literary style of Gabriel Garcia Marquez, one of the most celebrated Colombian writers. In *Narcos*, the quote frames this way of loosely relating to reality as a Colombian national trait.

unsuccessfully. A question can be therefore asked to what extent this exclusion from the cosmopolitan 'we' has been reinforced by the portrayal of the city's inhabitants as the violent and exotic Other.

These cultural dynamics have had a long presence in the debates in scholarly literature and have often been articulated through the concept of *orientalism*. Proposed by Edward Said (2019 [1978]: 201), orientalism critiques 'the varying degrees of projected inferiority and strength, the range of work done, the kinds of characteristic features ascribed to the Orient: all these testify to a willed imaginative and geographic division made between East and West'. Following a similar line of inquiry, the notion of Eurocentrism, coined by Egyptian economist Samir Amin (2009 [1988]: 7), refers to 'an apparently coherent and holistic theory based on the hypothesis that there are cultural invariants able to persist through and beyond possible transformations in economic, social, and political forces' that become the 'main driving force of inevitably quite different historical trajectories' between the West and the rest. Indian critical theorist Homi Bhabha (2004 [1994]: 94) found that the colonial world order spins around a practice of othering: 'An important feature of colonial discourse is its dependence on the concept of "fixity" in the ideological construction of otherness. Fixity, as the sign of cultural/historical/racial difference.' Recently, Yuval Harari (2011: 338) coined the concept of *culturism*, the assumption of 'contrasting merits of diverse human groups based on their historical differences'.

Orientalism and *othering*, facilitated by the economic and cultural dominance of Northern actors, inform the framing of *Narcos*. As Gokul (2019) points out, films that are appreciated in contemporary culture are 'Eurocentric or Hollywood-centric', and movies from the Global South 'seldom receive the kind of acceptance the Anglo-American English movies get across the world'. The exotic machismo present in *Narcos* has, furthermore, implications in the everyday lives of Medellín's inhabitants.

Immortalizing macho men, submissive women, and exotic others

The cultural influence of the Escobar's brand has by now penetrated deeply national cultural narratives. On 12 April 2022, the song "Tendencia

Mundial" ["Global Trend"], by Ovy on the Drums, became Colombia's fourth most popular song. Until that date, the song had been played 14 million times on Spotify, and its video had been watched 18 million times on YouTube. The song belongs to the popular genre of reggaeton. Like most songs in the genre, the lyrics tell the story of a man promising to *conquer* a woman, the way Pablo Escobar conquered Virginia Vallejo. The success of "Tendencia Mundial" signals the penetration of Escobar—the brand with its component of exotic masculinity—into Colombian pop culture. Escobar's macho persona became a role model to follow. How does *Narcos*' representation of masculinity affect the identities of the Colombians it seeks to represent?

In our fieldwork, seeking to capture what people usually do and how it relates to narco-shows, beyond observing the field, we talked with taxi drivers in Medellín. They gave us insightful views of the dynamics of the city via thick descriptions. They work between ten and sixteen hours a day, navigating all corners of the city, picking up passengers from all social groups, and observing the streets day and night. They map the city—geographically and symbolically. They have provided important insights into how narco-series shape the gender identities of the city inhabitants.[4]

We asked taxi drivers whether they thought that narco-shows shape how people behave in Medellín. We did not ask directly about gender roles or the exoticization of identities, but their responses invariably dealt with both phenomena. Juan, who had driven a taxicab for over a decade, told us that 'the boys behave differently, they have a taste for money and women . . . women are interested in the narco, in the criminal'. Guillermo, a driver in his fifties who moved to Medellín thirty-five years ago, said,

[4] Decades before us, Fred Davis (1959: 158), a member of the second Chicago School, proposed that because drivers 'act as if [they are] merely an extension of the automobile [they] operate', they have a 'splendid vantage point from which to witness a rich variety of human schemes and entanglements'. The position of taxi drivers, observed Davis, makes them approachable 'as someone to whom intimacies can be revealed and opinions forthrightly expressed with little fear of rebuttal, retaliation, or disparagement'. In other words, the anonymous nature of interactions with taxi drivers affords them 'glimpses of the private lives of individuals which few in our society, apart from psychiatrists and clergy, are privileged to note as often or in such great variety'. Flávio Silviera and Pedro Soares (2012) further documented that taxi drivers engage in mapping the cities in which they operate, due to their constant and extensive transit. The mapping carried out by taxi drivers is as geographical as it is symbolic: their trips around the city and their interactions with passengers of all walks of life put them in contact with the 'social imaginary'. Taxi drivers, by dint of their endless social and geographical trips around the city and beyond, encounter some widely shared—as well as deviant—social representations articulated by passengers from all social classes and backgrounds.

'young men watch these shows and they want to copy everything... they smoke a joint and believe they can replicate what Escobar did'. Guillermo also told us that 'girls from twelve years old and onwards go to the Lleras Park hoping to meet a man with money'. Angel, a middle-aged driver, elaborated:

ANGEL: Women want to find new narcos for the sake of money. They alter their bodies to attract men with money. Young men will do anything to get money and women.

DAVID: And do you think that the narco-telenovelas are to blame?

ANGEL: Yes, prostitution has skyrocketed. Girls from a very young age believe their virginity is worth a lot of money. Young women have that stuck in their heads now. They shape their personality around that belief, and that is because of the shows. That affects the society. And what do you think gringos come here for? For the prostitutes. They want to know Pablo's story and find themselves in a bedroom with two or three prostitutes just as Pablo did. And this is because the young had no experience of [Escobar's] era, and they don't know what things were like. They want to get easy money without much effort. Like yesterday, outside the Santa Lucia metro station, one kid entered a shop and killed two people. A boy just thirteen years old! The boys see all those shows and get ideas.

Many of our interviewees, not just the taxi drivers, expressed alarm about how *Narcos* immortalize violent macho identities for men and submissive and voluptuous roles for women. Valeria, the Colombian who worked as a set assistant on the production of *Narcos*, worries about how the portrayal of women in narco-shows affects society:

> I studied at a women's school in Bogotá. The school also had campuses in Barranquilla and Medellín. There were many problems on the Medellín campus: anorexia, girls dying because they underwent cosmetic surgeries... all that comes from a culture that sees women as trophies. That is something that has existed in society for a long time, but what is troubling is that we keep reproducing those models in *Narcos*.

Many other residents of Medellín, particularly those directly affected by violence, have expressed concerns about the impact of narco-series on the values of the younger generations. Alberto, the son of a prominent criminal justice official who, like his father, had to leave the country due to threats upon his life, was concerned about how the celebration of violent masculinity and the lack of other models might affect youth:

> Instead of so many cheap stories about shootings and women, about mafia and easily earned richness, we should see something else. I mean, what did those men give to the country? How is it helpful to us? Aren't portraits of those who gave their lives for the country more valuable? We don't find [media representations of those who advocated against narco power] because I think that is not commercially profitable. Virtue does not sell as well as we would like.

He was pained by the fact that bandits enjoy sex appeal among global audiences and lamented the fact that the assassinated judges have not been turned into heroes. He and his family addressed a letter of complaint to the *Netflix* producers: 'we said that [the show] was giving a bad example to the country's youth, and that we do not agree with that'.

Media scholars have highlighted the cultural importance of mediated portrayals of society—including depictions of violence (Rafter, 2007; Jewkes, 2015)—even though the effect films have on individuals is far from clear-cut and has been fiercely debated. It is methodologically difficult to 'rigorously establish straightforward causal relationships between images and effects' (Reiner, 2002: 377). This has led some to conclude that media do not play a significant role in the lives of the spectators (Reiner, 2002). Yet, numerous empirical studies have confirmed that media have an impact on the identities and perceptions of their audiences (Agrawal et al., 2021), and the whole field of marketing has developed based on the science of influencing buyers (Heath and Heath, 2010). The difficulty resides in assessing how an audience interprets the mediated messages. Members of the Chicago School have pointed out that how media affect audiences depends on their background and on how they consume messages (Buxton, 2008). According to Guillermo Orozco Gómez:

> 'Reception' cannot be understood as a mere receiving but as an interaction, always mediated by diverse sources and materially, cognitively and emotionally contextualised, which plays along a complex process situated in various contexts and includes strategies and negotiations from the subjects with a media referent and result in myriad appropriations that go from the mere reproduction to resistance and contestation. (2001: 23)

In other words, the consumption of messages disseminated by the media is relational and interactive (Barbero and Rey, 1999). People filter the media message through their identities and backgrounds. Other humans are thus central to the process of interpreting the mediated messages. A healthy approach to studying the effect of media on individuals and society is, therefore, to 'avoid trying to show that what people *believe* changes as a result of *particular media contents*' and instead investigate 'what people *regularly do*, and the conditions under which they are able to act' (Couldry, 2012: 84). We can then interpret the influence of media indirectly, by checking how it naturalizes 'certain dimensions, categorical features and "facts" that disable alternative accounts of the world' (ibid.).

As we shall see in the next chapter, the cultural narratives surrounding drugs and drug dealing, as well as the cultural roles ascribed to women and men, are an important legacy of the narco-series—something that a number of survivors care deeply about as narratives provided by entertainment corporations continue to shape the society they live in.

6
Dark consumerism and the trauma(tic) economy

'Kidnapped memory'

The profitability of the Escobar's brand is visible not only in the global popularity of *Narcos*, but also in Medellín's everyday economy which shapes the lived reality of the city's residents. The appropriation of the city's traumatic memories by the forces of commercialism goes beyond on-screen narratives about the violent past, and has become intricately intertwined with the lived materiality of the city. This chapter shows how Medellín's residents are surrounded by, and drawn into, a commercial web centred on the 'Escobar experience', which includes tours and souvenirs as well as a supply of drugs and sexual services. These practices and commodities are expressions of a popular culture that has a voracious appetite for stories about violence and sees them as a resource for commercial exploitation.

This chapter shows how the popularity of media productions has contributed to the growth of dark tourism in Medellín. We rely on statistical data provided by the mayor's office; ethnographic observation of narco-tours; and interviews with local residents and taxi drivers, who speak about the demands made by foreign visitors seeking to explore and re-enact Escobar's life. We also offer visual material from our visits to Escobar's shrines, such as his grave and residences, to show burgeoning dark tourism as well as the popularity of Escobar collectibles available on the market. What kind of impact do these commercial activities have on the personal and collective memories of the period of violence in the 1980s–1990s? What happens when a perpetrator becomes branded as an action hero, and inspires a global production of merchandise? How do these processes of global and local commercial appropriation of memory

Victimhood, Memory, and Consumerism. Katja Franko and David R. Goyes, Oxford University Press.
 DOI: 10.1093/oso/9780192874115.003.0006

affect the victims and residents who had experienced the violence first-hand? Moreover, how do they shape the present local identities of young generations?

Most societies address their traumatic, violent past through official discourses and by shaping the cultural memory of past events (Connerton, 1989). Cultural memory is different from both official and personal memory. It is shared outside formal historical discourse, and 'is entangled with cultural products and imbued with cultural meaning' (Sturken, 1997: 3). Popular culture, through films and televised images, contributes to the production of cultural memory, which in turn shapes historical narratives (ibid.). However, as Connerton (2011: ix) points out, what is conventionally referred to as cultural memory is charged 'with levels of meaning that reflect human sensory capacities more than cognitive categories'. If one wishes to explore cultural memory, it is equally important, for example, to examine bodily practices, such as tattoos, as it is to explore texts and documents. This is certainly the case when it comes to understanding Medellín's relationship to its violent past, which is embodied in a variety of material objects and practices, global and local.

Cultural memory is produced not only through images and representations, but also through objects which function as vehicles of representation (Sturken, 1997: 9). These objects can be seen as technologies that embody and generate memory. In this chapter, we will explore a variety of objects and cultural practices that embody and shape the memory of Medellín's violent past. We will see how images and representations created by *Narcos* continue to have their own lives and trajectories, particularly through the powerful forces of commercialism. Narratives about narco-violence, and its main perpetrator, become inscribed into the material fabric of everyday life through T-shirts bearing Escobar's likeness, coffee mugs, and keychain rings sold by local vendors. Moreover, these narratives continue to circulate on global commercial platforms and in the lives of thousands of people across the globe.

We will show how commercialism is a crucial structuring force in shaping cultural memories of Medellín's violent past. However, these commercially fuelled technologies of remembering also intersect, and are intertwined with, personal and official memory. Cultural forms of memory deeply affect individual memories of the period and challenge official forms of commemoration. Moreover, as commercial practices transform the city, which is home to those who had directly experienced the violence, they make it difficult to forget the traumatic events. The past is thus intricately woven into, and difficult to distinguish from, the present.

Dark tourism and the impossibility of forgetting

Several of Medellín's residents we interviewed resented the contribution of *Narcos* to what they perceived as the cultural decline of the city, mainly as a result of dark tourism. As one resident, a male engineer in his early forties, put it: '*Narcos* is bringing a wave of foreigners who come for sexual tourism, seek out all kinds of drugs, and want to live the life of Pablo Escobar.' Similarly, Nicolás, a seasoned journalist, saw the rise of dark tourism as directly connected to the release of *Narcos* and the growing U.S. interest in the city:

> There is a very important date, namely 2015, which is when the first season of *Narcos* aired; and between 2017 and 2018 narco-tourism exploded in Medellin: it was increasingly very common to see tourists visiting the same places, and a route was established. This interest was very curious, because it seemed like a resurrection of Pablo Escobar, who was more or less dead, who no longer had much prominence, and then resurfaced as a legend. At first, this had a lot of attraction for foreign tourists, and [. . .], who is a veteran *New Yorker* reporter with in-depth knowledge of Latin America, got interested in describing these narco-tours. He came, and I met with him. I spent four to five days with him. I did the narco-tour with him. I would have never done it on my own.

According to the data we obtained from city officials, the number of visitors to Medellín increased between 2008 and 2018 from 270,000 to 823,247, of whom 39 per cent were foreign.[1] Tours to landmark sites of Escobar's activity have been mushrooming in the city. A tour offered by Lonely Planet (2020), for example, is advertised thus:

[1] Email from vice-secretary in Medellín administration to the authors, 3 May 2019.

> Discover what life was like for the Colombian drug lord, Pablo Emilio Escobar Gaviria. Explore the mansion where he housed his hobbies, the site of his death and his final resting place. This private 3-hour tour will give you an in-depth look at the 'king of cocaine's' past and effects he left on his community. ... Head to 'Los Olivos', the neighbourhood where Pablo Escobar, one of the most well-known Colombian drug lords, was murdered. Visit the Monaco building where you will admire its elegant marble front.

Taxi drivers we interviewed reported frequent fares to sites associated with the cartels: '[When clients] ask about tourist spots, they obviously mean drug dealing, about where they can buy sex, buy drugs, where the clubs and the ladies are' (Ignacio). Tourists frequently choose Pablo Escobar as the topic of conversation, which, as one driver explained, is 'due to a lot of TV shows and movies that have portrayed Medellín as violent . . ., there are many foreigners wanting to learn more about that lifestyle' (Iñaki).

As part of our fieldwork, we took two guided tours themed around Escobar and drug violence. The tone of the fully scripted Pablo Escobar Family Tour was light, and the guides attempted to crack jokes. One of them, an Escobar lookalike, impersonated the drug lord. The emphasis was on glorifying Escobar's persona, highlighting his qualities and 'good deeds', and exalting him as 'the third richest man in the world'. Escobar was described as 'clever, crazy, and a polyglot', while the extreme violence was mainly blamed on his opponents. The tour included the site of the demolished Monaco building, where he had lived with his family; the site of his death; and a makeshift museum run by members of the Escobar family, with a gift shop well stocked with books about his life and collectibles.

One stop on the tour was the cemetery where Escobar is buried. Although dedicated to memory and mourning, its topography reflects the deeply stratified nature of Colombian society. It is deeply symbolic that Escobar's grave was placed right next to the church, while ordinary citizens rest farther afield (see Figure 6.1). The placement and size of Escobar's grave, as well as the fresh flowers and a presence of visitors, are indicative of his social status as well as the extent of public interest in,

Figure 6.1. Visitors to Escobar's grave, located next to the church.
Source: © Katja Franko.

even veneration of, him (Figure 6.2). The constant flow of visitors during our visit indicated that the grave has become a site of pilgrimage.

Dark tourism centred around Escobar is one of the most prominent features of Medellín's identity offered up to foreign visitors. Escobar tours, 'Things to Do in Medellín' and 'Cultural Tours' are, for example, among the most popular activities recommended by the global platform TripAdvisor. In addition to visits to the Escobar Museum and the *comunas*, the tour to his countryside property, Hacienda Nápoles

Figure 6.2. Pilgrims' offerings at Escobar's tomb. The epitaph reads: 'You were a conqueror of impossible dreams, beyond the legend that it symbolizes today, few know the true essence of your life.'
Source: © David R. Goyes.

(see Figure 6.3)—which, while located outside Medellín, is symbolically close to its imaginary—is among the most popular attractions (Vásquez, 2011). As in the case of several other 'Escobar experiences' offered to tourists, the focus is on excitement and enjoyment, making the term 'dark tourism' somewhat misplaced. The following advertisement of the Hacienda Nápoles on TripAdvisor gives the impression of a post-colonial experience staged for tourist enjoyment:

> This is a private VIP tour with a knowledgeable tour guide for up to five passengers in a high class vehicle. We collect from select hotels by arrangement. Breakfast and lunch are included. Hacienda Nápoles was one of the late Pablo Escobar's properties spanning 3,000 hectares and is currently a cultural, fauna and flora themed park located in the Colombian city of Doradal, Antioquia. It is located in the valley of the River Magdalena, 170 km from Medellín and is famous as a symbol of the Medellin drug cartel. We do a Safari around the park, viewing the

Figure 6.3. Visitors taking pictures at the entrance to the Napoles ranch, in front of the HK-617 Colombian airplane used by drug lord Pablo Escobar to transport his first shipment of cocaine to the United States.
Source: AFP PHOTO/Raul Arboleda/NTB.

> wild animals that Escobar imported into Colombia including, hippopotami, zebras, lions, leopards, pumas, elephants, crocodiles, and ostriches. Admire and swim in the Victoria Falls replica swimming pool, the Giant Octopus swimming pools and for the younger ones a ride into Jurassic Park. Visit the African cultural museum, and the Pablo Escobar Museum to learn about his life and history during the Medellin drug cartel.[2]

The violent history of the Medellín cartel has lost its darkness amidst the glamour of luxury, sunlight, Escobar's ostentatious living habits, and other exotic experiences.

There are, however, tours that offer a different tone and perspective. The guide on our second tour was an ex-police officer who shared his

[2] See 'Hacienda Napoles (Pablo Escobar) Theme Park Full Day Tour from Medellin', *TripAdvisor*, https://www.tripadvisor.com/AttractionProductReview-g297478-d18973531-Hacienda_Napoles_Pablo_Escobar_Theme_Park_Full_Day_Tour_from_Medellin-Medellin_Ant.html, accessed on 15 February 2023.

Figure 6.4. Mural in El Barrio Pablo Escobar in Medellín.
Source: © Katja Franko.

memories of the violent period. Although his account was quite different from the first tour, it was also part of the burgeoning Escobar tourism industry. Our guide had even appeared in a Netflix show on dark tourism.[3] The tour ran through the neighbourhood built by Escobar, where there is a large mural dedicated to him in the main street (see Figure 6.4) and a makeshift, community-built and run Escobar Museum. Although dramatically different in tone, the latter tour reveals how deeply embedded Escobar's story has become in Medellín's economy. Collectible items featuring Escobar's likeness were ubiquitous. T-shirts and coffee mugs (Figure 6.5) were even on sale at a local hairdresser's. The profitability of

[3] 'Latin America', *Dark Tourist*, episode 1, 20 July 2018, *Netflix*, https://www.netflix.com/watch/80189568?trackId=14277283&tctx=-97%2C-97%2C%2C%2C%2C%2C%2C%2C80189791%2CVideo%3A80189568%2CdetailsPageEpisodePlayButton, accessed on 3 June 2023.

Figure 6.5. A hairdresser's in El Barrio Pablo Escobar in Medellín.
Source: Raul ARBOLEDA/AFP/NTB.

the economy built on the Escobar myth is, therefore, not only a symbolic phenomenon but a prominent material and economic aspect of the city.

Although the commodification of pain for popular consumption is controversial (Ystehede, 2016), crime has a powerful appeal to tourists. Sometimes, 'the authorities intervene to deter morbidly curious tourists from visiting sites of crime' (Dalton, 2015: 1). Other sites, particularly those of genocide, mass murder, terrorist attacks, and state-sanctioned torture and human rights violations, are deemed so important that they warrant deliberate commemoration and memorialization, and become places where survivors, families, and the general public can grieve and heal (Dalton, 2015). Medellín does not belong to this latter category. While the gravity of Escobar's crimes would certainly warrant intervention to stem the flow of tourists morbidly fascinated by his violent entrepreneurialism, the 'Escobar experience' threatens to engulf the city and re-shape it through its narrative, causing great distress to those affected by his crimes.

Those directly affected by Escobar's violence find it offensive and trauma-inducing to encounter his image in public—something that Nicolás above described as Escobar's 'resurrection'. In chapter 3 we have seen how upsetting the commercial activities connected to Escobar were to the victims and survivors. Salomé, the journalist, on the other hand, was, in principle, not against the tours, but resented their commercial character, and thought they should have a different focus:

> I think that if those narco-tours had another focus and were operated differently, they could be part of a commemorative exercise that we would have to go through. I am not one to say how [it should be done] or what a tour guide's script should be like, but it seems unfortunate that [these tours] are in the hands of people who have only commercial goals in mind. They are feeding something morbid, which does no service to the construction of memory and history. I find it very regrettable.

Salomé's statement exemplifies the desire (also expressed by other interviewees) for an alternative narrative about the past that would not glorify the perpetrators of violence. Other interviewees, however, were also pained by the fact that the commercial boom has made it impossible to forget the traumatic events. All memories are, as Kundera observes, 'created' in tandem with forgetting (Kundera, 1980: 235 quoted in Sturken, 1997: 7). To banish something into oblivion has most often been seen as an expression of power that some social groups and societies have over others. Connerton states that 'when a large power wants to deprive a small country of its national consciousness, it uses the method of organised forgetting' (1989: 14). However, in the context of Medellín, the power aspects of social memory entail an amnesia of the lived experiences of some coupled with a simultaneous impossibility of forgetting. The constant reminders of the perpetrator's existence and, ultimately, his glorification, leave victims unable to escape a constructed reality that neither corresponds to their memories nor allows them to move forward.

Several interviewees recalled the outrage at encountering the images of Escobar, not only in Medellín, but also in other locations. Carlos, a judge whose life had been threatened by the cartel, recalled his anger upon seeing an Escobar T-shirt: 'I was in Spain and Italy two years ago, and I saw people out in summer wearing T-shirts with Pablo Escobar's image on it. So there you have it. . . . That is to say, as the story of the bandit is being told, he is raised to the altar of the heroes.' Similarly, Luciana recalled the outrage her husband, who had lost his father, felt when seeing friends wearing an Escobar T-shirt:

> We have some Spanish friends we adore, and they came to Colombia, with one of their first stops being in Cartagena. One of them was crazy about [*Narcos* and] bought the boss's T-shirt. My husband was outraged. But it's not just about being indignant, it's explaining what's behind the indignation. When the other understands your pain, he will understand that you don't like your country being associated with this.

The trauma(tic) economy

The episodes recalled by Carlos and Luciana reveal how commercialism and commodification of violence can be experienced as a form of re-traumatization by those directly affected by it. Encountering items promoting Escobar is painful to those who suffered and lost loved ones to drug violence. In the introduction, we introduced the concept of the *trauma economy* (Tomsky, 2011) in order to articulate the connections between memory and capitalism. The concept draws attention to how the privilege of narrating and re-narrating trauma is determined by 'economic, cultural, discursive and political structures that guide, enable and ultimately institutionalize the representation, travel and attention to certain traumas' (ibid.: 53). How past traumatic events are portrayed, narrated, and transmitted to future generations largely depends on economic and other structures of influence in a society. In her seminal study on memory and consumerism, Marita Sturken (2007: 1) describes the 'elaborate consumer networks of mass-produced goods that exist in American culture around events of national trauma'. Events such the Oklahoma City bombing or the 11 September attacks have not only produced sites of tourism and pilgrimage, but also a consumer culture of souvenirs (snow globes, teddy bears, T-shirts, and the like) in which people find comfort and a sense of history. Through these objects, they can relate to the tragedy without having to engage with the wider social, political, and economic context of violent events.

While the commercial structures surrounding Medellín's violent past, to some extent, resemble those practices in their material aspects, by incorporating tragedy into economic networks, they are, in key ways, also different. What is being consumed and commercialized, even though it triggers the victims' trauma, can hardly be described as representing tragedy and trauma. On the contrary. Every effort is being made to brand the objects and tourist experiences related to Medellín as entertainment. The focus is on light-hearted consumption and mischievous enjoyment of life, rather than on grief at the loss of life that took place in the city. Hacienda Nápoles, for example, is advertised like any other visit to a zoo or an exotic theme park, but with an extra touch of curiosity about Escobar's ostentatious lifestyle. Therefore, when appropriated by capitalist commercial networks and turned into a commodity, the meaning of Medellín's history becomes radically altered in the process. Trauma is erased and replaced with enjoyment. The question thus arises whether trauma economy can still be defined as such when, in the process of commercial exchange, traumatic events are commodified as entertainment.

Although in Medellín, like at Ground Zero, in Oklahoma City, and in other tourist locations, places associated with violence have been turned into sites of pilgrimage, the question can be asked what it is that the pilgrims are seeking there. The cheerfulness of our guides on the Escobar tours—one of them was a professional stand-up comedian—indicated that what they were offering to tourists was not an engagement with the collective trauma of drug violence, but rather satisfying an appetite for excitement and a curiosity about Escobar's life and persona. Tourism to sites of tragedy is often motivated by a wish for context and authenticity (Sturken, 2007). Numerous visitors' recommendations and comments on TripAdvisor about Escobar museums indicate that they perceive these sites as 'more authentic' than *Narcos*, because they give them more informative historical context than the series. Yet, herein lies a paradox. As Sturken points out, a tourist's search for authenticity comes from a position of detachment that demands no responsibility. The tourist is 'a figure who embodies a detached and seemingly innocent pose' (ibid.: 9). A tourist visiting sites of Escobar's activities might be motivated by the wish to get closer to the authentic lived reality behind *Narcos*, and yet remain unaware of the larger context of Colombian society and the effects that the drug trade (and its control) have had on it. The tourist is thus 'largely unaware of the effects of how tourist economies have structured the daily lives of the people who live and work in tourist locales' (ibid.: 10).

Few objects embody this position of light-hearted detachment better than Escobar T-shirt. T-shirts have become one of the most popular and recognizable material embodiments circulating in the commercial networks, particularly T-shirts printed with Escobar's mugshot (see Figure 6.6). Taken by the Colombian police on the occasion of his arrest in 1976, the photo shows a young Escobar with a defiant smile. Rather than hinting at the destructiveness and violence of his later deeds, the photo shows a young man full of life, roguish, and playful. It is also one of the most attractive real-life depictions of Escobar. It is telling that it is precisely this photo that should become his most popular posthumous representation.

During our visit, souvenirs bearing Escobar's mugshot photo and other images, including the popular trope '*plata o plomo* [*silver or lead*]', were easily available in shops and flea markets in Medellín (see Figure 6.7). The Escobar Museum also featured a number of other memorabilia, such as coffee mugs, pens, bookmarks, water bottles, and the like, as well as books authored by his associates.

Escobar-related merchandise is part of not only Medellín's local economy but is also available globally. A variety of items are available for purchase through major global retailers, such as eBay and Amazon. In addition to T-shirts and sweatshirts, customers can purchase an Escobar poster or even a costume and a mask. The fact that Carlos encountered a man wearing an Escobar T-shirt in Italy is therefore not surprising. Escobar has become part of a global iconography. His image has, moreover, become a popular subject of tattoos (Figure 6.8). Global image platforms, such as Pinterest, offer a variety of tattoo designs featuring Escobar, pointing at how cultural memory is in crucial ways embodied and inscribed in bodily practices.

As Connerton (2011: x) points out, tattoos 'are not merely decorative, but highly expressive of certain cultural interests and values: they literally embody, on the surface of the skin, matters that are normally considered to exist at the level of institutions, governments and family genealogies'. Existing both *on* and *beneath* the surface of skin, tattoos represent 'a form of powerful mnemonic code' (ibid.: 135). More than any other part of Escobar iconography and memorabilia sold and purchased at souvenir

Figure 6.6. A mug shot of Pablo Escobar taken by the regional Colombian control agency in Medellín in 1976.
Source: Colombia National Registry; Colombian National Police, 1976.

shops and flea markets, tattoos are, due to their immutability, most intimately connected to values and identity. They are literally inscribed into the body, and thus 'unambiguously part of you' (ibid.: 127).

The clue to the popularity of Escobar's police mugshot photo, and his memorabilia more generally, lies not only in its relation to the past, but in how it relates to present cultural values and issues of identity formation. According to Reuters, designer T-shirts produced by Escobar's son,

Figure 6.7. Souvenirs with the image of Pablo Escobar at a shop in Comuna 13 in Medellín.
Source: JOAQUIN SARMIENTO/AFP/NTB.

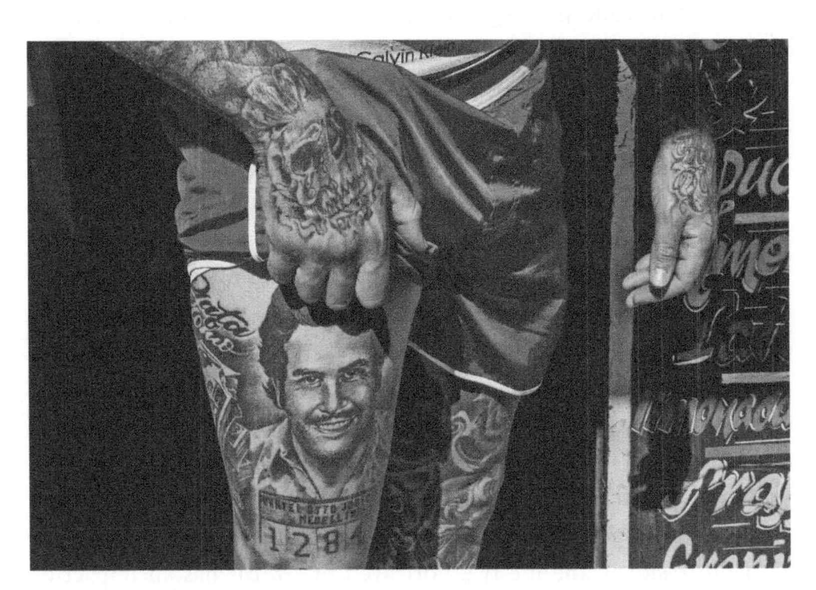

Figure 6.8. A tourist in Comuna 13 in Medellín showing off his Escobar tattoo.
Source: Photo by JOAQUIN SARMIENTO/AFP via Getty Images.

featuring his father, have become a hit in Mexican states that are on the front lines of the country's deadly drug war (Diaz, 2012). 'Featuring pictures from Escobar's student ID card, driver's license and other images, the shirts cost between $65 and $95—a small fortune in a country where about half of the population lives in poverty' (ibid.). Therefore, the consumption of objects related to Escobar is, crucially, about contemporary cultural values and the glorification of a specific type of masculinity.

Escobar's mugshot has become a symbol of transgressive masculinity and, in that respect, one could argue, it can be seen as a fetish. It has been imbued with specific meanings that are then transposed onto fashion items and other consumer goods. Fetishized consumer goods, such as clothing, may be consumed, because doing so allows individuals to experience more positive self-perception and self-presentation that may over time result in a sense of sexual empowerment (O'Donnell, 1999). An Escobar T-shirt or tattoo may thus create a sense of potency and a more positive self-image in the wearer. A large body of scholarship has pointed out the intimate connection between consumption (e.g., wearing) and being. Drawing on semiotics, Jean Baudrillard (2016) famously used the concept of sign/signifier to explain consumption not only in terms of purchasing products, but also as a language that expresses a sense of *who we are*. For Baudrillard, our purchases reflect our innermost desires so that consumption is caught up with our psychological production of self.

The commercialized signifiers of identity, such as Escobar T-shirts, may have quite a varied meaning for, and impact on, individuals around the globe. To foreign tourists in Medellín, these signifiers may represent an 'innocent', playful referencing and enjoyment of transgressive masculinity through the possession of things associated with it. This type of masculinity is increasingly challenged in mainstream Western cultural expressions; however, it can be, as with Escobar and *Narcos*, exoticized and outsourced to a foreign culture. To residents of Medellín, these objects and practices represent signs of pernicious influence on their local culture, particularly youth culture. According to one long-time Medellín resident, the lifestyle portrayed by *Narcos* has an impact on the local youth: 'Young people want that [thing] and they want the easy life. . . . Because they [Narcos] teach them their ways of being and acting, so I think they [*Narcos*] do have a great impact on youth.'

Therefore, the resentment that Carlos and Luciana's husband expressed at seeing people wearing Escobar T-shirts not only relates to the impossibility of forgetting a traumatic past because of constant reminders on the streets. Their outrage was also related to a sense of transformation of culture where people fetishize and wear signifiers indicating approval of the main perpetrator of serious crimes. In Carlos' mind this was 'as if someone went and bought a T-shirt with Hitler'[s picture]'. Several other interviewees referenced Hitler when mentioning Escobar, partly to convey how unacceptable it would be for U.S. or European consumers to wear a T-shirt of an actual mass murderer in their cultural context. Emiliano, who had lost his father to drug violence, compared narco-tours to the glorification of Nazism:

> We should tell visitors not to do this. Do not encourage those narco-tours because it is as if Germany set up Nazi tours that went through all the concentration camps to promote the German National Socialist ideology of the 1930s–1940s, and Latinos were taking those tours to visit Nazi death camps. I think that if a German comes, he will not like us to take him to the drug tours.... They are showing something that hurts us. And it hurts because they show precisely one thing that is not good. That is nothing to be proud of. So, when they come we should ask, do you know what you are doing? It's the same as if you were looking for a Nazi tour. I think that with that it is much easier for them [the tourists] to understand the resentment that narco-tours produce.

In the eyes of those directly affected by drug violence, consumerism and tourist activities related to *Narcos* and Escobar have a direct connection to their local culture and historic memory of their society. Many also see these activities as an expression of differential treatment of their own trauma with the ways trauma is dealt with and remembered in other, particularly Western, societies.

Memory and branding in an unequal society

Memory is crucial to understanding culture and national identity (Sturken, 1997, 2007). There is a dialectical relationship between the past and the present, between memory and identity, that is also clearly present in our findings. The commercialism surrounding *Narcos* and Escobar is not simply about the creation of a consumer brand concerning one individual, but in crucial ways also about the branding of Medellín and Colombia, more generally. Several residents of Medellín we talked to felt that *Narcos* contributed to a negative branding of the city as well as of them as Colombians. A long-time Medellín resident pointed out the negative stereotyping of *paisas* (i.e., people from the northwest of Colombia, including Medellín):

> I think it influences the way Colombians are perceived in the world and even the *paisas* within the country. To that extent it has an impact on me, because we end up being seen as stereotypes of drug traffickers, no matter how different I might physically be from a man like Pablo Escobar. And then the *paisas* end up being the *culebreros* [sycophant] who sell anything, who ask for a discount, for everything, that we want to win at all costs, pure stereotypes of assholes, even though I personally am quite far from that.

Asked whether the series had an impact on his life, another resident said:

> Yes, totally. Yes . . . look at how they treat us. When you're at an airport: "Are you from Colombia?" The kind of faces they make when you say you are Colombian: "Drug trafficker?" Why do you have to remember those things now? If they already saw us differently [because of the war], why do they have to run that series … and air it in Colombia and then pass it on to other countries, then they say "look at the Colombians."

This association of *Narcos* with Colombian identity and national psyche is not accidental. The series skilfully incorporates not only the imagery of the city and the country's landscape, but also its music and cultural history. The soundtrack for the series was composed by award-winning composer Pedro Brofman and includes a number of beloved traditional Colombian songs. This creates an impression of authenticity, one of the highlights of the series, as well as intricately connects the Escobar brand to Colombian culture and identity.

According to Alejandro Herrero-Olaizola (2022: 1), narco-series are among several global cultural products that perpetuate the perception that violence is 'intrinsically ingrained in Colombia's national fabric'. In addition to narco-series and narco-stories, mass-marketed cultural products include captivity memoirs, gritty travel narratives imbued with exoticism, and a number of cinematic representations. Such cultural expressions have a strong global commercial appeal. Although, to a large extent, alluding to the Latin American social reality as a whole, global cultural representations have a particular focus on Colombia and:

> espouse the idea that there is such a thing as 'Colombian violence'—a rather homogenizing category in which very different iterations of violence are lumped together in a rather simplistic fashion … it attaches violence to a country's identity and, in doing so, it relays that there is a specific, homegrown violence that implicitly defines and becomes the identifier of Colombia. (ibid.)

As we saw in chapter 2, the genealogy and trajectory of violence in Colombia is complex and varied. Drug-related violence, in particular, has been shaped by the U.S.-inspired 'war on drugs' and fuelled by the voracious appetite for drugs among consumers in the Global North. Drug violence in Colombia can, therefore, not simply be described as homegrown. Ironically, the growth of dark tourism became possible precisely because of the overall 'pacification' of Medellín—a euphemism for state-sponsored mass killings in some regions of the city (Maclean, 2015)—and the decrease in the visibility of Colombian's internal armed conflict through the signing of the peace accords (even though the country is far from being a 'post-conflict society').

How do nations, regions, and cities get 'branded' with a particular image? The processes of branding are most often a result of strategic national reputation management, which has become an increasing concern for governments due to globalization, growth of tourism, demands of the economy and a number of other social dynamics (Angell and Morhorst, 2015). The term 'nation branding' originates from corporate consulting (Anholt, 1998) and refers to how nations actively use branding tools from business-reputation management to promote their image in the world. Rather than simply aiming to be known, nations, regions or cities must aim to 'become world famous' and 'megabrands' if they want to maximise the nation branding effect (Anholt, 2006: 102).

Although branding of nations and places can also be negative (Gammeltoft-Hansen, 2017), most literature sees branding as an active process through which various actors actively choose to shape their national and regional identities and create a particular image of themselves in the world. In the case of Medellín, however, its 'brand' is not the result of active self-representation, but rather an identity imposed by powerful global actors and then commercialized by local and international entrepreneurs. Medellín's global image, and the related tourist industry, are connected to the notoriety—and branding—of one of its inhabitants. The power of the Escobar brand springs to a large extent from the commercial power of Netflix and its ability to globally promote its products. Faced with the branding power of Netflix, many inhabitants of Medellín and (as we shall see in the next chapter) the city's political authorities experience a considerable level of powerlessness and frustration.

One of our interviewees from the communes saw the series as a direct form of foreign influence that should be resisted:

> There is another thing: we cannot identify with what they are selling us. That is what the outsiders are selling us, and what the gringos and the Europeans are telling us? Even if you are not a drug dealer, or a drug addict, or anything, you will be seen from the outside: 'This must be a drug dealer, he comes from the land where marijuana is grown, and where they snort a lot of cocaine," and things like that. So, they're selling a negative image [of Colombians].

In addition to the negative stereotyping of their city and their country, our interviewees resented the narco-series for their perceived corrosive impact on future generations. Asked how he feels about the series, one resident said:

> Angry. Many people are trying to highlight the technical level of cinematography. And they present our history as if it were dominated by drug trafficking. I am angry, also because these stories have been normalized.... [Escobar] has brought down all these planes, as if it was the most normal thing in the world, as if this was an achievement.

> Because you hear children say that they want to be like this or that character, or that they want to live this story and that they want to have money at any cost. It makes me furious! ... And the fact that even in 2019 he is such a strong and forceful influence on everything.

The narratives of the past are thus perceived to be crucial to shaping the outward image of the city as well as its present values. Our interviewees also expressed concern about how the heavily gendered portrayals of characters in narco-shows affected young people. A lawyer in his late forties said: 'Boys just want to become hit men.' As we have seen in chapter 5, gender stereotypes permeate the narratives of *Narcos*. Some of our interviewees thought that the heroic cinematic portrayals of Escobar were particularly harmful to the poorer parts of the society:

> People do like to watch all that, the telenovelas, the news ... people socialize and educate themselves in front of the TV. Whatever they're told on the TV becomes a fact ... [Television] really creates a reality and transforms history. Then the city buys the story about a heroic character [Escobar], who helped the poor and end up forgetting everything else. Because there is also that part of the culture which believes that the man was a leader, and he helped the hungry and gave them houses and markets. But this should be disregarded, since these are the tricks of the trade.

One of our respondents from the communes, described television as a form of education: 'I think television is a kind of school, isn't it? It is like a classroom for many young people.'

These observations reveal that narco-series are seen as an important vehicle of education not only about the past, but also in terms of transmission of values to future generations, particularly when it comes to portrayals of gender roles and the normalization of violence. The impact of narco-series, therefore, lies not only in terms of forming the city's outward identity, but are very much woven into its self-perception. Most of our interviewees considered the negative self-image to be a pressing concern in view of the pervasive nature of the drug economy and violence. The creation of stereotypes by foreign actors was thus intricately intertwined with the social forces that support the drug economy and hence also create an ambiguity about Escobar's legacy. One of our respondents from the communes, who had lost two cousins who had been involved in the drug trade, pointed out Escobar's ambiguous legacy:

> I think you see him more as a hero, because people who were close to him adored him, and he built neighbourhoods and managed a lot of money and ... I think they remember him more for that. Even foreigners come to Colombia to take the tours, see where he lived, what he did.... It seems to me that this should not exist.

This ambiguous nature of Escobar's legacy is stamped on the city through the existence of an entire neighbourhood named in his honour. A large mural with Escobar's image welcoming visitors to the Barrio Pablo Escobar (Figure 6.4) is a potent material testimony of the positive image of the drug lord's legacy projected by the neighbourhood. In a makeshift museum next to the mural, images of members of the Medellín cartel are prominently displayed next to religious symbols (Figures 6.9 and 6.10). The site is not merely a place of local worship, but increasingly and due to the commercial agreements between tour entrepreneurs and the locals, also a must-see landmark on an 'Escobar experience' itinerary.

Several of our interviewees pointed out that Escobar's legacy is viewed differently by different segments of the population. When asked how Escobar should be remembered, one resident said:

> Here, in Medellín, there are many people who idolize him, because he brought money to impoverished places left behind by the authorities. But I think that if you rejoice in that and endorse it, you are having a double standard, because you cannot be good to some people, on the one hand, while, on the other, murdering and torturing left and right, and terrorizing thousands. No, the man is nothing but a murderer, period, there is no in-between.

This statement points to the importance of class and social inequalities in the shaping of collective memory. The idolization of Escobar is not only a result of the global popularity and profitability of his brand of violent masculinity among tourists and Netflix viewers, but also a way out of poverty aspired to by local youth seduced by a Robin Hood narrative.

Figure 6.9. The statue of a saint in El Barrio Pablo Escobar.
Source: © Katja Franko.

Issues of class and social inequality were brought up by several of our interviewees who situated the violent events of that period into a context of great social inequality and class conflict between the rich and the poor. José, for example, talked about 'upper-class children who went to work

Figure 6.10. Portraits of prominent members of the Medellín cartel in El Barrio Pablo Escobar.
Source: © Katja Franko.

with Pablo Escobar and gave information on who had to be kidnapped'. He was perplexed when his brother became a victim of the violence even though he did not belong to the upper classes nor lived in the communes: 'Honestly, when the massacre occurred, we asked ourselves, why us? Why my brother? If we are middle class people, we have no enemies.'

One resident, who described himself as a working-class man, on the other hand, expressed indignation at the damage that the narco-economy and violence did to his neighbourhood:

> [A]t that time, Pablo Escobar did a lot of damage to the youth. Although I was very young also at that time, I was affected in my neighbourhood when he and his henchmen arrived at the corners where the boys were to give them dollars to talk and he said, 'Come, come', and he took them away. I have been working class all my life. Even my school friends, they [henchmen] took them to give them shooting lessons, to train them as hitmen and that hurt me a lot. Two cousins of mine, first cousins, died in that time of violence.

> So, for me, it was a very dire time, I wouldn't even want to remember that. And I don't watch those movies. If I see that they are going to screen those series I turn off the TV. In my house, they are not watched, not at all ... They should put on something more constructive and cultural, well ... worthwhile things.

The testimony reveals the complexity and paradoxes of Escobar's impact on some of the most impoverished neighbourhoods: the temptation of easy money in an environment of scarcity and exclusion, and the simultaneous heavy death toll of the drug economy on the local youth, as well as the discomfort brought on by Escobar's recent 'resurrection' in popular culture.

In his trilogy *Memory of Fire*, the Uruguayan writer and novelist Eduardo Galeano remarks that, throughout centuries, the memory of Latin America has been kidnapped and the Latin American voices silenced. The continent has not only been 'despoiled of gold and silver, nitrates and rubber, copper and oil: its memory has also been usurped. From the outset it has been condemned to amnesia by those who had prevented it from being' (Galeano, 1987: 203). In several ways, the findings of this book are also a story of the usurpation of memory by powerful actors. We have documented how the processes of the creation of collective memory of Medellín's violent past in the media and cultural portrayals have left its residents with a sense of loss of control. The strength of commercial forces and storytelling about Escobar has overshadowed the processes of local memory construction. The conjunction of the symbolic power of narco-shows, and the dark tourism taking place in the city, indicate that transnational actors have taken over Medellín's narrative, trapping it in the role of deviant city.

This chapter has documented the difficulties that dark tourism poses for victims and those directly and indirectly affected by the violence. The shock experienced by a man who had lost his father to drug violence at the sight of a Spanish friend wearing an Escobar T-shirt can be described as a trauma trigger, and in the long run is inscribed in a dynamic of re-victimization. The trauma(tic) economy feeding on the 'Escobar experience' creates global cultural narratives about violence in Medellín and offers a number of items and products to consumers and tourist experiences to those eager to immerse themselves in narco-culture. These commercial activities not only brand the city but also shape its local culture in intricate ways. Brands are about identity. And by becoming a global brand, Escobar has been brought back to life, and continues to haunt the city, particularly through his influence on younger generations. In the next chapter, we show how the city and its local authorities have attempted to take back control of its outward image and its historic narrative.

7

The quest for recognition

The battle to control memory

The iconization of Escobar and the commercialization of violence described in the previous chapter have not gone unchallenged. In 2016, more than two decades after Escobar's death, the public portrayal of the drug lord was put on the political agenda and concerns were raised about the global narratives that had been constructed about Medellín. In this chapter, we examine the local initiatives and struggles to shape the story of the city's violent past. The chapter describes the dynamics of a campaign initiated by the newly elected mayor of Medellín to inspire the city to embrace its history, and reclaim ownership of its memory, by challenging the stories imposed by commercial actors. We shall see that while these struggles brought greater attention to victims of drug related violence, they also introduced a new dynamic into the processes of profiting described in this book, namely, *political profiting*. The chapter critically appraises the interplay between the aims of the local authorities' campaign to acknowledge victims' experiences and the desire for political gain.

We then explore how these local attempts to regain control of Medellín's memory intersected with global narratives. We show how the memory-creation in the context of the Holocaust served as a source of inspiration for Medellín's efforts to commemorate its losses which, ultimately, remains elusive to victims of drug violence.

Netflix and the writing of history

As we have seen in previous chapters, for the survivors of drug violence and residents of Medellín the question of memory is a central concern.

Victimhood, Memory, and Consumerism. Katja Franko and David R. Goyes, Oxford University Press.
 DOI: 10.1093/oso/9780192874115.003.0007

Although some of our interviewees expressed stronger indignation about Netflix's portrayal of Medellín's past than others, most were concerned that narratives created by narco-series would become the main story about what happened to their loved ones and their city. Salomé, who described herself as a survivor, said:

> I don't understand why we are leaving the construction of memory, of the history of what had happened and continues to happen, up to fiction scriptwriters and above all to outsiders' visions ... based on research and studies of what audiences want to see in fiction. That worries me. I am not against narco-series as such ... It seems to me that they are also important, very important when it comes to building memory and delivering, let's say, those episodes from a time in history. I worry that they are the only voices.

Salomé's comment alludes to the power that Netflix and other commercial actors have as writers of history and creators of collective memory. The creators of *Narcos*—Eric Newman, Doug Miro, and Carlo Bernard—explain that their goal with was 'to depict [the people and the personalities] as they really were, and while much of what they did seems too strange to believe, one of the great strengths of *Narcos* is that the stories we tell are almost always the truth' (2018: 6). Several other interviewees also expressed similar ambitions. Particularly those involved in the creation of the Colombian production, *El Patrón del Mal* saw the series as an opportunity to write history and shape cultural memory. Diana argued that doing the series was 'like a different way of telling the story of Colombia. ... In a palatable way, if you will, that everyone can understand. ... In a universal and popular language of the world, which I believe is what television is.' Although she saw the risks of focusing on the perpetrator, she also saw the series as a part of a healing process:

> That is part of what we are as Colombians, it is part of what the city of Cali, Medellín, Bogotá is, of what we are and what we are living as a country. We would be wrong not to tell the story, not to talk about what many people pretend does not exist: 'that's already happened, you don't need talk about that'. In my opinion, if you have to talk about it, like

> when you go to the psychologist, you undergo therapy, and you talk and talk about your experiences.

Diana's observation alludes to drug violence as a repressed part of Colombia's history, as something that was 'not talked about'. The burgeoning of narco-series ruptured this layer of silencing and thus took the place previously occupied by artistic films as the most important narrative about what happened to the city and its inhabitants.

Although many of the victims and those directly affected by drug violence were concerned about the silence imposed on their experiences, they did not see the commercial narratives as a solution. Many saw the shows as the most prominent public narrative that has emerged about the terrible events, and were deeply upset by the historical inaccuracies, particularly when those pertained to their loved ones. Valentina, who had lost her father, remembered:

> I asked a friend to send me the episode where they recreate the attack on my dad. I was outraged. It bothered me because my dad never ran. . . . If you want to do a series, try to get closer and try to investigate. . . . Try not to offend the victims and try not to mutilate the history of a country. Because it can get confusing. Although they say, 'this series does not correspond to reality', it makes me angry; it bothers me. . . .

Most of our interviewees were deeply upset by the focus on Escobar which they saw as a creation of a misguided historic narrative. Alberto, for example, described narco-series as a falsification of history: 'National and international series have shown him practically as a hero, as a rising hero. I think it is a falsification of national history. I think it is a spoof of history.'

Asked about how the violent period should be remembered, the words 'education' and 'healing' were a common thread in the answers. One resident, for example, said: 'I think [drug violence] should be remembered as the worst thing that the country has experienced, and it should have been learned from.' Another resident similarly expressed exasperation at the approach chosen by narco-series:

> I don't know what [those] who make [narco-]series have in their heads. ... I don't think they are teaching anyone anything. I don't know, I'm very radical about that. I find it very sad. It seems to me that things should be approached in a different, educational, and healing manner.

The concern about education was particularly strong because the drug economy continues to be a concern for the city. Many of our interviewees wished to create a more positive narrative about the future. Isabella pointed out that the story of violence in Medellín should be studied as part of national history, as a positive example of resilience:

> I think everyone should study it, but with the aim of avoiding its repetition and of remembering the city which had suffered so much and was reborn ... because Medellín is an example of the rebirth of Colombia in general. It also seems to me that [this history] should be studied, that it should not be forgotten, and it should not be left in the past.

Likewise, Nicolás, a journalist involved in local projects of commemoration:

> The story told about Medellín's neighbourhoods is not only the story of its victims; it is also the story of the successful ones. The appeal lies in the stories of success and these stories have an impact [on people] as a model to follow; as a life option for many people. Many people keep doing it [dealing with drugs]; they have not stopped; they have not stopped despite having fifty thousand victims. It is possible that [the violence] will not stop in the short term.

As we have seen in chapter 3, several survivors of drug violence felt compelled to write blogs, books, and other types of public interventions to make their story heard, and to weave the story of drug violence into a broader historic narrative, but without the element of entertainment. These attempts at 'grassroots storytelling' were motivated not only by the desire to introduce a different narrative—one not focused on entertainment and iconization of Escobar—but also to include aspects that were silenced by narco-series. However, not only the victims' side of the story gets obscured due to the overwhelming focus on Escobar, but also the political forces behind the violence and the role of the state in it. Our focus-group interviews in the communes reveal the widespread desire to know the truth about the role of the state in the violent encounters that took place. One resident said:

> I want to know the history of Medellín, but the history that is hidden, not the history that is being presented to us at the moment. The history that is hidden from how the *combos* [hitmen gangs and paramilitary groupings] were organized with the participation of the government … [I'd like to know] how that truce was declared and peace was concluded.

Mentions of corruption that permeated state institutions at the time, and continues to do so, were common in our interviews. Sandra, who had lost her husband in the plane bombing, remembered:

> Well, when we came to find out that the people from the DAS [Administrative Department of Security] were all involved [in acts of corruption]. So, what did we expect? They were in the game. So, what confidence can authority give us? And I'm ashamed to say it: we cannot trust our institutions, something that is very difficult and is still happening today. The issue of corruption has not been resolved. So, what confidence can you have in the authorities if you are seeing that there is a lot of corruption? And what percentage of those [corrupt people] were authorities at that time?

This deeper level of understanding of the society, and the role of political actors in the drug violence, certainly eludes the narratives presented in narco-series. Netflix is a very powerful, yet partial narrator of history, one who has the ability to focus the narrative according to its own, commercially determined, preferences. *Narcos*, as we discussed in chapter 4, is essentially narrated through the eyes of two U.S. law enforcement agents. Medellín's authorities were thus faced with a dilemma of how to resist the power of such a prominent global actor in order to define the historic memory of the city through eyes of its residents.

Political profiting and local resistance

Issues surrounding the public portrayal of drug violence in Medellín were put on the political agenda in 2016 with the election of Federico Gutiérrez as mayor of Medellín. During his time in office (2016–2019), Gutiérrez repeatedly tried to establish contact with Netflix. In a letter sent to the company, entitled 'Encounter with Memory', he referred to the period when Medellín was the most violent city in the world, and pointed out:

> [N]obody escaped the tragedy: journalists, judges and attorneys, public servants, police officers and soldiers, athletes, artists, entrepreneurs, citizens, thousands of men and women died due to narco-terrorism.... That tragedy has become an almost-fictional commodity.[1]

Medellín's tragic history, he argued, had become an action movie that turned drug dealing and the mafia culture associated with it into 'a cultural revolution'. Gutiérrez finished by calling for a new narrative: '[L]et us tell this story again to defeat the power that narco-culture and illegality have today.'

Gutiérrez's efforts are revealing of the strategies that local and national actors have used to resist the power of Netflix, and other global media outlets, to narrate their story. Gutiérrez's letter was part of a broader political effort to limit and undo the mythmaking surrounding Escobar. Gutiérrez also sent letters to international artists, who had used Escobar in their work, declaring that 'endorsing drug trafficking, Pablo, and his violence is a huge act of irresponsibility'. He made several unsuccessful attempts to shut down Casa Museo Pablo Escobar, a museum operated by Escobar's brother, and to curtail narco-tours in the city. He also wrote an official letter to the former Colombian ambassador to France, asking her to campaign for the closure of the Parisian restaurant Le Baron, which offered dishes named after Escobar's hitmen and ceremonies called '*plata o plomo*' and 'the death exchange'.[2]

[1] Letter from Federico Gutiérrez to Netflix on 'Encuentro con la Memoria' [Encounter with Memory] (n.d.). Gutiérrez's personal secretary sent us via email this and other private communications from the office of the mayor.

[2] Letter from Federico Gutiérrez to Farruko and Víctor Manuelle (n.d.); Letter from Federico Gutiérrez to Vivian Morales (2018).

In a similar effort to curtail Escobar's notoriety and that of his associates, Sandra recalled how she intervened in a radio program:

> When Popeye [one of Escobar's associates] came out of jail, it was as if a hero was released. There is a radio program that I like very much, 'Vox Populi'. They began to create a character with the voice of Popeye that was even encouraging people. I said, 'but what is this?' as if it was fine to make jokes about that topic when violence had such a devastating impact on us. And they used that as a joke. It seems to me that it is not the way to go.

Sandra's intervention and initiatives by private NGOs and public civil servants were motivated by the desire to change the tone of public narratives about violence from one of amusement to seriousness, and to curb the hyper-visibility given to perpetrators at the expense of the victims. The authorities sought to highlight the names of some of the victims, to emphasize the fact that hardly any of them were well known, while Escobar and his hitmen enjoyed notoriety.

The political efforts and local strategies of resistance took place at several levels. They aimed to curtail the global commercial appropriation of Medellín's history and create a more dignified and victim-focused account of its past. They also tried to limit the corrosive impact of narco-series on the cultural values of the city, particularly those of its younger generation.

The city launched a project called 'Medellín abraza su historia' [Medellín Embraces Its History], which had as one of its main objectives creating a different narrative about the city's past, one where victims would have a prominent voice. These initiatives began to remove the layers of internal silencing and repressed memories of the traumatic events. For many survivors, this period was the first time they publicly told their stories. Luciana recalled how emotional it was to witness her husband and her mother-in-law speaking about their loss for the first time:

> My husband is about to turn fifty, and he had never broached the subject of his father, not even among the family. When he first opened up about it in 2016, in an interview with the BBC reporter from London,

> I wept. . . . I understand he did it as a personal catharsis. . . . I had been with him for twenty-four years, and I had never heard him tell the stories he told the BBC. Many of his reactions, words that I had never heard from him, not only the stories, surprised me a lot. His mother and brothers were surprised to see the interview. It opened the door for them to talk about what had happened during those times. . . . It is not easy. In 2018, as part of 'Medellín Embraces its History', when my mother-in-law [name redacted] was interviewed, I cried. Words, stories, and memories that were kept silent for so long.

Although commercial actors were among the first to break through the layers of repressed memories, often showing a lack of sensitivity that was hurtful to the survivors, the process that followed was for some a healing experience. The public discussion that ensued as part of 'Medellín Embraces its History' brought not only different narratives into the public domain but, on a personal level, helped some to deal with the pain.

The most visible symbolic expression of the mayor's campaign was the demolition of the Monaco building, one of Escobar's luxurious residences (see Figure 1.2). The building was seized by the government in 1990 and had become a popular tourist destination due to its connection to Escobar. Gutiérrez and his team decided to demolish the building and replace it with a memorial dedicated to the victims (see Figure 7.1). According to his personal secretary, Manuel Villa Mejia, the mayor

Figure 7.1. Parque Conmemorativo Inflexión.
Source: © Susana Valdés Builes.

decided 'to make the demolition a symbolic event and to build a space there to honour the victims of the tragedy; a space to build memory'.

Gutiérrez's approach is a classic example of political figures harnessing the symbolism of victimhood to promote their message and garner political support (Green, 2008). By calling the Monaco building a 'symbol of evil' and employing an emotive, moral language, he managed to attract popular support. This form of 'political profiting' is a trend that has been observed in many Latin American countries registering high crime rates (Krause, 2009). Although he was not explicitly supported by a political party during the 2015 mayoral elections, Gutiérrez drew on a long tradition of politicians turning crime into an electoral trump card. His political career had an upswing, and he became, albeit unsuccessfully, the right-wing candidate in the 2022 presidential election (see further Daniels, 2022).

Not surprisingly, the mayor's approach provoked some controversy, and not all of the victims we interviewed were supportive of his efforts. José described the campaign as using the victims 'as a bargaining chip to win prizes and votes'. He recalled with regret how the mayor, rather than honour the victims, took centre stage himself at the demolition of the Monaco building:

> On the first day, we met on the seventh floor of the Continental Hotel to mingle; there was enough food catered to feed all the Medellín communes. The Continental is a luxury hotel. That was not just nonsense, the menus there were impressive. What did Federico do? Allowed the media in, let the people in, let the whole world be there. He was the last one to arrive, so that everyone would say, 'Federico, the saviour is here.' Everything was planned down to the last detail: the controlled demolition of Monaco was perfectly timed. I think it must have been rehearsed. Federico finished his speech, lowered the curtain. Boom! Implosion.

José, therefore, felt he was taken advantage of, and that the victims were also being silenced by political authorities:

> This is all politics, and people do not realize that they are being used. During the demolition of the Monaco building, Gutiérrez asked us to

> go on the stage for a photo op. I thought we would have the chance to use the microphone and tell our stories. But it was only him [Gutiérrez] who got to talk. That event was business for a lot of people, and Gutiérrez profited politically from it. He used us; he used the victims.

Nicolás was also critical of the mayor and saw him as 'taking advantage of a situation to boost his own visibility'. Several of our interviewees were critical of the economic wastefulness of these measures. A taxi driver, Raúl, pointed out: 'Well, I don't know, there are people who say that this building would have been taken over to house people, there are so many people out there who need help.'

In a telling example, one of our interviewees, who had lost her husband to the violence, described a disagreement with a taxi driver on her way to a ceremony at the Monaco building. The taxi driver was worried that the demolition might mean loss of income from tourism:

> I told him that drug tourism is not good for you and your children, for your grandchildren, that is not good, [that] you have to look for other sources of income, you have to look at alternatives. No, he did not agree with that, and criticized the mayor for having gone through with it. I, however, agreed [with the mayor] and I congratulated him. I told him, 'Your idea seems very good to me.' You have to get rid of [the building], knock it down, because you have to remove that shadow. It seemed to me [the tours of the building] showed a lack of respect. Unconsciously, everyone was getting involved in that.... There were a number of people living around it and living off it. So, I don't agree with [dark tourism].

While we were conducting research, the Monaco building was still standing and continued to attract Escobar aficionados. On one of the tours we took, the guide vehemently declared: 'This will never be a peace park, this place will always belong to Pablo Escobar!'

Despite the controversy, most of our informants expressed support for the demolition. Luis, who had lost his father, saw it as a historic turning point and an important symbolic step towards proper commemoration of his family's losses:

For almost thirty years, we were just anonymous victims left alone with our own tragedy. In 2019, the state made symbolic reparations to the relatives of those victims who died as a result of the war against the government, against the policemen who persecuted that criminal, and finally against the journalists [who died] among whom was our father. What had been the site of narco-tour for many years, has now become part of the 'Medellín Embraces its History' tour, which takes people to places where crime had been promoted by businessmen who profited from the pain of the families, of the victims of this criminal.

To start with, the Monaco building, where Escobar had lived with his family, was torn down. Shortly thereafter, the Parque Conmemorativo Inflexión [Inflexión Memorial Park] was established in its place. It sends the message to the world that Medellín is finally turning a new leaf and putting that horrible, dark history behind. We felt a surge of conflicting emotions, sadness and joy, when that infamous building collapsed, and we felt that a symbol of wilful violence had been felled to the ground. And, finally, on the day of the inauguration of the Inflexión Memorial Park, we felt great joy, because after everything we've been through, our loved ones were able to see themselves as heroes. . . .

Luis expressed a wish that the name of his father, Roberto Sarasti Obregon, be printed in our book as an acknowledgement of the victims and a way to have their names remembered by future generations.[3] Federico Arellano also asked us to have his father honoured this way.[4]

[3] Roberto Sarasti Obregon. Padre, esposo y periodista colombiano asesinado en Medellín al finalizar el año más sangriento en la historia reciente de este país. Salió la mañana del martes 10 de octubre de 1989 de su hogar, besó a su esposa y no regresó. Email communication to the authors on 19 March 2021.

Su partida prematura trunco los planes de vida de sus hijos. No obstante, lo sembrado en ellos fue suficiente para que ambos se convirtieran en personas útiles a su comunidad.

El silencio sobre las causas de su muerte es un grito que aún estremece a su familia y a muchas otras familias, a una ciudad, y a una sociedad entera.

La voz que aclama ser escuchada ahora, la que se debe reivindicar, es aquella que con estridencia silencie el ruido de las armas, la que arrulle la cuna de sus nietos, la que proclame que no debemos permitirnos olvidar a nuestros seres queridos, que debemos celebrar sus vidas y evocar su memoria.

Detrás de cada historia de muerte y crimen, hay otras tantas más de vida y amor. Eso fue lo que nuestro padre nos enseñó.

[4] Gerardo Arellano Becerra: un hombre que, con su carisma y su voz, ondeaba la bandera de la paz por el mundo.

'Respect our pain, honour our victims'

Although situated within Colombia's fraught and divisive political landscape, Medellín's local strategies of resistance were motivated by a sense of anger and unease at the way the city was represented and, ultimately, stigmatized in global narratives, as well as by tourists and international visitors. According to Manuel Villa Mejia, the intention of the city's authorities was to send a message to the world: 'Respect our pain, honour our victims.' Inspired by Holocaust commemorations, Medellín's authorities tried to develop a more dignified and sober narrative. The mayor's speech before the demolition of the Monaco building was clear about these ambitions:

> It is important to know what has happened in the world, in order to have a clear perspective [of the conflict in Medellín]: the memorial in Hiroshima, the 9/11 memorial in New York, the memory of Auschwitz, the memorial to the Jews in Berlin, the memorial to the veterans in Washington.[5]

The local policies developed by the mayor's office, although critical of the narratives disseminated by the entertainment industry, were as such not anti-global but, in fact, strongly shaped by global influences and intended to be a part of a global discussion. Holocaust commemorations were a particularly strong source of inspiration. Manuel Villa Mejia told us:

> I do have a dream and that is that this continues, that just as in Jerusalem there is Yad Vashem, which is the national authority for the remembrance of the Holocaust, here there is the museum of memory as the authority for the remembrance of the memory of the victims of narco-terrorism.

[5] Intervención del alcalde de Medellín: Homenaje a Héroes y Víctimas del Narcoterrorismo y Derribo del Edificio Mónaco [Intervention of the mayor of Medellín: Homage to Heroes and Victims of Narco-Terrorism and Demolition of the Mónaco Building] (2019), https://www.youtube.com/watch?v=ch10A9Dw5d4, accessed on 17 June 2023.

Figure 7.2. Museo Casa de la Memoria, Medellín.

In that respect, the city's efforts were not only driven by symbolic politics, but represented a sustained effort to create a different historic tradition inclusive of victims of drug violence.

The most visible step in the attempt to tell an alternative story of the city was the upgrading of the Museo Casa de la Memoria. Though architecturally considerably smaller, the museum resembles the Jewish Museum in Berlin. (See Figure 7.2.) As stated on its website, the museum's aim is not only to remember the past, but to become a space for developing alternative visions of the future as part of society's peace-building efforts:

> Our memories are alive. We remember in order to contribute to the prevention of future violence. This space is a house for gathering and dialogue to understand what has happened and is still happening in our society—it also offers a chance for us to be hopeful again and create other possible futures without violence.[6]

[6] Museo Casa de la Memoria (n.d.), https://www.sitesofconscience.org/membership/museo-casa-de-la-memoria/, accessed on 5 June 2023.

During the process of expanding and upgrading the museum, Medellín officials visited Holocaust museums around the world. According to Villa, the policy of the city authorities has been to 'look back, retell the story, and change the referents. To retell the story from the side of the truth, from the side of the victims, from the side of the heroes.' Their objective has been to build a narrative that competes with that of the entertainment industry and 'generate interest in those individuals who stood up and resisted'.

However, according to Nicolás, a journalist involved in projects of local memorialization, the story of the victims of drug trafficking, at first, had difficulties fitting into the museum and into the general historic narrative about violence in Colombia:

> Museo Casa de la Memoria, which is about ten years old, had done a job of reconstructing the armed conflict, but drug trafficking had been somewhat marginalized from that first wing of the museum.... Drug trafficking was excluded a little spatially, and I think strategically, in a first stage, to be able to count the actors of the conflict, above all because that museum was in the framework of the Victims' Law and that law does not consider the victims of [drug violence] as victims. It only considers the victims of the armed conflict as victims. There is something very strange going on here, because drug trafficking is excluded from the armed conflict. His peace agreement tried to include it, but it is still very confusing. The victims of drug trafficking do not have any official recognition.

Nicolás' comment alludes to the Victim's Law, which is discussed in the next chapter, as an important mechanism of marginalization and exclusion of victims of drug violence from official recognition. The Museum was built primarily to address the wider history of armed conflict in Colombia, in which victims of drug violence do not play a prominent role. Their victimhood thus remains difficult to categorize, in legal discourse as well as in official practices of historic commemoration.

However, efforts to develop an alternative narrative of drug violence have also been obstructed by the same dynamic that motivated drug violence in the first place: the strength of global commercial and cultural forces promoting a fascination with Escobar. When trying to find the

Museo Casa de la Memoria during our field work, we discovered that it was largely unknown to locals, taxi drivers, and residents. This alternative narrative was, in fact, not easy to locate. Our observation was confirmed by statistics provided by the City Hall showing that in 2018 only 1.7 per cent of visitors to the city's museums went to the Museo Casa de la Memoria. A cursory examination of popular websites, such as TripAdvisor, at the time of our fieldwork showed that, while the privately run Museum Pablo Escobar was the third most popular attraction in the city in visitors' rankings, Museo Casa de la Memoria was ranked eleventh.

The struggle for recognition and the cosmopolitan exclusion

It is not surprising that many of our interviewees and city officials named Holocaust commemorations as a model for constructing a respectful memory tradition. The Holocaust has not only become, as Jeffrey Alexander observes (2009: 3), 'a generalized symbol of human suffering and moral evil', but also one of the most powerful examples of the creation of collective memory of a shared past. For some interviewees, it was an example of how atrocities *should be* remembered, and how nations should respectfully acknowledge the losses suffered by other nations.

In their seminal work on collective memory and the Holocaust, Daniel Levy and Natan Sznaider (2002, 2006) coined the term 'cosmopolitan memory'. They argue that, in a global age, global media representations, in particular, create new memory traditions and memory cultures. Levy and Sznaider use the stories and the evolving memories of the Holocaust as an example of how societies transition from national to cosmopolitan memory cultures, and, in the case of Europe, the creation of a common European cultural memory. This cosmopolitan process carries with it new sensibilities and moral obligations, as well as 'the mutual recognition of the history of the "Other"' (Levy and Szneider, 2002: 103). The creation of global and local memory is thus intertwined and symbiotic.

Memories and narratives of extreme violence, therefore, do not exist in isolation but co-exist in the public sphere and, ultimately, shape one other (Rothberg, 2009). The memories of individual histories are thus not easily separable from one another, but emerge dialogically, and, as described above, have in recent decades been seen to contribute to cosmopolitanization (Beck, Levy, and Sznaider, 2016). José saw the efforts to tell the truth about the violence in Medellín as parallel to other international historic efforts to write history, yet far less successful:

> In Europe, citizens have built their narrative of the concentration camps, of … the two world wars, and [their society has] been rebuilt, revived because people have had that awareness. The Spanish Civil War … is in the middle of [the world] wars and then remains isolated, but it is an impressive civil war. What about the people [of Colombia]? They build their story, they build their law of victims, they keep fighting. There are the mothers of the Plaza de Mayo in Argentina, sixty, eighty years old, still there. And here the Colombians do nothing, the Antioqueños [people living in Antioquia] who are so entrepreneurial, are not able to pick up a microphone and start denouncing as one denounces.

Cosmopolitan memory tradition is, according to Levy and Sznaider (2002: 103) 'based on the mutual recognition of the history of the "Other"'. Medellín's struggle to re-write its history, and to re-frame it on the global stage, can thus be understood within the framework of the 'politics of recognition'. The term was coined by Charles Taylor (1992), and has since been further developed by key critical thinkers (see, e.g., Honneth, 2021; Butler, 2021). Although most often referring to the political struggles of sexual, racial, and ethnic minorities, the concept of recognition in its most basic sense addresses 'the experience of depending on others in one's relation to oneself, for better or worse' (Ikäheimo, Lepold, and Stahl, 2021: 1). In the case of Medellín, this means that, in order to 'embrace history', the city has been also dependent on the world to acknowledge its struggle.

Global responses to, and ideas about, drug violence are key to achieving a sense of recognition. Carlos, the judge who witnessed the assassination of his colleagues by Escobar's hitmen and was forced into exile, remembered how important international support and truth-telling in the international domain were for their struggle:

> [W]e were obliged to denounce these events [violence and threats to the judges], but no longer among ourselves, because we were clear about

> what was happening and where the bullets were coming from, but to get this information out of the country. And then, in 1991, when we took on the task of denouncing [the violence] in Europe, and we were invited by the German judges, and the Dutch invited us and we were invited to Sweden, because we said, quoting Eduardo Galeano in *Open Veins of Latin America*, that if we were keeping silent that was quite similar to stupidity.

Despite Medellín's efforts to join the cosmopolitan discourses on memory and mourning, city officials found their efforts to be largely unsuccessful. Due to the enduring influence of the global entertainment industry and the powerful forces of commercialism, they were unable to stem the tide of dark tourism. Nor did they manage to challenge the global commercial mythmaking surrounding Escobar and establish an alternative cultural experience focused on the victims and survivors. For that reason, the mayor's personal secretary angrily compared Medellín's situation to that of similar places where large-scale violence had taken place, arguing that, while victims in Northern societies receive sympathy and solidarity, Medellín is treated as a source of entertainment:

> The United States had their twin towers destroyed; in Europe, there have been recent [terrorist] attacks; and in the Second World War, there was a brilliantly evil character. [Similarly], thirty years ago we had planes bombed, we had explosions, we had a charismatic drug lord. Why does the whole world feel solidarity with the Jews, with the Germans, with the United States, with France, Spain, and England, but not with us?

Nicolás saw the process of joining the cosmopolitan victim community as fraught with difficulty. However, he saw these difficulties as partly connected to the ambiguous nature of victims of drug violence. Having visited Holocaust museums in Germany and the United States, he concluded:

> I was able to make these visits during these two years, trying to understand how they showed the victims, but the problem with the victims of drug trafficking is that many of them are also perpetrators. In other words, one could consider that the assassins are victims of a system that

> forced them to become victimizers. In drug trafficking, there are many beneficiaries who are difficult to identify. We have no way of telling [them apart], because it didn't seem to us that the history of drug trafficking is a history of victims.

Both statements point to the ambiguous position of victims of drug-related violence. They also indicate a belief in a global hierarchy of victimhood (Franko, 2021), where some victims are more deserving of recognition than others. For Nicolás, this lack of recognition is connected to the ambiguous status of victims of drug violence; while Villa sees it as a sign of global inequality where tragic events in the countries of the Global North are given a different kind of attention and commemoration (see also Franko, 2021).

The difficult path to recognition

When, after more than two decades of neglecting the topic, the local authorities finally turned their attention to honouring the victims, the memorial tradition they tried to create was inspired by cosmopolitan models of commemoration, and stood opposed to the story of gangsterism focused on Escobar. Yet, the narrative power of the global entertainment industry has created a seemingly unsurmountable challenge to the local struggles for recognition. The city authorities have felt marginalized and excluded from global memory traditions and unable to make their story heard in the cacophony of voices narrating Escobar's story. These dynamics challenge Rothberg's (2009: 3) hypothesis that 'memory works *productively* through negotiation, cross-referencing, and borrowing; the result of memory conflict is not less memory, but more—even of subordinated memory traditions'. In the case of Medellín, it seems that rather than working productively, the narrative power of the entertainment industry has 'won' among the competing voices.

These global dynamics support observations of critical analysts of social struggles for recognition, who point out that recognition is intimately connected with relations of domination and power. As Butler (2021: 43) points out, recognition entails not only attribution of a normative status to the one who is recognized by the recognizer, but also that they both emerge as subjects. These processes of subjectification mean that the struggle for recognition is bound up with the problem of dependency and carries a certain ambivalence (ibid.: 44). Recognition does not take place in a social vacuum. How do people and social groups emerge as subjects to be recognized to begin with? Therefore, a question that inevitably arises is 'To what extent are people's specific claims for recognition *themselves* shaped by politics?' (Ikäheimo, Lepold, and Stahl, 2021: 8).

As we showed in this chapter, although it had taken more than two decades before the process of political involvement took pace in Medellín, politics and victimhood became inextricably connected. Consequently, as Jacoby (2015) observes, when victims are incorporated into broader political campaigns, it becomes nearly impossible to separate the victim from politics. While many of our interviewees strongly welcomed this attention to their struggle, a few others were critical of the political profiting that they observed taking place. Rather than seeing the political involvement as a form of recognition, they experienced it as a form of silencing.

The struggle for recognition of victims and survivors of violence in Medellín has thus been taking place in a complex arena with a variety of actors, some presenting outwardly competing claims, while others advancing claims only superficially more compatible. Further adding to this complexity has been the ambiguity of the category of victim of drug violence. If an essential part of any struggle for recognition, as Butler (2021) observes, is that the subject become 'understandable' or 'intelligible' to others, then the question can be asked to what extent this has taken place in Colombia. Nicolás, the journalist involved in projects of local memorialization, thought that the process of joining the cosmopolitan victim community was fraught because of the ambiguity surrounding victims of drug violence.

In a sense, victims of drug trafficking could be described as 'difficult victims', or not quite the right kind of victims, which has affected their social recognition. They depart from Nils Christie's (2018 [1986]) description of the 'ideal victim' discussed in the next chapter. While the victims of the HK-1803 plane bombing have been among those that have had the greatest success in achieving a distinct voice, victim identity, political influence, and social recognition, this position has proven more elusive for others. This ambiguity and difficulty in categorizing the victims of cartel violence will be further explored in the next chapter, where focus will be on questions of legal recognition. According to Axel Honneth (2021: 11), recognition can take several forms: love and care, social esteem, as well as what he terms 'legal respect'. We shall, therefore, proceed to examine how legal respect is connected to questions of intelligibility (mentioned by Butler), categorization, as well as global and national relations of power and domination.

8

Global hierarchies of victimhood

The Victims' Law

When the Colombian Congress drafted its Victims' Law in 2011,[1] it came as a surprise to many that victims of violence in Medellín were excluded from the recognition and benefits that the law accorded to victims. The Congress decreed that the law would only cover 'direct victims of the conflict: those affected by the guerrillas, paramilitaries, or agents of the state' (Unidad para la Atención y Reparación Integral a las Víctimas, 2018: 7). The law further specifies that 'those whose rights have been harmed as a consequence of *common criminality* will not be considered as victims' (art. 3, para. 3; italics added). Several of our interviewees were perplexed by the lack of official recognition. Emiliano, son of a judge executed by the Medellin cartel, said:

> It's incomprehensible why the victims of drug trafficking are not regarded as victims (forgive the redundancy), but makes no sense. From a legal point of view, it is absurd to say that victims of drug trafficking are not victims of the armed conflict in Colombia, when it was common knowledge that the cartels were financing the guerrillas. They financed the storming of the Palace of Justice. This is a proven fact. They financed the protection of their crops and promoted guerrillas and paramilitaries. It is incredible that a law was passed that does not apply to victims of drug trafficking.

Emiliano's statement points to the complex intertwining of drug trafficking and other forms of political violence taking place in the country.

[1] Law 1448 of 10 June 2011 by which measures of attention, assistance, and integral reparation are set forth for the victims of the internal armed conflict and other provisions are established. English translation available at https://en.unesco.org/creativity/sites/creativity/files/law1448v18jun20.pdf, accessed 5 May 2023.

Victimhood, Memory, and Consumerism. Katja Franko and David R. Goyes, Oxford University Press.
 DOI: 10.1093/oso/9780192874115.003.0008

Yet, the law created a distinct separation between these categories of violence as well as a distinction between those affected by the different types of violence.

Reacting to his exclusion from the official category of victim, Federico Arellano—son of the musician Gerardo Arellano, who died in the HK-1803 flight—began to engage in strategic litigation trying to force the state to recognize that drug cartels are also political actors in Colombia's internal conflict. After all, the main target of the HK-1803 attack was the presidential candidate, César Gaviria, who had promised to extradite drug lords should he win the election. In the end, Gaviria was not on the plane that killed Federico's father. Twenty-two years after the bombing, Federico founded the Fundación Colombia con Memoria [Colombia with Memory Foundation] as a platform for his fight. The foundation declares on Facebook: 'In 2009, when the criminal investigation was about to conclude, a group of families gathered to avoid the case remaining in impunity and being forgotten by the history of our country.'[2]

Immediately after Congress had ratified the Victims' Law, Federico, together with other members of the foundation, issued a public statement denouncing the limitations imposed by the law. They argued that the law 'left victims of criminal organizations—such as cartels—and victims of political violence in a grey area' (Galán Pachón et al., 2011: 6). Next, Federico filed a lawsuit challenging the Victims' Law as unconstitutional and arguing that the limitation of the law 'excludes a universe of victims [including] the victims of narco-violence' (Arellano Mendoza, Pulido Caro, and Arellano Becerra, 2011: 3). The Colombian Constitutional Court eventually rejected the lawsuit, defining as victims only those affected by violence related to the internal armed conflict.[3]

Yet, Federico continued his fight for recognition by the Colombian state. Next, he filled a legal request with the Unidad para la Atención y Reparación Integral a las Víctimas [Unit for the Attention to and Integral Reparation for Victims of Crime]—an organization created by the Victims' Law, which was given the task of identifying victims and issuing

[2] For more information, see Fundación Colombia con Memoria, Facebook, https://www.facebook.com/people/Fundaci%C3%B3n-Colombia-con-Memoria/100064883462567/, accessed 5 May 2023.

[3] See Corte Constitucional [C.C.] [Constitutional Court], 18 May 1995, Sentencia C-781, C-225/95; C.C., 29 March 2012, Sentencia C-781/12; and C.C., 12 June 2015, Sentencia T-364/15.

reparations. Federico argued that in the attack on the airplane, in which his father died, paramilitary leaders Carlos and Fidel Castaño allied with Pablo Escobar. 'They were the material authors of that crime, funded by Escobar and other co-financers not yet caught by justice' (Arellano Mendoza, Pulido Caro, and Arellano Becerra, 2011 quoted in Reyes, 2013). The Unit for Victims agreed that the attack against HK-1803 'was a terrorist act with political motives related to the internal armed conflict' (Arellano Mendoza, Pulido Caro, and Arellano Becerra, 2011 quoted in Reyes, 2013), and therefore granted Federico, in 2018, the category of a victim. Although the Colombian legal community considered this a milestone (Unidad para la Atención y Reparación Integral a las Víctimas, 2018: 7), the Unit for Victims warned that not all the victims of Pablo Escobar will get the status of victims or receive reparations, but rather 'the Unit will have to analyse case by case to see if the facts are related closely enough with the conflict' (Arellano Mendoza, Pulido Caro, and Arellano Becerra, 2011 quoted in Reyes, 2013). Federico's grit and intellectual and social resources placed him in a special category among victims of drug violence—a position that is largely unobtainable to others. So far, few other victims of drug violence have achieved such recognition. They are still considered the *wrong type of victim*.

Internationally, the approach of the Colombian state is not an anomaly. Processes of transitional justice initiated in the aftermath of armed conflict do not generally include victims of drug-related violence. This is the case despite the fact that in several Latin American countries deaths caused by cartel violence easily exceed the common 1,000-battle-deaths-per-year criterion of civil war (Lessing, 2015: 1487). In this chapter, we will show that distinctions between victims of war and victims of what is often termed conventional crime are have a great impact on the notion of legitimate victimhood and on legal recognition. While we showed in chapter 3 how social inequality within Colombia, and the strength of global commercial forces, shape victims' ability to have their voices heard, this chapter shows that victims of mass drug violence also face deeply engrained structural and legal obstacles to their recognition.

Drawing on previous scholarship on hierarchies of victimhood (McEvoy and McConnachie, 2012, 2013), we argue that the position of victims of drug violence in Medellín reflects a globally established hierarchy, which distinguishes between victims of war and victims of 'conventional crime', and gives the former greater priority. Colombia, and Medellín in particular, was the first Latin American region to experience drug violence on a massive scale. It therefore serves to show that hierarchies of victimhood have serious legal, symbolic, and material implications for those who find themselves in the less favoured category. Victims of drug-related violence struggle to achieve recognition, to access justice, and to make their voices heard in public discourses about violence.

The chapter begins with an overview of the existing scholarship on hierarchies of victimhood. While research on the issue has brought significant advances over the past decade, we point out that there has not yet been an examination of how global epistemological power imbalances contribute to our understanding of victimhood. We then continue to discuss the distinction between war and crime and the relevance of scholarly perspectives on the coloniality of knowledge to understanding its genealogy. Drawing on the empirical findings presented in chapter 2, about what it was like for Medellín's inhabitants to live in an environment where violence was so widespread that it seemed like a war, we argue that current binary distinctions between war and crime do not offer sound conceptual tools for understanding the situation in Medellín. Nor are they useful for understanding the empirical realities of mass violence and atrocities in many other societies in the Global South. Such distinctions have a distinct Northern bias which, when used uncritically, can be counterproductive for understanding Southern contexts.

The chapter then asks why the experiences of victims of mass drug violence are not considered important for transitional justice processes and what the implications of this exclusion from legitimate victimhood have been for those affected by violence in Medellín.

Hierarchies of victimhood

A large body of scholarship has shown the importance of the construction of victimhood in transitional societies and those that have experienced mass victimization. Questions of victimhood are, as Jankowitz (2018: 236) points out, central 'to better equip societies to address violent pasts and secure a more peaceful future'. One of the most salient findings in previous studies on victimology, transitional justice, and criminology has been that victims are accorded unequal value and legitimacy. Examples range from von Hentig's classic study (1948), in which victims were classified according to the nature of their involvement in the criminal act, to Christie's (2018 [1986]: 20) influential concept of the ideal victim. The 'ideal' victim generates the most sympathy from the society: typically, an old lady mugged by a big man, who uses the stolen money to buy drugs. However, Christie also points out that ideal victims must have power and visibility if they are to gain legitimacy as victims (ibid.).

In transitional contexts, the category of victimhood has proved to be highly contentious. According to Ferguson, Burgess, and Hollywood (2010: 860), 'legitimate identification as the victim may be used to attract resources and international support to the ingroup while strengthening ingroup solidarity and moral superiority over the outgroup'. The label of victim has been contested particularly fiercely because it is closely associated with notions of blame. This, as McEvoy and McConnachie (2012, 2013) show in their seminal studies, leads to the creation of *hierarchies of victimhood*, which are based on a distinction between deserving and undeserving victims. Such hierarchies may be problematic in that they are based on standards and criteria that reflect the narrative or ideology of the group making the ranking and may lead to further conflict and re-victimization by privileging certain victims' needs and experiences over those of others (Jankowitz, 2018).

The growing scholarly engagement with the politics of victimhood found in contexts of internal armed conflict shows that the notion of innocence is central to the social understanding of victimhood. 'Innocent' victims are 'at the apex of a hierarchy of victimhood' and become 'a symbol around which contested notions of past violence and suffering are constructed and reproduced' (McEvoy and McConnachie, 2012: 532). Van Wijk's (2013) and Schwobel-Patel's (2018) studies show that notions of innocence and ideal victimhood also inform how international crimes are understood. Conflicts where distinctions between 'good guys' and 'bad guys' (Van Wijk, 2013: 169) are clear and simple attract greater media attention and enable victims to publicize their experiences, and thus 'benefit' from their status as victims.

Although the innocence paradigm has been by far the most influential approach to the understanding of legitimacy in transitional contexts, some commentators identify further elements to explain and predict differential ranking of legitimacy. Brewer and Hayes (2015), for example, find that ideological and religious convictions affect perceptions of innocence. Moving beyond the 'innocence paradigm', Jankowitz's study of the conflict in Northern Ireland distinguishes between two meta-types of hierarchies: normative, which 'communicate beliefs about how victim experiences should be prioritized or distinguished against one another', and descriptive, which reflect 'beliefs that certain victim experiences are treated as more profound or deserving than others' (2018: 224). More specialized studies have investigated the creation of hierarchies of victimhood in national legislation. Hearty (2016: 334) points out that the meta-conflict positioning of legislators—i.e., the 'continuing political disagreement over the causes and consequences of conflict'—determines who is recognized as a victim and which victims are prioritized. Consequently, even regulations intended to end the conflict end up being 'war by other means via restrictively ascribing blame for suffering in accordance with meta-conflict positions on the (il)legitimacy of certain violence' (ibid.: 335). Similarly, Killean (2018: 227) shows how processes leading to inclusion in the category of victimhood are permeated by political interests, particularly the desire to 'limit the extent of this [the state's] accountability'. Prosecutorial and judicial selectivity and visibility in the courtroom may also shape hierarchies of victimhood (ibid.).

In the global domain, scholars have pointed out that the hierarchy of victimhood is also shaped by international politics (Carrabine et al., 2020), and have stressed the importance of victims' ability to attract the attention of politicians, international NGOs, and, above all, international media. Christie's model of the ideal victim seems largely appropriate in the context of international crimes, although in crucial ways it is shaped by media attention (Van Wijk, 2013). Here we also encounter the paradox described by Christie (2018 [1986]): victims have to be vulnerable in order to seem deserving of victim status, yet strong and powerful enough to gain it and fend off counterclaims (see also Schwöbel-Patel, 2018).

Most existing scholarship on hierarchies of victimhood focuses on victims' characteristics, particularly their perceived innocence, relationship to perpetrators, and ability to attract international support and media attention. For the purposes of our discussion, however, Van Wijk's (2013) study is important because he also draws attention to the characteristics of conflicts. Not all conflicts are able to endow victims with legitimate victimhood. An important factor determining legitimate victimhood is whether a conflict is defined as war or as a conventional crime. As exemplified by the Colombia's Victims' Law, distinction between the two has important legal and symbolic consequences for victims. It helps create structural conditions in which victims of mass drug violence are placed at the bottom of the hierarchy of victimhood, although they have other qualities usually associated with 'ideal victims'. In what follows, we shall first explore the origins and nature of the distinction made between war and crime and examine how it may be seen as a reflection of deeper epistemological inequalities between the Global North and Global South. We will ask to what extent the conceptual placing of mass drug violence in the category of 'ordinary crime' represents a Northern perspective on violence.

Mass drug violence: A civil war or an 'ordinary crime'?

In many Latin American countries today, the casualties of drug-related violence far exceed accepted definitions of civil war. According to Lessing (2015: 1487), militarized conflict between cartels and states has particularly afflicted Latin America's three largest countries (Brazil, Mexico, and Colombia) 'arguably supplanting revolutionary insurgency as the hemisphere's predominant form of conflict'. Next to the war in Syria, Mexico's cartel–state conflict has been, so far, the most violent subnational conflict of the twenty-first century (ibid.). According to the official government count, 70,000 people were killed between 2006 and 2012 in inter-cartel and state–cartel conflicts. This is 'more than four times greater than the median death toll of all civil wars in the second half of the twentieth century' (Trejo and Ley, 2020: 2).

It is commonplace in political speeches, media reports, and academic writing to describe the situation in Mexico and elsewhere as a 'drug war' (Gibler, 2011; Shirk, 2011). For example, in 2006, Mexico's President Felipe Calderón famously declared war on the cartels (Trejo and Ley, 2020). The term is also used to convey the level of militarization found in the fight against illegal narcotics. Brands (2011: 230) argues that, due to its propensity to attack state institutions, 'illicit activity in Latin America begins to straddle the demarcation between non-political and political violence, between crime and insurgency'. The numbers of drug violence casualties not only match conventional definitions of war but also represent a threat to the central functions of society (Trejo and Ley, 2020).

The blurred line between criminal and military actors has long been acknowledged as a feature of many conflicts. Terms such as 'civil war' (Schedler, 2013), 'criminal war' (Trejo and Ley, 2020), 'irregular warfare', and 'criminal insurgency' (Brands, 2011) have been used by scholars to describe the scale and gravity of violence in cartel–state conflicts. Other observers, however, have been more reluctant to challenge the established distinction between crime and warfare. Lessing (2015) acknowledges the severity of the threat of cartel violence and its magnitude, but argues that it should be distinguished from war because of 'differences in underlying logics of violence': 'cartels do not seek to topple the government and seize formal power' (ibid.: 1488).

Our main objective is to examine the implications such conceptual distinctions have for those affected by large-scale drug violence. While studies of transitional justice, international criminal law, victimology, and criminology have paid increasing attention to the position of victims of war (McGarry and Walklate, 2015), they have mostly overlooked victims of drug violence. Similarly, the fields of international relations and criminology have been striving to bridge the divide between studies of crime and war, the 'inside' and the 'outside' (see, inter alia, Loader and Percy, 2012; Jamieson, 2014; McGarry and Walklate, 2015); however, the categorization of mass drug-related violence as a crime has largely remained unchallenged. This means that we have a growing body of knowledge about the nature and causes of drug violence, the damage it causes to state institutions, and how it challenges national security (Lessing, 2015; Durán-Martínez, 2018; Trejo and Ley, 2020), but know far less about the impact of mass drug violence on victims and their ability to access justice.

Neither has a more nuanced understanding of such violence informed international and national legal frameworks. Colombia's Victims' Law is not only an example of national legislation, but also an expression of an international legal consensus. The militarization of Mexico's drug war has sparked debate about whether the conflict should be classified as non-international armed conflict (Bergal, 2011; Sassoli, 2019); but, so far, drug-related crimes have not been included in internationally agreed definitions of mass atrocity crimes, even though they may involve widespread, systematic attacks on civilian populations (Robinson, 2015). Interestingly, the negotiation of the Rome Statute of the International Criminal Court was originally initiated by Trinidad and supported by several other small states that wanted an international tribunal to try drug trafficking offences. This argument was later lost in the negotiation process due to the influence of powerful (Northern) actors, particularly the United States (Boister, 2012).

In sum, much of the scholarship on the hierarchies of victimhood stresses the importance of moral considerations, particularly perceptions of victims' innocence (McEvoy and McConnachie, 2012, 2013). Although victims of drug violence in Medellín meet the criteria of 'innocence' and 'respectability', and have undoubtedly experienced grievous harm, our findings show that they feel neglected and impotent in terms of having their voices heard and being able to access justice. Their public standing and the legitimacy of their claims are defined by the fact that they are victims of 'conventional crime' rather than of war or political violence. The question therefore needs to be asked why acts such as civilian massacres, systematic assassinations of politicians, judges, and other state representatives are classed as 'conventional crime'. In chapters 2 and 3, we tried to convey the sensory experience of these forms of violence, which our interviewees often likened to war. Ultimately, as Gray observes (1989: 11 quoted in McGarry and Walklate, 2011: 900), while 'the magnitude of violence may vary with the object and means of war, the violent essence of war will never change'.

Unlike war, however, much crime is non-violent. This applies particularly to countries of the Global North, many of which have witnessed a steady decline in recorded crime, including homicide. According to the United Nations Office on Drugs and Crime's *Global Study on Homicide* (UNDOC, 2019), the homicide rate in Europe has declined by 63 per cent since 2002 and is now at 3.0 per 100,000. Although drug-related crimes continue to feature prominently in crime statistics in Northern societies, they produce few fatalities. By contrast, the homicide rate in the Americas is the highest recorded in the region since reliable records began being kept in 1990. Central America and South America, at 25.9 and 24.2 per 100,000, respectively, were in 2017 the subregions with the highest homicide rates in the world, followed by the Caribbean, with 15.1 per 100,000 (UNODC, 2019). Large-scale loss of life related to drug activities thus takes place predominantly in the countries of the Global South. The conceptualization of drug-related violence as ordinary violence fits Northern realities much better than it does the extreme type of crime found in Latin American countries. To what extent, then, are current understandings of 'ordinary crime' shaped by epistemological inequalities at the global level? As we have seen, several of our interviewees ascribed the lack of recognition and respect for losses to the fact that they were not from affluent Northern societies.

A growing body of scholarship has, in the past decades, drawn attention to the connection between geopolitical position and knowledge production. Connell's influential critique of Northern theory (2006) is particularly relevant here as it points out how vast global inequalities of resources shape all academic disciplines, including the social sciences. These inequalities 'may also be embedded *within* a discipline, in the way intellectual workers define their problems and carry out their work' (ibid.: 237). Because, overwhelmingly, social theory is produced in the Global North, scholars are socialized into what Connell terms 'reading from the center': metropolitan theorists, building on personal knowledge or local research, 'generalize the specific experience of metropolitan countries' (ibid.: 259). The seeming universality of contemporary social theory thus results from the generalization of Northern experience.

Connell's work draws on a long tradition of social critique of Eurocentrism and the coloniality of knowledge (see, inter alia, Amin 2009 [1988]; Said, 2019 [1978]; Hall, 1992). The Latin American decolonial movement has also brought attention to the mutually constitutive power relations 'between the international division of labour, the global racial/ethnic hierarchy and the hegemonic Eurocentric epistemologies in the modern/colonial world-system' (Grosfoguel, 2007: 95). The notion of coloniality highlights the role that knowledge systems play in neo-colonial practices and in the way Northern influence shapes how Southern realities are understood. The Southern embrace of Northern views of reality blinds scholars to dynamics that may contradict or nuance existing academic understandings. Santos (2014) calls this phenomenon *epistemological blindness*, or 'the conscious or unconscious preference to accommodate only that which accords with our existing epistemological and methodological configurations, leaving other possibilities or data ignored' (Goyes and South, 2017: 168). This results in inadequate, decontextualized readings of reality. Moreover, as this book also shows, the impact of metropolitan academic worldviews goes beyond the definition of research issues, concepts, and methods, also shaping the issues included on states' agendas, the concepts guiding how the issues are understood, and the public policy adopted to confront them (Goyes, 2019).

A war seen 'from below', but not 'from above'

The scope of violence in Medellín in the 1980s and 1990s, as we have seen in chapter 2, was extreme in terms of the number of casualties, and the modalities of the assault on state institutions and their representatives, as well as the militarized nature of the state's response. The cartels openly challenged the supremacy of state institutions, and the state responded with increasingly military means. We have also shown that it was not only the objective elements (such as the number of casualties) that made the conflict war-like, but also the subjective experiences of the civilian population affected by it. Many people referred to the situation as a war.

Our respondents from the communes, in particular, often used the term 'war' to refer to drug violence. The term designated not just the situation in the 1980s and 1990s, but a persistent conflict that stretched into the following decades. Speaking of narco-series, one resident, who was deeply engaged in community work, said:

> For me, these TV programs take us to the time of war, when we lived in the communes, where those wars killed many people, adults and children alike. You must keep that in mind: there were many children between 2000 and 2008 who were left traumatized. And [narco-shows] bring back traumatic memories, make the viewers recall the time you couldn't go outside to exercise, because you might cross paths with a bullet.

She pointed out that the safety continues to be a problem in some communes: 'In commune one, the war is over, but in commune thirteen, you can still see the war ... it is the drugs, that is the silent war that is in the communes.'

These accounts point to the pervasiveness of violence that affected both impoverished population residing at the outskirts of the city as well as economically privileged citizenry, such as judges and other prominent state representatives. Recalling this period, the inhabitants of the city we interviewed described car bombs, executions, homicides, kidnappings, and many other forms of destruction and violence they had witnessed, as well as the pervasive fear that affected all segments of the population and the young in particular. Luciana, a relative of a kidnapped politician, noted: 'There wasn't a single person who would feel completely safe in this city.'

Our interviewees described the deadly assault on social institutions such as the courts and the police and noted that the society they lived in had been 'brought to its knees'. Therefore, the question of why these social conditions should be classified as 'ordinary crime', rather than a form of political violence, becomes even more pertinent. This classification reveals the underlying tendency to separate drug violence from the realm of politics. As mentioned in the introduction, 'drug violence' is difficult to define. The label has been used by the Colombian government to delegitimize certain actors in the conflict; the framing of violence as an attack of 'narco-terrorists' on the state and citizens has led to a denial of the political aspects of the conflict. The label has been employed as part of a strategy of de-politicization as well as legitimization of militarized responses. A re-politization of the phenomenon, therefore, implies an awareness that 'drug violence' is not simply violence 'brought on by drugs', but it is deeply intertwined with political processes and actors.

Many of our interviewees were acutely aware of the involvement of the political system. Alberto, son of a prominent politician, remembered how drug trafficking infiltrated the political system due to the money involved: 'So many sectors of society participated in this environment. They bowed, bowed to the power that drug traffickers wielded at that time. Politics was not alien to that because they laundered money in politics.' Carlos pointed out how drug trafficking was connected to local political parties and enabled by policies towards the marginalized parts of the society:

> Drug trafficking, which had managed to penetrate the traditional parties as well as social and political regional leadership, quickly became strong. First, they began to penetrate marginalized sectors of society as a kind of Robin Hood. They built sports fields for them, held events for the citizens, guaranteed the payment of burials, but they [cartels] also formed an army of hitmen mainly made up of young people. In the case of Medellín, [hitmen were] young people from the communes who had been completely marginalized and who had been subjected to the state's punitive approach to poverty.

It was not only the shift of attention from the victims to the perpetrators that our interviewees saw as an unfortunate effect of narco-series, but also the obscuring of the social and political forces within the Colombian society that were enabling drug trafficking, especially the political elites that have profited and continue to profit from it. Carlos saw the current focus on Escobar's personality as essentially connected to the misguided responses to drug trafficking:

> By responding with violence to a phenomenon that is above all social, without making an agrarian reform that guarantees that the peasant has the right to land, the only option left to the peasant is to eradicate [drug crops] or leave [the land]. There is no productive alternative that guarantees the right to live in dignity. I think that we have to analyse the phenomenon of Pablo Escobar in this context. It is a mistake and a horror to personalize it.

An additional political aspect (obscured in *Narcos*) is how the 'war on drugs' is to a large extent a prohibition regime created by the countries in the Global North, particularly the United States (del Olmo 1998; Andreas and Nadelmann, 2006; Goyes and South, 2017; Franko, 2020) with a deeply destructive impact on Southern societies. Carlos argued that '[w]hat the Colombian state does is almost like serving as a jailer for people who, from the U.S. perspective, should be sentenced for committing the crime of drug trafficking.' He saw the extradition regime imposed on the cartels, which led to the escalation of drug violence, including the Avianca plane bombing, as 'a mechanism for imposing a one-way street' with few other avenues of actions open to the Colombian state. Some of our other interviewees were also critical of the global drug prohibition regime. Nicolás, the journalist investigating memory and violence in Medellín, said:

> Medellín continues to pay the price for a global business, which is responsible for many local deaths, also for corruption, deinstitutionalization, and a generation that is poorly educated. [The war on drugs] has many impacts beyond the dead.

Both Carlos and Nicolás were proponents of some form of legalization of illicit drugs and therefore critical of the current global and national militarized drug policies 'which feed violence'. Carlos thus concluded that, '[a]s long as there is prohibition, there will be cartels, and there will be death and violence against people.'

The cartel's most prominent attempt at political involvement was Escobar's short spell in Congress. However, the cartel's political ambitions were also transparent in its intentions of changing specific policies, such as the extradition agreement between Colombia and the United States. As mentioned earlier, the signing of the agreement was an important turning point in the escalation of violence in Medellín and Colombia, more generally. Moreover, the violence posed a direct threat to state institutions and individuals (and their families, who were performing central public duties). Our interviews with former members of the judiciary and their relatives describe a national criminal justice system that was broken and unable to cope under the pressure. Judges and police officers were among the most exposed targets. Several of our interviewees were relatives of judges who had been assassinated. Alberto, son of a prominent criminal justice official, described his family's situation as 'institutionally abandoned':

> I do believe that those who stood up to [drug violence] have been abandoned. They were institutionally abandoned. In other words, they were neither imagined nor were they presented as the men who really faced the forces threatening the democratic stability of the country. They weren't really considered to be true heroes.

Similarly, Carlos, a prominent member of the judicial union, described those who had resisted as 'absolutely alone':

> In other words, the government only limited itself to counting the dead, issuing communiqués, and talking about exhaustive investigations. But the legitimacy of the state to prosecute crime was always in question, and we never saw it.

Carlos' sense of abandonment referred not only to the Colombian state but also to the international community: 'The victims were not honoured by the Colombian state or the international community, since all [the international community] did was observe from a distance what was happening in Colombia.'

These testimonies reveal not only how deep the wounds inflicted on state institutions were, but also why recognition through the state criminal justice system was unavailable to victims of cartel violence.

'An ignored death': The elusiveness of justice

Paying homage to Richard Quinney, Sandra Walklate (2012: 173) points out that are three interrelated narratives on criminal victimization—the academic, the cultural, and the political—and suggests that there are remarkable similarities between the victims we 'see' and the victims we fail to see in each of these narratives. Our interviewees experienced a sense of invisibility at all these levels.

As in other post-conflict situations (McEvoy and McConnachie, 2012, 2013; Jankowitz, 2018), in Colombia the political issues surrounding victimhood are fiercely contested. The Victim's Law was drafted in 2007 as a response to the intense criticism that was directed at the Justice and Peace Law. In 2005, the former Colombian president, Álvaro Uribe Vélez, negotiated a peace agreement with the main paramilitary group operating in the country (the United Self-Defence Armies of Colombia). The Peace and Justice Law granted substantial benefits to paramilitary combatants who chose to demobilize. While the declared aim was to replicate the truth, justice, reparation, and guarantees of non-recurrence frameworks found in international war transition experiences (Uprimny Yepes et al., 2006), commentators condemned the law for imposing insufficient sentences on combatants who had committed appalling atrocities. The controversial Justice and Peace Law added to the '*parapolítica* scandal', which exposed close ties of many high-ranking elected officials to the paramilitaries (Counter, 2018: 127; see also Goyes, 2015). The controversies surrounding the Justice and Peace Law then spurred the creation of the Victims' Law, whose proponents wished to put an end to 'the government's undue deference to paramilitaries and subsequent neglect of conflict victims', while its opponents objected that the law would treat 'terrorists [members of guerrilla groups who were also victims] as equals to police and soldiers' (Counter, 2018: 127). Despite such opposition, the Colombian Congress ratified the Victims' Law in 2011. The Law 'transformed the small-scale reparation mechanisms embodied in the Justice and Peace Law into a large-scale transitional justice process' (Sandvik and Lemaitre, 2015: 259) and offered victims the right to benefit from a program to protect a dignified life (including economic support until they cease being in a vulnerable situation), family reunification, a safe return to the place they were displaced from, and re-possession of their land (should they have lost it).[4]

The law is explicitly founded on the principle of justice, promoted by international institutions, and symbolically endorsed by the international community through the presence of the UN Secretary-General Ban Ki Moon at the adoption ceremony (Sandvik and Lemaitre, 2015).[5] It is beyond the scope of this book to give a comprehensive overview of the Victims' Law and the national debates surrounding it. Our primary point of interest here is not the overall analysis and efficacy of the Law, but rather how the binary distinction between war and crime in the Law may have contributed to the systematic and structural exclusion of victims of mass drug violence from transitional justice processes. Although excluding victims of drug related violence from legitimate victimhood may have been motivated by the state's desire to limit its own accountability (Killean, 2018), it is also in line with internationally established traditions of thinking about transitional justice.

[4] For more information, see 'Preguntas Frecuentes', *Unidad para las victimas*, https://www.unidadvictimas.gov.co/es/preguntas-frecuentes/90, accessed on 26 October 2021.

[5] In addition to the transformative influence of the norms of international law, the internationalization of peace processes in Colombia had three other components: a *political* one, in which Western nations became facilitators of the processes; an *economic* one, in which the international community funded the peace dialogue; and a *theoretical* one, in which the Colombian peace processes followed Western models (Cujabante Villami, 2016: 216).

As Counter (2018: 128) points out, the Victims' Law specifies that the category of victim is reserved for individuals who were victimized by officially recognized actors, and who had been subjected to one of twelve officially recognized 'victimizing acts'. 'These acts, however, must be related to armed conflict (as opposed to "common crime")' (ibid.). One of our interviewees, who had tried to obtain legal recognition as a victim, spoke of her experiences:

> Because, when the Victims' Law was enacted, [a friend] said to me, 'you could be among the victims'. So, I began to go through the whole process, and was told: 'No, you do not classify as a victim because you did not suffer at the hands of the guerrillas or paramilitaries.' But, in the end, there is no difference between the two. Because later, in 1994, they saw that that some of the guerrillas had a close relationship with Pablo Escobar's people. So, if asked if I'm a victim, I answer, 'Yes, I am'. Victims of drug trafficking, of the guerrillas, paramilitaries, they are the same.

The distinction made between different categories of victim seemed incomprehensible to her, because of how intertwined the two forms of conflict were. Similarly, Federico Arellano, who, as we have seen, was the first victim to eventually receive recognition, told us:

> Lawmakers misunderstood the meaning of the so-called 'internal armed conflict'. For them, it meant a conflict between guerrillas and the paramilitaries, which left out important elements, such as the drug cartels. Drug-dealing has fuelled the conflict.

Due to the strict demarcation of the 'field of recognizability' of victims, as Counter (2018: 129) points out, 'certain lives are erased from consideration for reparations'.

The ultimate objective of most of our interviewees was not necessarily to achieve victim status or material reparation; many preferred to describe themselves as survivors, and wished to convey an impression of resilience. Sandra, who had lost her husband in the plane bombing, certainly identified as a victim, but rather than financial reparation she wished for acknowledgement and psychological support:

> We are already victims of violence. That we had a recognition about two years ago, that we have a judgment where you recognize us as victims. For us, for me, for my daughter, that document does not mean much. Supposedly with that document the reparations will come but we know we will not receive them. And I know of victims who need them more than we do. But we've never had any support from the government. I don't know if this is because it was a long time ago and the displacements came later and they began to handle the subject of displacements much more. But our people, our loved ones died on that plane. At no time did the government call us and said, 'Look, we can offer support. They are going to need psychological support.' Well, one would not have asked for financial support, but for psycho-social support, and we did not have it. We have supported one another. That made us create the foundation ... But really, the government, to us—the victims of the plane—has given no support.

Isabella, on the other hand, did not see herself as a victim, but thought—in collective terms—that anyone 'who walked through the streets of Medellín every day was a survivor. Bombs were going off at every turn; going to a shopping centre was a risk, an adventure. I believe that anyone who dared to go outside at that time is a survivor.' Several other interviewees disapproved of victimhood as an individualistic project and stressed the importance of collective memory. Some resented individual victims promoting their stories because, as Isabella observed, 'many people have got a lot of [financial] advantage from that position of victim.'

Despite differences regarding the victim label and status in legal terms, our interviewees had common concerns, which had to do with *truth*, *impunity*, and *memory*. These concerns resonate with victims' needs in other transitional justice and post-conflict settings. As Brants and Klep (2013: 36) observe, '[t]ruth, collective memory, and history-telling have become buzzwords in the transitional justice debate, conceptual keys to reconciliation, democracy, and peace in conflict-ridden nations.' The importance of finding the truth was forcefully argued by the daughter of a judge who was assassinated by the Medellín cartel:

> I feel that there was no one, no one from the justice system, who took my father's case forward. And that hurts a lot, you know. His is like an

> ignored death. I don't think he deserved it. Just as he gave his best efforts and his own life to carry out a judicial process, they should have done the same for him. So, thirty-five years have passed. That's what hurts me the most, you know. I believe that impunity is one of the things that affects me the most. Look, nobody's going to bring him back, nothing can fix that. In other words, a family was broken. Six lives—of my grandparents, my uncles—were broken, many days were broken, and more than the personal process, absolutely nothing can be done about that. But the least I hope for, and what I sincerely want ... is that they [the State] will make some effort to at least investigate what happened. Years go by and the opportunity to learn the truth is increasingly lost.

The importance of truth-telling emerged as one of the central concerns for our interviewees. Sometimes it was related to the fate of individual victims: the desire that their death not be ignored and to find out learn the truth and make it known. For Federico Arellano, truth was a necessary precondition for achieving a number of objectives, such as justice, reparations, and non-repetition.

> That is why one talks about truth, justice, reparation, and guarantees of non-repetition. One can't exist without the other two: without truth, there is no justice; without justice, there can be no reparations; and once truth, justice, and reparations are done, the precedent is set so that what happened is not repeated. That is to say, guarantees of non-repetition, that's where we talk about comprehensive reparations, that's what I mean by reparations.
>
> In our case, we have neither truth nor justice, much less reparation, and we are very far from non-repetition. So that's why impunity is so serious, which is nothing more than the earliest stages of the opening of a criminal investigation. Nothing has happened there! And thirty-one years have passed. There is a lot of evidence, a lot of things that should have been asserted, and have not been asserted.

As we have seen in the chapter 3, some survivors started blogs or wrote books to counter official disinterest and lack of recognition. José, whose brother was killed when he was in his teens, dedicated his life to independently investigate the involvement of various state actors in his brother's murder. This project left him deeply disillusioned with state authorities and the political system for covering up the truth. 'We build the story, we transform reality. We have to empower ourselves, stop fear and shit.' Similarly, Carlos argued that the truth was the most important precondition for achieving a symbolic reparation for the victims, especially since this would mean uncovering the complicity of state elites in drug trafficking: 'If those elites who were compromised by drug trafficking are afraid of anything, it is the truth.'

Truth-telling was also frequently described as a project that would contribute to collective memory and help repair the damage done to the community. In that respect, communities affected by mass drug violence resemble other communities in post-conflict settings. The need for truth-telling and ability to shape collective memory are seen as necessary steps to social recognition. This recognition must take place not only at the level of the community as a whole (as described in the previous chapter), but also at a personal level where individuals make sense of their experiences.

Our interviewees stressed the importance of acknowledging the seriousness of the crimes committed, and were afraid that their losses would be forgotten. Alberto, whose family lived under a direct death threat for a number of years, reflected that the glorification of perpetrators of such violence made him wonder about the meaning of his and his family's sacrifices: 'Then one might say, why did we sacrifice so much? I say that, as a family, my father never asks that question, because that was his duty to do that. These lonely struggles occurred and are not fairly recognized.'

Such feelings resemble those emerging in the aftermath of other atrocities and have been presented in scholarly literature as an argument for truth commissions (rather than traditional criminal justice trials) as the preferred response. As Brants and Klep (2013: 36) point out:

> The primary concern of truth commissions is to bring justice to victims through publicly establishing what happened to them. But this obvious difference hides a significant similarity: such truth-finding also promotes the development of a collective memory by establishing a version of history that informs, and is informed by, the memories of those involved – a shared truth about crime and injustice that allows sense to be made of a traumatic past and is a prerequisite for a stable future.

However, few such avenues to social recognition and collective repair have been available to those affected by drug violence in Medellín. No truth commissions were established to learn the truth. The national criminal justice system was severely damaged by the onslaught of violence. And the task of truth-telling has, in the last twenty years, to a large extent, been taken over by the global entertainment industry.

Unequal victims and the obliteration of pain

In this chapter, we critically engaged with the conceptual distinctions between war and crime, and explored their implications for affected individuals and communities. Conceptualizations of violence, including the violence of war, are historically and contextually contingent. For example, conflict-related sexual violence has only in recent years received proper recognition as an element of wartime violence. This has led to efforts by the international community to fight impunity related to wartime rape and sexual assault (Houge and Lohne, 2017). Because the prevailing view is that drug-related violence is conventional crime, it is excluded from discussions of mass atrocities and transitional justice, irrespective of the scale of its casualties. Consequently, when scholars and practitioners refer to 'fighting impunity'—a powerful slogan used by contemporary justice movements (Lohne, 2019)—this does not include victims of mass drug violence. A strong resentment of impunity of the perpetrators, and the political elites supporting them, was expressed by several of our respondents.

The strength of victims' voices and social perceptions of legitimacy of their claims depend on a number of factors. In chapter 3, we argued that victims differ in terms of their social capital, where class plays an important role. Nicolás was, for example, critical of the political processes of selection of victims' voices in the 'Medellín Embraces its History' campaign:

> It was a project between journalism and public relations, a very strange mix, zero universities, academia, zero other actors, a manipulation of the victims by treating them as heroes, very selected, generally upper-class victims, generals, victims of politicians and judges who were used.

Moreover, we have argued that the position of victims of mass drug violence is shaped by unequal epistemological relations. The hierarchies of victimhood are, in addition to class, perceptions of innocence, and other forms of capital, also shaped by global inequality and the nature of the conflict. Drug-related mass violence is mostly found in societies in the Global South, and especially in Latin America. The prevailing binary distinction between warfare and crime does not adequately capture the reality on the ground in Southern societies. This conceptual distinction fails to address the needs of victims of this type of mass violence by creating a structural divide, and thus a hierarchy among victims, which ignores the severity of suffering undergone by the affected communities. A sensory approach has enabled us to describe drug violence in Medellín not from a (detached) analytical perspective, but as it was experienced by the survivors and the city's inhabitants. Our aim was to get closer to individual and communal realities, rather than accepting existing conceptualizations and analytical perspectives, which mostly define drug-violence as 'ordinary crime', thus exhibiting a distinctly Northern epistemological bias. According to critics, the contrast between the peaceful North and the violent South—where violent loss of life is normalized—has been one of the defining features of colonial imaginaries, which continue to influence contemporary scientific approaches (Morrison, 2006).

However, our objective has not been simply to critique Northern epistemological influence, but rather to show its consequences for the affected communities. A sense of justice has remained permanently elusive for victims of drug violence in Medellín. If we are to advance conditions for social justice in countries of the Global South, we need a more nuanced conceptual understanding of mass violence. In recent years, scholars have made great advances in understanding how modern technologies, such as drones, have individualized warfare and taken it out of its collective frame (Di Nucci and Santoni de Sio, 2016). Along the same lines, in the case of mass drug violence, crime needs to be lifted out of its individualized, criminal-justice frame and attention needs to be paid to collective understandings and responses to match those accorded to victims and survivors of war and mass atrocities.

Drug violence is deeply intertwined with politics in terms its causes and responses (Durán-Martínez, 2018). There is an 'intimate connection between political change and large-scale criminal violence' in several

Latin American countries (Trejo and Ley, 2020: 3). An a priori placement of this form of violence in the category of 'ordinary crime', rather than that of political violence, obscures the involvement of political actors and closes off other, potentially productive, ways of understanding it. As we have seen in chapter 3, several of our interviewees felt that victims of drug violence were invisible. Valentina reflected on this:

> There is nothing to make her [the victim of drug violence] visible and to also respect her experiences and memory. . . . I think that such an important incident as drug trafficking is left out because that would uncover truths and realities that not everyone is willing to reveal. Because of corruption and impunity this [violence] has not been taken into account. It is an intentional exclusion. . . . In other words, drug trafficking would uncover many things at different levels of society, especially at political levels. So, I believe that [drug trafficking] was strategically excluded, so that the facts about those who hold or have held power would not be uncovered.

Valentina, the daughter of a judge murdered by the cartels, points to a commonly held belief that political conditions have been conducive to the invisibility of victims of drug related violence, because of the ways the drug economy permeated and continues to permeate the existing political system and power structures in the society.

9
Conclusion

Memory, voice, identity, and power in a global society

On 10 October 2018, Netflix released the movie *22 July* about the terrorist attack on the Norwegian island of Utøya and government buildings in Oslo. The producers offered the victims' support group the opportunity to watch the movie before its public release; health personnel were available during the screening for victims' families and survivors.[1] The director, Paul Greengrass, had several meetings with the victims' support group during the production, and several of the actors met and even befriended the survivors they were portraying. The movie's focus, explained Greengrass, was the aftermath of violence—not a depiction of the violent event itself: 'When filming stories of violence like this one', he said, 'one has a responsibility to make a truthful movie, but at the same time restrained and decent. It is difficult to balance these objectives, but I think it is necessary' (Enge and Storrusten, 2018). Erik Poppe directed *Utøya: 22 July*, also about the attacks. Poppe acknowledged the ethical difficulties inherent in depicting such an event, and explained that he intentionally refrained from focusing on the perpetrator, since much is already known about him through the criminal trial and books that have been written (ibid.). This is an example of how Western productions might respond to trauma taking place on Western soil.

When traumatizing episodes happen in North America and Europe, the concept of trauma is deeply entrenched in the intellectual and emotional responses of the society (Fassin and Rechtman, 2009). The acknowledgment of trauma and the fear of re-traumatization shape the social

[1] For more information, see C. Enge and K. Storrusten, 'Nå kommer Netflix-filmen om 22. juli' ['Now comes a movie about July 22nd'], *Aftenposten* (4 September 2018), https://www.aftenposten.no/kultur/i/21xdpB/naa-kommer-netflix-filmen-om-22-juli, accessed on 15 February 2023.

Victimhood, Memory, and Consumerism. Katja Franko and David R. Goyes, Oxford University Press.
 DOI: 10.1093/oso/9780192874115.003.0009

understanding of victimhood and the responses to public portrayals of violence. However, this sensitivity to victims' experiences in depictions of violence has been far from the case in Medellín.

We have shown how the survivors and victims' families of drug violence in Colombia have faced numerous obstacles to obtain social recognition of their trauma. Following the explosion of commercial appropriation of the period of violence, the story of Medellín has been framed in terms of exotic gangsterism and violent masculinity, and the survivors have been confronted with the commercial branding of one of the main perpetrators. Victims' and survivors' tragic story has been turned into entertainment. The sense of re-victimization has been further strengthened by the reshaping of the city's life by entrepreneurial actors—simultaneously also impacting younger generations. Ana, a widow who chose to define herself as a survivor rather than a victim, stressed the importance of personal strength and resilience. Yet, she described the commercialism surrounding Escobar as something that prevented her from moving on with her life:

> I am unable to put [the painful experience] behind me, and it festers like an open wound. [To] see that Pablo Escobar's son is selling something; Pablo Escobar's brother selling something else; they are using his name as the glory. That is, he is an idol. That hurts and hurts me because I say [it] is not based in reality. That is harmful. It is deeply painful and all this has not allowed me to have closure. And perhaps I would have progressed further in my life without this permanent reminder.

More than three decades after the peak of violence in Medellín, many of our interviewees said that the violent events were still alive in their consciousness and shaped their everyday experiences. Victims and survivors have received little remedy from the national criminal justice system, which has been paralysed and been unable to deal with the destructive attack on its own members and functions. Nor do the victims feel included in the global discourse about mass atrocities, which could potentially offer them a respectful acknowledgment of the tragic losses they had suffered.

Truth-telling and collective memory were very important to most of our interviewees. The narrative and epistemic power of the global entertainment industry and the stories promoted by it are, therefore, an obstacle in terms of achieving a greater sense of social justice (Goyes and Franko, 2021). As McEvoy and McConnachie (2013: 496) point out, giving victims a voice is key to achieving justice in post-conflict settings. One of the main arguments of the present book is that, in the case of Medellín, this voice is drowned out (if not entirely silenced) by the cacophony of narratives about Escobar promoted by various commercial actors. These actors not only have a louder voice but also promote different values and see the past as a something to be exploited commercially, to be enjoyed, rather than as a tragedy to be commemorated.

The transformation of Medellín's story into entertainment demonstrates how Southern victims of drug violence differ from victims in the Global North. While victims and victim groups in Northern societies increasingly function as the 'representation of the world through pain' (Walklate, 2016: 5), the element of pain in the South has been airbrushed out of the narratives presented by narco-series. Violence committed against the local population of Medellín is primarily put in a framework of entertainment. Entertainment was an explicit objective named by our interviewees from the entertainment industry. By transforming pain into entertainment, victims were left with a feeling that their loss was being made fun of. As Ana said, 'I think that these series should not make fun of the pain of others.' There was a pervasive sense of a loss of agency among our interviewees: they felt unable to shape the narrative about what had happened to them, or shape their present environment, the city they live in without being constantly confronted with a glorified image of the perpetrator.

In order to show the inequality that exists between groups of victims in contemporary global society, we have framed our argument through the concept of *hierarchies of victimhood*. These hierarchies are shaped by a number of factors, such as class, gender, age, as well as perceptions of innocence and blameworthiness (McEvoy and McConnachie, 2012, 2013). We argue, moreover, that these hierarchies are also shaped by racial and global inequality (Franko, 2021). There are differences between social responses to victimization in the Global North and the Global South. However, these inequalities do not simply refer to geographical locations, but are in central ways informed by the post-colonial continuities and epistemic differences in power they entail. There are substantial differences between the treatment of victims of mass violence in societies of the Global North and the Global South. This is particularly the case when it comes to victims of large-scale drug violence in the Global South, whose position is marked by the lack of access to justice on the national level (both criminal justice as well as transitional justice processes). They also feel excluded from practices of global solidarity extended to victims of mass atrocities. In this book, we have shown the resentment felt by Medellín's political authorities and its inhabitants at the lack of respect for their suffering and the perceived denial of their cosmopolitan aspirations.

Historically, as Karstedt (2010) observes, groups of victims have been often silenced immediately after a conflict but have eventually achieved recognition. Since World War II, victims in transitional justice have been on a road from absence to presence, and from invisibility to visibility (ibid.: 9). This has been far from the case in Medellín. Here, the extraordinary violence of the 1980s and 1990s has been, over the past decade, marked by the hyper-visibility and global fame of the perpetrators. The entertainment industry has achieved enormous commercial success by framing the story of Medellín's violence as the story of Pablo Escobar, based on a recognizable narrative template of a mafia boss. Not only Escobar, but also other associates have become household names in Colombia and across the world. Their fame has opened doors to lucrative contracts. For the survivors of the violence, on the other hand, the road to having their voice heard has been filled with obstacles. Victims' narratives have been 'eaten up' by powerful global, as well as national and local, commercial and political actors. According to Zelizer (2011), the influence of Western media outlets leads to the minimization of local memorial impulses in favour of formulaic and accessible narratives, which results in the 'cannibalization of memory'.

Although the international community has been supportive of the Colombian peace process (Cujabante Villamil, 2016; Goyes, 2015), on the assumption that reconciliation with its legacy of large-scale abuses is possible, Colombia's violence is also a source of profit for both local and international actors. The global political economy grants the entertainment industry a privileged position in the narration of history and, as a by-product, undermines the local aspiration to participate in cosmopolitan discourse on human rights and transitional justice. Although collective recognition of trauma can be conducive to social solidarity and provide acknowledgement of shared responsibility (Alexander 2004), in Medellín these processes have been undermined by commercial and cultural forces which silence the suffering of its inhabitants and promote the image of violent Latino otherness.

We argue that policies and legal and institutional frameworks aiming to achieve justice in transitional contexts should transcend binary distinctions between crime and warfare, and become more aware of the hierarchies of victimhood that rigid distinction might produce. Large-scale violence inflicted by state and criminal actors leaves local populations with few forms of redress. We are mindful, though, of suggesting that such redress should come from more criminalization and that 'drug violence' should become an international crime on par with others within the jurisdiction of the Rome statute. The primacy given to criminal justice responses has been rightly criticized as an approach preferred by Northern states to a variety of violent conflicts (Lohne, 2019). Therefore, a legitimate victim status should not automatically mean a punitive approach. Our interviewees were not primarily concerned with punishing the guilty. In several hundred pages of our interview transcripts, the word 'punish(ment)' appears four times. Instead, victims and survivors expressed a desire for recognition and truth—truth not determined by commercial interests.

For more than half a century, the global war on drugs has been waged allegedly in the name of victims of drug violence. Its harmful consequences for Colombia and other countries in Latin America were acknowledged by several of our interviewees who hoped for a more holistic way of dealing with the problem that would include political, rather than simply militarized and penal, solutions. An acknowledgement of the need to find different political approaches to trade in illegal narcotics has in recent years influenced the peace process in Colombia between the government and the guerrilla group FARC-EP (Fuerzas Armadas Revolucionarias de Colombia—Ejercito del Pueblo, The Revolutionary Armed Forces of Colombia—People's Army), which has been quite unique in trying to tackle the underlying causes of illicit economies (Goyes, 2015).

Unlike in peace negotiations with the paramilitaries, victims played an important role throughout the peace negotiations with the guerrillas.

The agreement between the FARC-EP guerrillas and the Colombian government stated that in order to guarantee the maximum participation of Colombian citizens in the peace dialogue, a procedure would be established whereby citizens could submit their proposals and suggestions regarding any of the items under discussion. Representatives from all regions, communities, ethnicities, social and economic classes, sectors of industry, and political affiliations in Colombia were called to take part in the process. They were chosen based on their knowledge of a specific topic to be discussed and for their ability to represent their background or provenance. From late August 2012 until January 2013, the peace dialogue called for four different forums. All of these forums were conducted according to the terms defined by the peace dialogue. In total, these forums were attended by 4,244 people from nineteen community-based organizations. Those attending represented peasants' organizations, indigenous peoples' organizations, women's organizations, victims' organizations, *raizales* organizations (Afro-Caribbean ethic group), youth organizations, *afrodescendientes* organizations (Afro-descendants), human rights activists, gay communities, churches, scholars, environmental activists, labour unions, private entrepreneurs, peace organizations, political parties, universities, community associations and experts on drug issues (Goyes, 2015). The points on the agenda were: (i) comprehensive agrarian policy reform; (ii) political participation; (iii) conflict termination; (iv) solution to the problem of illegal drugs; (v) victims' reparations; and (vi) implementation, verification, and popular countersignature of the final agreement reached by the parties.

The approach used in the 2012 peace process shows that the issue of trade in illegal narcotics is inherently connected to peace and is a political and economic issue rather than simply a question of criminal justice.

Narcos and the epistemic power of the North

Even though the punitive, militarized prohibition model promoted by the United States may today look weaker than ever, its definitional and epistemic power is still upheld by the narratives promoted by the entertainment industry. The war on drugs is the backdrop for the heroic narrative of the two U.S. law enforcement agents who are the main narrators of *Narcos*. Viewers are invited to see the world through their eyes. As we have seen in chapter 5, Colombian participants had only a minor role in the production. The inequality between the Global North and the Global South, and the pervasive influence of the United States, which has for a long time determined the global management of narcotics are, at a cultural level, reflected in the narrative power of U.S. corporations and the fascination with violent Latino gangsterism. Consequently, Medellín and its culture have been transformed from victims to collective culprits. By equating the city, and Colombia more generally, with violent Latino criminality, the violence experienced by the inhabitants becomes a sign of their exotic otherness and, therefore, reinforces their abjection and exclusion from the cosmopolitan 'we'.

In this book, we have tried to challenge the pervasive focus on Escobar and the framing of violence as entertainment by foregrounding the sensory memories of local inhabitants. By focusing on the silent stories of the people who lived through that time—the smell of corpses on the streets, the noise of sirens and bombs—we have attempted to place the story of Medellín within the so-called geographies of trauma (Coddington and Micieli-Voutsinas, 2017), incorporating individual stories of loss and vulnerability in a collective story of the city. The language of trauma is used to describe the loss of life and the thwarted future experienced by many of our interviewees. However, this is by no means intended to undervalue the enormous resilience of the city and its residents. Medellín is a vibrant and resourceful city. With its growing urban population and burgeoning economic and cultural life, its story should undoubtedly be told as a story of resilience and success. This was clearly expressed by many of our interviewees, several of whom preferred to describe themselves as survivors rather than victims. We have also shown how the city authorities have exercised their agency and taken action to challenge the global branding of the city and the processes of collective memory construction.

Yet, the ultimate failure of the city authorities to curtail dark tourism and to challenge the global branding of Escobar shows that the global market economy allots very uneven power to those engaged in processes of memory construction. Although successfully initiating several local history projects, the local actors have had little influence over the global narratives of their traumatic past. They have been unable to prevent the transformation of their experience into a profitable source of entertainment for global audiences or to counter tourists' fascination with Escobar. Moreover, the powerful symbolic representations produced by the entertainment industry target not only global audiences, but also shape the aspirational identities of Medellín's younger generations, preventing, as noted many interviewees, the creation of more positive, future-oriented identities and role models. The findings in this book reveal several paradoxical, socially problematic consequences of the influence of the global entertainment industry on memory building in the Global South and reflect the complexity of contemporary global interconnections (Franko, 2020). Dark tourism is a source of income to local entrepreneurs. Escobar's aura may give the city a sense of excitement that is attractive to foreign visitors. Yet, the power of his brand and the power of Netflix as a global narrator of history make it almost impossible for local actors to challenge. Butler et al.'s (2009) research, for example, shows that learning history by watching historically based movies inhibits people's ability to correct misinformation presented on the screen, even when faced with correct information in textual forms.

Medellín's challenge of competing with Netflix, one of the most powerful contemporary narrators of history, is not unique. Netflix's role in narrating popular British history has been the subject of heated debates, most recently, in relation to its popular series *The Crown*. The critique has eventually resulted in the inclusion of a disclaimer saying that the show is a 'fictional dramatization', albeit 'inspired by real-life events' (Glynn and Bushby, 2022). However, Netflix's portrayal of Medellín's history has received relatively little international criticism. While there are many highly competent academic and popular writers who would be able to correct the historic inaccuracies of *The Crown*, the epistemic power of Netflix is far more difficult to challenge in the case of Medellín. Who will be able to rectify the portrayal of Valentina's father, a judge who had dedicated his late career to prosecuting Escobar, as someone who fled before his assassins? For Valentina and her family, the acknowledgement of the judge's heroic death is extremely important, but their pain was made even greater by seeing the perpetrator portrayed as a hero. There have been alternative Colombian cinematic portrayals of drug violence, significantly better crafted than *Narcos* and with a deeper understanding of Medellín's history (Liévano, 2018);[2] few, however, have reached the global and national influence of *Narcos*.

This book reveals a strong concern among the city's inhabitants about the historic portrayal of the events and the impact of Escobar's branding on younger populations. Asked about how he felt about the popularity of narco-series, Emiliano, the son of a judge murder by the Medellín Cartel, said:

> A little bit of sadness. Because [these shows] distort reality too much. They show things that did not happen. They extol or idolize a person who doesn't really deserve it. You might say that [Escobar] has harnessed great economic resources, was an innovative entrepreneur.... But the damage he did to society is not to be idolized. You have to be very careful with that, and if you want to distort reality. That's why I say [these shows] are fictions. You can't sell these series. Nor can they be classified as a historical series because they are not.

When the narrative about the past is shaped by commercial actors, they also exert influence over individuals and collective identities and their expectations for the future, which raises issues about the ethical and moral responsibilities of commercial actors and the narratives they promote.

Do no harm: Crime drama and the global consumer culture

Social responsibilities of business and corporations are increasingly being put on the agenda in a number of fields. At the time of writing of

[2] For example:

- Patricia Castaño and Adelaida Trujillo, directors. *La ley del monte*. Estudios América, 1988.
- Víctor Gaviria, director. *Sumas y Restas*. Latin Cinema Group, 2004.
- José Antonio Dorado, director. *El Rey*. Eucoriné, 2004.
- Margarita Martínez and Scott Dalton, director. *La Sierra*. First run/Icarus Films, 2005.
- Felipe Aljure, director. *El Colombian Dream*. Sonica, 2006.
- Margarita Martínez, director. *La selva en blanco*. La Sierra Producciones, 2010.
- Ciro Guerra and Cristina Gallego, directors. *Birds of Passage*. Mer Film, 2018.

this book, the world is embroiled in debates about the FIFA World Cup 2022 in Qatar. Football fans across the world are wondering whether they can ethically watch the games, considering the grave human rights violations in the country and the exploitative conditions under which the tournament facilities have been built. Consumer goods, indicating for example the support of LGBTQ rights, are used actively by those attending the tournament to express a moral stance (Topping, 2022).

Such debates are a vivid acknowledgment that consumer actions matter also when it comes to media consumption. On a smaller scale, but closer to the examples discussed in this book, other victim groups have expressed public criticism about 'true crime' media depictions. In 2022, the drama about the U.S. serial killer Jeffrey Dahmer became one of Netflix's most watched shows. Family members of Dahmer's victims have publicly spoken out against the series, saying it had re-traumatized them. Their criticism resonates with the experiences of many of our interviewees and shows that there is room for a broader discussion about the social consequences of 'true crime' media productions and related commercial products. Kaplan and LaChance (2022) have aptly termed the mass media consumption of 'true crime' as 'crimesploitation'. The phenomenon captures the mass cultural 'desire to consume and appropriate the criminal to satisfy one's own needs', particularly the need to alleviate boredom (ibid.: 44). If applied to the case of *Narcos*, the argument of exploitation acquires an additional dimension as the patterns of consumption uncomfortably parallel the historic colonial *extraction of resources from the colonies* for the consumption in the imperial metropoles. In the trauma(tic) economy described in this book, it is Southern trauma that is being processed for the consumption of (mostly) Northern audiences.

However, as McGarry and Walklate (2015: 5) observe, when pitted against corporate victimization, even widespread victim movements with global recognition struggle against 'being subsumed by legalese, obscured from public view, or hidden in plain sight'. Dark tourism in Medellín, driven by the search for an 'authentic Escobar experience', can be experienced as hurtful and disrespectful of the local population, particularly by those with direct experiences of violence. Yet, few have a voice strong enough to challenge it. Such trauma(tic) economy may feel safe and sanitized to tourists; but the locals who are profoundly affected by it, both materially and symbolically, do not see it that way. The Pablo

Escobar Museum, operated by Escobar's brother, was proclaimed by TripAdvisor in December 2022 to be the number two tourist attraction in Medellín, with almost 2,000 reviews, most of them extremely positive.[3] The seemingly a-moral commercial machinery thus keeps perpetuating interest in Escobar's persona, yet also serves as a source of history telling. Most user comments describe the museum as 'informative' and 'offering a new perspective on history'.

Commercial products and practices are not produced nor consumed in a social vacuum. Campaigners have raised awareness about harmful practices involved in the production chain, such as environmental issues, lack of animal welfare, labour rights, and child labour. Others have gone further and argued that businesses should not simply try to minimize the damage and 'do no harm', but aim to 'renew and repair' and be 'a source for good' (Crane et al., 2008). While producers of commercial products discussed in this book might argue that their position is a-moral, this lack of acknowledgment of moral responsibility also entails a moral stance on the side of profit—a phenomenon termed by Brisman and South (2018) 'econocentrism'. As Zygmunt Bauman succinctly observes, living in a globalized world entails sharing a moral and ethical universe, whether we like it or not. Global interconnectedness makes the social distance between countries smaller, and therefore maintaining a moral distance becomes increasingly impossible:

> However local their intentions might be, actors would be ill-advised to leave out of account global factors, since they could decide the success or failure of their actions. What we do (or abstain from doing) may influence the conditions of life (or death) for people in places we will never visit and generations we will never know. (Bauman, 2009: 71)

Although some might binge-watch *Narcos* in their spare time or wear an Escobar t-shirt with a sense of detached irony, Bauman's argument challenges the perception of such practices as innocent fun. The findings of the present book raise questions about the role of the global

[3] See 'Museum Pablo Escobar', TripAdvisor, https://www.tripadvisor.com/Attraction_Review-g297478-d12144209-Reviews-Museum_Pablo_Escobar-Medellin_Antioquia_Department.html, accessed on 15 February 2023.

community of consumers in fuelling the commercialization of violence. We ask whether a globally aware ethics of consumer responsibility can challenge the power of global entertainment corporations. Although far from advocating censorship, and keenly aware of the potential for cultural elitism, we see room for discussion about alternative representations of drug violence that could foster a healing process in the affected societies. These alternative representations should at least seek to address the current epistemic imbalance and pave the way for more sensitive, democratic ways of narrating violence.

This book has not only been concerned with mass media consumption, but also with the consumption of other cultural products and material objects. Consumer items and commercialism play an important role in processes of memory construction in contemporary societies (Sturken, 2007). The commercial production of what is often termed as 'kitsch' (coffee mugs, pens, keychains, etc.), has faced accusations of representing a superficial way of mourning the loss of life (ibid.: 20). Yet, in the case of Medellín, the consumer culture has flooded the city and global commercial platforms with mass-produced kitsch items depicting one of the main perpetrators of violence rather than the sites of loss. Global commercial platforms, such as AliExpress and Etsy, also offer T-shirts, iPhone covers, and coffee mugs featuring Saddam Hussein and many other disreputable historic figures, although few have reached the levels of commercialism associated with Escobar. These objects are not value-neutral and often carry with them political messages. As Sturken points out, 'kitsch' objects should not simply be seen as cultural objects but as essentially enmeshed in political discourse. They are related to sentiment and to the idea of universal emotions that political discourse can tap into (2007: 25). The political message these objects convey may be much more obscured in the case of Escobar souvenirs, although their political force may lie precisely in *de-politicizing* the war on drugs and turning the attention to one person, rather than focusing on the politics of the 'war on drugs'.

It is important to note, though, that Escobar's life has been depicted not only in mass culture. In addition to alternative cinematic representations of the city, Fernando Botero, one of the most beloved and influential Colombian artists, depicted his death in several works, including *La muerte de Pablo Escobar* (1999) and *Pablo Escobar muerto* (2006) (see Figure 9.1). Botero's paintings present a sombre, unglamorous image of the drug lord with his inflated belly and his large body hanging over the city's roof tops. Exhibited in the Museum of Antioquia in Medellín, the paintings offer a powerful cultural portrayal of Escobar's dark legacy. Juan Carlos Botero, the son of the artist, explains that '[Escobar's] image is monumental compared to the rest of the elements in the composition, to show the dimension [the tragedy] had acquired' (2016). Next to that oversize figure of Escobar, *Pablo Escobar Muerto* also shows a small figure of a policeman and an even smaller figure of a woman. The officer's size, compared to Escobar, seems to indicate the decades-long powerlessness of the law.

Today, Botero's works compete with the mass-produced cultural items that show Escobar in a very different light: as smiling, youthful, defiant, and glamorous. And it is these items that have the strongest visual impact

Figure 9.1. *Pablo Escobar Muerto* by Fernando Botero, 2006. Oil painting on fabric, 135cm x 164cm. Property of the Museo de Antioquia permanent collection, Colombia. Registry number: 4016.
Source: © Carlos Tobón.

on Medellín and can also be found in marketplaces, pubs, and restaurants around the world. We have framed these commercial practices as a form of haunting of the city. Escobar's ghost keeps returning to the place where he, in his lifetime, had left such a tragic imprint. His presence and his story refuse to fade with the passage of time, and have instead become ever stronger, amplified by powerful commercial forces.

The fear of oblivion

The story presented in this book is one among several competing cultural visions and ways of remembering. According to the painter's son, Botero's intention behind his paintings of Escobar was the creation of memory: 'My dad did not make them to change reality, but to keep these episodes so that they are never forgotten. The intention was to tell the brutal Colombian reality' (Miranda, 2018). For a number of years, the losses experienced by our interviewees were covered in layers of silence, as one of them put it, 'closed in a capsule of oblivion'. The fear of erasure, that the loved ones lost to the violence will be forgotten, is what motivated many of them to contribute to this book. In the face of structural impunity and a criminal justice system brought to its knees, memory becomes of central importance. As María, the daughter of a judge Escobar had killed, reflected:

MARÍA: Sometimes you fantasize. When Popeye [Escobar's associate] was in the news, I said to myself: my God! I even want to go find him and get him to tell me the truth, to know what happened. I do not want to hold these people accountable or sue them for what had happened. Pablo Escobar already lost his life, you see what I mean? The many years he spent in prisons where he also caused terrible pain to his family, to his daughter. I do not wish to punish or condemn anyone. What I need is to know the truth.

DAVID: In other words, the truth is what matters the most to you?

MARÍA: Yes, and no impunity, you know? In other words, things stayed as they are because everyone was threatened, and nobody wanted to take the case.

María was deeply upset by the lack of response and acknowledgement on the part of the legal system, including the Victims' Law. However, she also expressed a strong need to know the truth and to remember in a dignified and respectful way.

This need for the truth in the aftermath of a murder is beautifully expressed in the memoir of Héctor Abad, whose father was killed in Medellín by paramilitary forces, appositely titled *Oblivion* (2006). Like a Shakespearean character, the son feels implored by his dead father not to avenge his death but to tell the truth:

> It is possible that all this will be for nought; no word can bring him back to life—the story of his life and his death will not give new breath to his bones, will not bring back his laughter, or his immense courage, or his persuasive and vigorous words—but in any case I need to tell it. His murderers remain at large, every day they grow in strength, and I cannot fight them with my fists. It is only with my fingers, pressing one key after another that I can tell the truth and bear witness to the injustice. I use his own weapon: words. What for? For nothing, or for the most simple and essential reason: so it will be known. To extend his memory a little longer, before the inevitable oblivion. (ibid.: 243)

Abad's work is marked by a deep belief in the power of words to create and keep memory alive. This has also been one of the intentions of this book. Yet, its findings also show the reverse side of Abad's positive belief: they reveal the power of visual culture to shape society's memory in negative ways. Through television, movies, and consumer items distributed across the world by the forces of capitalism, images of Escobar pubs and commercial products, embellished with his grinning face, still keep appearing on our phones and in our mailboxes from friends and acquaintances across the world. For the time being, these global commercial practices appear unstoppable. However, the resilience and vigour shown by the city of Medellín as it recovers from the tragic period may also point to the strength of local communities and the possibility of forging a different type of memory.

References

Abad, H. (2010). *Oblivion: A Memoir*. A. McLean and R. Harvey, trans. Farrar, Straus and Giroux.

Adams, D. (2011). 'Vínculos entre paramilitares y drogas: Antes y después de la desmovilización' ['Links Between the Paramilitaries and Drug Trafficking: Before and After the Demobilization']. In E. M. Restrepo and B. Bagley (eds.), *La desmovilización de los paramilitares en Colombia: Entre el escepticismo y la esperanza* [*The Demobilisation of Paramilitaries in Colombia: Between Scepticism and Hope*] (pp. 69–87). Universidad de los Andes.

Agrawal, S., Khandelwal, U., and Bajpai, N. (2021). 'Anthropomorphism in Advertising: The Effect of Media on Audience Attitude'. *Journal of Marketing Communications, 27*(8), 799–815, https://doi.org/10.1080/13527266.2020.1771403.

Alarcón, A. V. M. (2014). 'Latin American Culture: A Deconstruction of Stereotypes'. *Studies in Latin American Popular Culture 32*, 72–96.

Alcaide, C. L., Pie, É. P., and Puig, M. R. (2018). 'Cocaína, violencia y realismo mágico: Qué sucede cuando Netflix explica Colombia' ['Cocaine, Violence, and Magical Realism: What Happens When Netflix Explains Colombia?']. In S. G. Luque (ed.), *¿Por qué amamos a Pablo Escobar? Cómo Netflix revivió al narcotraficante más famoso del mundo* (pp. 201–18). Editorial UOC.

Alexander, J. C. (2004). Toward a theory of cultural trauma. In J. C. Alexander, R. Eyermain, B. Giesen, N. J. Smelser, and P. Sztompka (eds.), *Cultural Trauma and Collective Identity* (pp. 1–16). University of California Press.

Amin, S. (2009 [1988]). *Eurocentrism*. Monthly Review Press.

Andrade, X., Forero, A. M., and Kraus, D. (2021). 'Ensamblajes y experiencia museal: La ingorbernabilidad de "lo narco" en un museo policial' ['Assemblances and Museal Experiences: The Ungovernability of "the Narco" in a Police Museum']. In D. Santos López, A. Vásquez Mejías, and I. Urgelles Latorre (eds.), *Narcotransmisiones: Neoliberalismo e hiperconsumo en la era del #narcopop* [*Narcotransmisions: Neoliberalism and Hyper-Consumerism in the Era of the #narcopop*] (pp. 213–32). El Colegio de Chihuahua.

Andreas, P., and Nadelmann, E. (2006). *Policing the Globe: Criminalization and Crime Control in International Relations*. Oxford University Press.

Angell, S. I., and M. Mordhorst (2015). 'National Reputation Management and the Competition State'. *Journal of Cultural Economy 8*(2), 184–201, https://doi.org/10.1080/17530350.2014.885459.

Anholt, S. (1998). 'Nation-Brands of the Twenty-First Century'. *Journal of Brand Management 5*, 395–406, https://doi.org/10.1057/bm.1998.30.

Anholt, S. (2006). 'Editorial: Why Brand? Some Practical Considerations for Place Branding'. *Place Branding and Public Diplomacy 2*, 97–107, https://doi.org/10.1057/palgrave.pb.5990048.

APA (2013). *Diagnostic and Statistical Manual of Mental Disorders: DSM-5*. American Psychiatric Association.

Arellano Mendoza, F., Pulido Caro, É. J., and Arellano Becerra, L. A. (2011). 'Demanda de Inconstitucionalidad contra la Ley 1448 de 2011' ['Unconstitutionality Lawsuit against Law 1448 of 2011']. Bogotá.

Aristizábal Uribe, A. C. (2018). *Medellín a oscuras: Ética antioqueña y narcotráfico* [*Medellín in the Dark: Antioqueña's Ethics and Drug Dealing*]. Universidad Pontificia Bolivariana.

Armenta, K. T. (2017). 'Narcotelenovelas: La construcción de nuevos estereotipos de mujer en la ficción televisiva de Colombia y México a través del retrato de una realidad social' ['Narco Telenovelas: The Creation of New Stereotypes of Femininity in the Fiction TV of Colombia and Mexico Through the Portrayal of a Social Reality']. Doctoral Thesis, Universidad Autónoma de Barcelona, https://ddd.uab.cat/pub/tesis/2017/hdl_10803_459153/kta1de1.pdf.

Arratia Sandoval, E. (2022). 'From "Failed State" to Exporter of Security? Colombia and the Diplomacy of Security'. *AUSTRAL: Brazilian Journal of Strategy & International Relations 5*(10), 148–72, https://doi.org/10.22456/2238-6912.67313.

Ballvé, T. (2012). 'Everyday State Formation: Territory, Decentralization, and the Narco Landgrab in Colombia'. *Environment and Planning D: Society and Space 30*, 603–22, https://doi.org/10.1068/d4611.

Barbero, J. M., and Rey, G. (1999). *Los ejercicios del ver: Hegemonía audiovisual y ficción televisiva* [*The Excercise of Seeing: Audio-Visual Hegemony and Fictional Television*]. Gedisa.

Barker, C., and Wiatrowski, M. (2017). 'Introduction'. In C. Barker and M. Wiatrowski (eds.), *The Age of Netflix: Critical Essays on Streaming Media, Digital Delivery and Instant Access* (pp. 1–9). McFarland & Company.

Bartsch, A., and Mares, M.-L. (2014). 'Making Sense of Violence: Perceived Meaningfulness as a Predictor of Audience Interest in Violent Media Content'. *Journal of Communication 64*(5), 956–76, https://doi.org/https://doi.org/10.1111/jcom.12112.

Bassil-Morozow, H. (2020). 'The Soviet Woman in Bond Films'. In S. Gerrard (ed.), *From Blofeld to Moneypenny: Gender in James Bond* (pp. 91–101). Emerald.

Baudrillard, J. (2016). *The Consumer Society: Myths and Structures*. C. T., trans. Revised edn. SAGE.

Bauman, Z. (2009). *Does Ethics Have a Chance in a World of Consumers?* Harvard University Press.

Beck, U., Levy, D., and Sznaider, N. (2016). 'Cosmopolitanization of Memory: The Politics of Forgiveness and Restitution 1'. In M. Rovisco and M. Nowicka (eds.), *Cosmopolitanism in Practice* (pp. 111–28). Routledge.

Benavides, H. (2008). *Drug, Thugs, and Divas: Telenovelas and Narco-Dramas in Latin America*. University of Texas Press.

Berg, C. R. (2002). *Latino Images in Film: Stereotypes, Subversion, and Resistance*. University of Texas Press.

Bergal, C. (2011). 'The Mexican Drug War: The Case for Non-International Armed Conflict Classification'. *Fordham International Law Journal 34*(4), 1042–88.

Bhabha, H. (2004 [1994]). *The Location of Culture*. Routledge.

Bibliowicz, A. (1980). 'Be Happy Because Your Father Isn't Your Father: An Analysis of Colombian *Telenovelas*'. *The Journal of Popular Culture 14*: 476–85, https://doi.org/10.1111/j.0022-3840.1980.1403_476.x.

Boister, N. (2012). 'International Tribunals for Transnational Crimes: Towards a Transnational Criminal Court?'. *International Law Forum 23*, 295–318.

Bolívar Moreno, G. (2006). *Sin tetas no hay Paraíso*. Oveja Negra.

Botero, J. C. (2016). *El arte de Fernando Botero* [*The Art of Fernando Botero*]. Planeta Colombia.

Bourdieu, P. (1986). 'The Forms of Capital'. In J. G. Richardson (ed.), *Handbook of Theory and Research for the Sociology of Education* (pp. 241–58). Greenwood Press.

Boville, B. (2004). *The Cocaine War in Context: Drugs and Politics*. Algora Publishing.

Brands, H. (2011). 'Crime, Irregular Warfare, and Institutional Failure in Latin America: Guatemala as a Case Study'. *Studies in Conflict and Terrorism 34*(3), 228–47.

Brants, C., and Klep, K. (2013). 'Transitional Justice: History-Telling, Collective Memory, and the Victim-Witness'. *International Journal of Conflict and Violence 7*(1), 36–49.

Bredal, A. (2007). 'Den "spesielle" volden. Vold mot minoritetsjenter på sidelinjen' ['The "Special" Violence. Violence Against Minority Girls on the sideline']. In K. Storberget, B. Bråten, E. Rømming, K. Skjørten, and A. Aas-Hansen (eds.), *Bjørnen sover: Om vold i familien* [*The Sleeping Bear: About Violence in the Family*] (pp. 57–60). Aschehoug.

Brewer, J. D., and Hayes, B. C. (2015). 'Victimhood and Attitudes Towards Dealing with the Legacy of a Violent Past: Northern Ireland as a Case Study'. *British Journal of Politics and International Relations 17*(3), 512–30.

Brisman, A., and South, N. (2018). 'Autosarcophagy in the Anthropocene and the Obscenity of an Epoch'. In C. Holley and C. Shearing (eds.), *Criminology and the Anthropocene* (pp. 25–49). Routledge.

Britto, L. (2016). 'Car Bombing Drug War History'. *NACLA Report on the Americas 48*(2), 177–80, https://doi.org/http://dx.doi.org/10.1080/10714839.2016.1201278.

Brodzinsky, S. (2014). 'From Murder Capital to Model City: Is Medellín's Miracle Show or Substance?'. *The Guardian* (17 April), https://www.theguardian.com/cities/2014/apr/17/medellin-murder-capital-to-model-city-miracle-un-world-urban-forum.

Brown, M. (2009). *The Culture of Punishment: Prison, Society, and Spectacle*. New York University Press.

Brown, M., and Rafter, N. (2013). 'Genocide Films, Public Criminology, Collective Memory'. *British Journal of Criminology 53*(6), 1017–32, https://doi.org/10.1093/bjc/azt043.

Bruner, J. (1996). 'A Narrative Model of Self Construction'. *Psyke & Logos 17*, 154–70.

Bull, B. (2021). *Latin-Amerika i dag: Nye interesser og gamle bånd til USA, Kina, Russland, Midtøsten og Europa* [*Latin America Today: New Interests and Old Ties to USA, China, Russia, the Middle East, and Europe*]. Cappelen Damm Akademisk.

Butler, A. C., Zaromb, F. M., Lyle, K. B., and Roediger, H. L. (2009). 'Using Popular Films to Enhance Classroom Learning: The Good, the Bad, and the Interesting'. *Psychological Science 20*(9), 1161–8, https://doi.org/10.1111/j.1467-9280.2009.02410.x.

Butler, J. (2021). 'Recognition and the Social Bond: A Response to Axel Honneth'. In H. Ikäheimo, K. Lepold, and T. Stahl (eds.), *Recognition and Ambivalence* (pp. 31–54). Columbia University Press.

Buxton, W. J. (2008). 'From Park to Cressey: Chicago Sociology's Engagement with Media and Mass Culture'. In D. Park and J. Pooley (eds.), *The History of Media and Communication Research* (pp. 345–62). Peter Lang.

Caballero, A. (2014). *Historia de Colombia y sus oligarquías (1498–2017)* [*History of Colombia and its Oligarchies (1498–2017)*]. Ministerio de Cultura.

Cabañas, M. (2012). 'Narcotelenovelas, gender, and globalization in *Sin tetas no hay paraíso*'. *Latin American Perspectives 39*(184), 74–87.

Campion, C. (2015). 'I Shot Pablo Escobar: Narcos' José Padilha on His New TV Series'. *The Guardian* (24 August), https://www.theguardian.com/tv-and-radio/2015/aug/24/i-shot-pablo-escobar-narcos-jose-padilha-on-his-new-tv-series.

Caple James, E. (2004). 'The Political Economy of "Trauma" in Haiti in the Democratic Era of Insecurity'. *Culture, Medicine and Psychiatry 28*, 127–49.

Carbado, D., Crenshaw, K., Mays, V., and Tomlinson, B. (2013). 'INTERSECTIONALITY: Mapping the Movements of a Theory'. *Du Bois Review: Social Science Research on Race 10*(2), 303–12, https://doi.org/10.1017/S1742058X13000349.

Carpenter, T. G. (2003). *Bad Neighbor Policy: Washington's Futile War on Drugs in Latin America*. Palgrave Macmillan.

Carrabine, E. (2014). 'Seeing Things: Violence, Voyeurism and the Camera'. *Theoretical Criminology 18*(2), 134–58, https://doi.org/10.1177/1362480613508425.

Carrabine, E., et al. (2020). *Criminology: A Sociological Introduction*. Routledge.

Carrington, K., Dixon, B., Fonseca, D., Goyes, D. R., Liu, J., and Zysman, D. (2019). 'Criminologies of the Global South: Critical Reflections'. *Critical Criminology 27*(1), 163–89.

Carter-Visscher, R. M., Naugle, A. E., Bell, K. M., and Suvak, M. K. (2007). 'Ethics of Asking Trauma-Related Questions and Exposing Participants to Arousal-Inducing Stimuli'. *Journal of Trauma and Dissociation 8*(3), 27–55.

Castro Caycedo, G. (2012). *Operacion Pablo Escobar* [*Pablo Escobar Operation*]. Planeta.

Centro Nacional de Memoria Histórica. (2017). *Medellín: Memorias de una guerra urbana* [*Medellín: Memories of an Urban War*]. Centro Nacional de Memoria Histórica.

Christie, N. (2018 [1986]). 'The Ideal Victim'. In M. Duggan (ed.), *Revisiting the 'Ideal Victim': Developments in Critical Victimology* (pp. 11–23). Policy Press.

Clark, R. P. (2016). *Writing Tools: 55 Essential Strategies for Every Writer*. Little, Brown & Company.

Coddington, K., and Micieli-Voutsinas, J. (2017). 'On Trauma, Geography, and Mobility: Towards Geographies of Trauma'. *Emotion, Space and Society 24*, 52–6.

Connell, R. (2006). 'Northern Theory: The Political Geography of General Social Theory'. *Theory and Society 35*(2), 237–64, https://doi.org/10.1007/s11186-006-9004-y.

Connell, R. (2014a). 'Margin Becoming Centre: For a World-Centred Rethinking of Masculinities'. *NORMA: International Journal for Masculinity Studies 9*(4), 217–31, https://doi.org/10.1080/18902138.2014.934078.

Connell, R. (2014b). 'Rethinking Gender from the South'. *Feminist Studies 40*(3), 518–39, https://www.jstor.org/stable/10.15767/feministstudies.40.3.518.
Connell, R. (2016). 'Masculinities in Global Perspective: Hegemony, Contestation, and Changing Structures of Power'. *Theory and Society 45*(4), 303–18, http://www.jstor.org.ezproxy.uio.no/stable/44981834.
Connell, R. W. (1995). *Masculinities*. Polity.
Connerton, P. (1989). *How Societies Remember*. Cambridge University Press.
Connerton, P. (2011). *The Spirit of Mourning: History, Memory, and the Body*. Cambridge University Press.
Córdoba Laverde, P. N. (1980). 'Paro de dos días en el Poder Judicial, por asesinato de la juez Ana Cecilia Cartagena' ['Two-Day Strike in the Judiciary Due to the Murder of Judge Ana Cecilia Cartagena']. *El Colombiano*, 7B.
Couldry, N. (2012). *Media, Society, World: Social Theory and Digital Media Practice*. Polity.
Counter, M. (2018). 'Producing Victimhood: Landmines, Reparations, and Law in Colombia'. *Antipode 50*(1): 122–41.
Crane, A., Matten, D., McWilliams, A., Moon, J., and Siegel, D. S. (eds.) (2008). *The Oxford Handbook of Corporate Social Responsibility*. Online edn. Oxford University Press, https://doi.org/10.1093/oxfordhb/9780199211593.001.0001.
Csikszentmihalyi, M. (1990). *Flow: The Psychology of Optimal Experience*. Harper Perennial.
Cujabante Villamil, X. A. (2016). 'La comunidad internacional y su participación en los procesos de paz en Colombia' ['The International Community and Its Participation in the Colombian Peace Processes']. *Equidad y Desarrollo 26*, 207–22.
Dalton, D. (2015). *Dark Tourism and Crime*. Routledge.
Daniels, J. P. (2022). 'Has Colombian Left's Time Come at Last as Ex-rebel Closes in on Presidency?'. *The Guardian* (28 May), https://www.theguardian.com/world/2022/may/28/colombia-election-president-gustavo-petro-leftwing.
Davis, F. (1959). 'The Cabdriver and His Fare: Facets of a Fleeting Relationship'. *American Journal of Sociology 65*(2), 158–65, http://www.jstor.org/stable/2773022.
de Zubiría Samper, J. (2016). 'La guerra nos ha insensibilizado' ['War Has Made Us Numb']. *Agencia de Noticias Univalle* (8 November), https://www.univalle.edu.co/universidad-y-region/la-guerra-nos-ha-insensibilizado.
Debord, G. (2002). *The Society of the Spectacle*. M. Imrie, trans. Hobgoblin Press.
del Olmo, R. (1987). 'Aerobiology and the War on Drugs: A Transnational Crime'. *Crime and Social Justice 30*, 28–44.
Del Olmo, R. (1998). 'The Ecological Impact of Illicit Drug Cultivation and Crop Eradication Programs in Latin America'. *Theoretical Criminology 2*(2), 269–78.
Di Nucci, E., and Santoni de Sio, F. (2016). *Drones and Responsibility: Mapping the Field*. Routledge.
Diaz, L. (2012). 'Pablo Escobar T-Shirts a Hit in Mexico Drug War States'. *Reuters* (2 October), https://www.reuters.com/article/life-mexico-escobar-idUSL1E8L1WCK20121002.
Downes, C., Harrison, E., Curran, D., and Kavanagh, M. (2013). '"The Trauma Still Goes On ... ": The Multigenerational Legacy of Northern Ireland's Conflict'. *Clinical Child Psychology and Psychiatry 18*(4), 583–603, https://doi.org/10.1177/1359104512462548.

Duarte, M. (2014). '*El cartel de los Sapos*: Illness, Body, and Nation'. *Latin American Perspectives 41*(2), 144–60, https://doi.org/10.1177/0094582x13509070.

Dudash, S. (2021). 'Meta Consumerism: Holiday Gifts, Digital Goods, & Virtual Expression'. *Forbes* (31 December), https://www.forbes.com/sites/greatspeculations/2021/12/31/meta-consumerism-holiday-gifts-digital-goods--virtual-expression/.

Duke, S., and Gross, A. (1999). *America's Longest War: Rethinking Our Tragic Crusade against Drugs*. E-reads.

Duncan, G. (2013). 'Una lectura política de Pablo Escobar' ['A Political Reading of Pablo Escobar']. *Co-herencia 19*, 235–62.

Durán-Martínez, A. (2018). *The Politics of Drug Violence: Criminals, Cops, and Politicians in Colombia and Mexico*. Oxford University Press.

Edgerton, G. (2000). 'Television as Historian: An Introduction'. *Film & History 30*(1): 7–12.

El Colombiano. (1984). 'Una dama pereció al explotar carro-bomba' ['A Lady Died in a Car Bomb Explosion]. (27 November), 16A.

El Colombiano. (1990). 'Brutal atentado dinamitero en El Poblado' ['Brutal Dynamite Attack in El Poblado']. (15 June), 15C.

El Espectador. (1987). 'Asesinado Pardo Leal' ['Pardo Leal Killed']. (12 October), 1.

El Tiempo. (2008). 'Virginia Vallejo, ahora testigo en el caso del Palacio' ['Virginia Vallejo, Now a Witness in the Palace Case']. (17 August), https://www.eltiempo.com/archivo/documento/MAM-3056983.

El Tiempo. (2019). '"Narconovelas" con las que Caracol y RCN también han subido el rating' ['Caracol and RCN use "Narconovelas" to Boost Their Ratings']. (7 February), https://www.eltiempo.com/cultura/cine-y-tv/las-narconovelas-que-han-sido-duenas-del-rating-del-pais-323832.

Enge, C., and Storrusten, K. (2018). 'Nå kommer Netflix-filmen om 22. juli' ['Now comes a movie abot July 22nd']. *Aftenposten* (4 September), https://www.aftenposten.no/kultur/i/21xdpB/naa-kommer-netflix-filmen-om-22-juli.

Escobar, J. P. (2016). *Pablo Escobar: My Father*. Thomas Dunne.

Escobar, J. P. (2019). *Det faren min aldri fortalte* [*What My Father Never Told Me*]. Cappelen Damm.

Escobar, R. (2010). *Escobar. Drugs. Guns. Money. Power: The Inside Story of Pablo Escobar, the World's Most Powerful Criminal*. Hodder.

Espinosa, J. M. (1876). *Memorias de un abanderado: Recuerdos de la Patria Boba, 1810–1819*. [*Memories of a Standard-Bearer: Memories of the Patria Boba, 1810–1819*]. Imprenta de El Tradicionista.

Evans, L. (2020). '"How Godfather Part II of You": The Gangster Figure and Transnational Masculinities in Marlon James's *A Brief History of Seven Killings*'. *Interventions 22*(1), 49–70, https://doi.org/10.1080/1369801X.2019.1659161.

Fassin, D., and Rechtman, R. (2009). *The Empire of Trauma: An Inquiry into the Condition of Victimhood*. Princeton University Press.

Ferguson, N., Burgess, M., and Hollywood, I. (2010). 'Who Are the Victims? Victimhood Experiences in Postagreement Northern Ireland'. *Political Psychology 31*(6), 857–8.

Fiddler, M. (2019). 'Ghosts of Other Stories: A Synthesis of Hauntology, Crime and Space'. *Crime, Media, Culture 15*(3), 463–77.

Fileborn, B., and Loney-Howes, R. (2019). 'Introduction: Mapping the Emergence of #MeToo'. In B. Fileborn and R. Loney-Howes (eds.), *#MeToo and the Politics of Social Change* (pp. 1–18). Springer International Publishing, https://doi.org/10.1007/978-3-030-15213-0_1.

Fineman, M. A. (2010). 'The Vulnerable Subject and the Responsive State'. *Emory Law Journal 60*, Emory Public Law Research Paper No. 10-130, https://ssrn.com/abstract=1694740.

Fishman, G. (1979). 'Patterns of Victimisation and Notification'. *British Journal of Criminology 19*(2), 146–57, https://doi.org/10.1093/oxfordjournals.bjc.a046979.

Franko, K. (2019). *Globalization and Crime*. Sage Publications.

Franko, K. (2020). *Globalization and Crime*. 3rd edn. Sage.

Franko, K. (2021). 'Lives that Matter: Criminology and Global Security Inequality'. *International Criminology 1*, 20–7, https://doi.org/10.1007/s43576-021-00007-0.

Franko, K., and Goyes, D. R. (2023). 'Drug Violence, War–Crime Distinction, and Hierarchies of Victimhood'. *Social and Legal Studies 32*(1), 75–95, https://doi.org/10.1177/09646639221091226.

Fraser, A., and Li, E. C.-Y. (2017). 'The Second Life of Kawloon Walled City: Crime, Media and Cultural Memory'. *Crime, Media, Culture 13*(2), 217–34.

Fricker, M. (2007). *Epistemic Injustice: Power and the Ethics of Knowing*. Oxford University Press.

Galán Pachón, J. M., Arellano Mendoza, F., Pulido Caro, É. J., Jaramillo Zapata, B., and Lara Restrepo, R. (2011). *Comunicado: Grupo de acuerdo generacional* [*Public Statement: Group of Generational Agreement*], http://www.indepaz.org.co/wp-content/uploads/2011/07/633_demanda-3.pdf.

Galeano, E. (1987). *Memory of Fire: Genesis*. Vol. 1. Open Road.

Galeano, E. (1997 [1971]). *Open Veins of Latin America: Five Centuries of the Pillage of a Continent*. Monthly Review Press.

Gammeltoft-Hansen, T. (2017). 'Refugee Policy as "Negative Nation Branding": The Case of Denmark and the Nordic', https://ssrn.com/abstract=3902589.

García Hernández, A. (2017). 'Jaime Pardo Leal, el candidato presidencial que murió por querer transformar el país' ['Jaime Pardo Leal, the Presidential Candidate Who Died for Wanting to Transform the Country']. Prospectiva en Justicia y Desarrollo Blog (11 October), https://projusticiaydesarrollo.com/2017/10/11/jaime-pardo-leal-el-candidato-presidencial-que-murio-por-querer-transformar-al-pais/.

Gerrard, S. (2020). 'Introduction'. In S. Gerrard (ed.), *From Blofeld to Moneypenny: Gender in James Bond* (pp. 1–8). Emerald.

Gibler, J. (2011). *To Die in Mexico: Dispatches from Inside the Drug War*. City Lights Books.

Giddens, A. (1990). *The Consequences of Modernity*. Polity Press.

Gilman, N., Goldhammer, J., and Weber, S. (2011). *Deviant Globalization: Black Market Economy in the 21st Century*. Continuum.

Giraldo, I. (2015). 'Machos y mujeres de armas tomar. Patriarcado y subjetividad femenina en la narco-telenovela colombiana contemporánea' ['Machos and Women of taken weapons. Pathriarchy and Female Subjectivity in the Contemporary Colombian Narco-Telenovelas']. *La Manzana de la Discordia 10*(1), 67–81.

Giraldo, M. L. (2011). *Estudios sobre memoria colectiva del conflicto. Colombia 2000–2010* [*Studies About Collective Memory of the Conflict. Colombia 2000–2010*]. Universidad de Antioquia.

Glynn, P., and Bushby, H. (2022). 'Netflix Adds Disclaimer under The Crown's Trailer for Series Five'. *The Guardian* (21 October), https://www.bbc.com/news/entertainment-arts-63341010.

Gokul, D. R. (2019). 'Global South and Political Oppositional Cinema'. *Global South Colloquy: e-Journal of the Institute for Global South Studies and Research* (23 June), https://globalsouthcolloquy.com/global-south-and-political-oppositional-cinema/.

Goyes, D. R. (2015). 'Land Uses and Conflict in Colombia'. In A. Brisman, N. South, and R. White (eds.), *Environmental Crime and Social Conflict* (pp. 75–93). Ashgate.

Goyes, D. R. (2019). *Southern Green Criminology: A Science to End Ecological Discrimination*. Emerald.

Goyes, D. R., and Franko, K. (2021). 'Profiting from Pablo: Victimhood and Commercialism in a Global Society'. *The British Journal of Criminology 62*(3), 533–50, https://doi.org/10.1093/bjc/azab078.

Goyes, D. R., and South, N. (2017). 'Green Criminology before "Green Criminology": Amnesia and Absences'. *Critical Criminology 25*(2), 165–81, https://doi.org/10.1007/s10612-017-9357-8.

Goyes, D. R., South, N., Abaibira, M. A., Baicué, P., Cuchimba, A., and Ñeñetofe, D. T. R. (2021). 'Genocide and Ecocide in Four Colombian Indigenous Communities: The Erosion of a Way of Life and Memory'. *The British Journal of Criminology 61*(4), 965–84, https://doi.org/10.1093/bjc/azaa109.

Goyes, D. R., South, N., Ramos Ñeñetofe, D. T., Cuchimba, A., Baicué, P., and Abaibira, M. A. (2023). '"An Incorporeal Disease": COVID-19, Social Trauma and Health Injustice in Four Colombian Indigenous Communities'. *The Sociological Review 71*(1), 105–25, https://doi.org/10.1177/00380261221133673.

Grajales, J. (2013). 'State Involvement, Land Grabbing and Counter-Insurgency in Colombia'. *Development and Change 42*(2), 211–32, https://doi.org/10.11111/dech.12019.

Grant, A. (2017). *Originals: How Non-Conformists Move the World*. Penguin Books.

Gray, A. M. (1989). *Warfighting*. United States Marine Corps.

Green, D. A. (2008). *When Children Kill Children: Penal Populism and Political Culture*. Oxford University Press.

Greenberg Research (1999). *The People on War Report: ICRC Worldwide Consultation on the Rules of War*, https://www.icrc.org/en/doc/assets/files/other/globalreport.pdf.

Greer, C., and McLaughlin, E. (2017). 'News Power, Crime and Media Justice', in A. Liebling, S. Maruna, and L. McAra (eds.), *The Oxford Handbook of Criminology* (pp. 260–83). Oxford University Press.

Griffin, M. G., Resick, P. A., Waldrop, A. E., and Mechanic, M. B. (2003). 'Participation in Trauma Research: Is There Evidence of Harm?'. *Journal of Traumatic Stress 16*(3), 221–7.

Grosfoguel, R. (2007). 'World-System Analysis and Postcolonial Studies: A Call for a Dialogue from the "Coloniality of Power" Approach'. In R. Krishnaswamy and

J. C. Hawley (eds.), *The Postcolonial and the Global* (pp. 94–104). University of Minnesota Press.

Grupo de Memoria Histórica. (2013). *¡BASTA YA! Colombia: Memorias de Guerra y Dignidad* [*ENOUGH IS ENOUGH! Colombia: Memories of War and Dignity*]. Imprenta Nacional [National Print], http://www.centrodememoriahistorica.gov.co/micrositios/informeGeneral/descargas.html.

Gutiérrez de Pineda, V. (1975). *Familia y cultura en Colombia* [*Family and Culture in Colombia*]. Instituto Colombiano de Cultura.

Gutiérrez-Rexach, J. (2012). 'José Padilha: Elite Squad/Tropa de elite'. In I. M. Queipo (ed.), *Socio-Critical Aspects in Latin American Cinemas* (pp. 136–8). Peter Lang.

Hachenberger, C. (2019). 'Narcos and the Promotion of an U.S. (Informal) Cultural Empire Based on Processes of Stereotyping and Comparison'. *Forum for Inter-American Research 12*(1), 43–55.

Hall, S. (1992). 'The West and the Rest: Discourses and Power'. In S. Hall and B. Gieben (eds.), Formations of Modernity (pp. 184–227). Polity Press/Blackwell Publishers/the Open University.

Hamburger, A., Hancheva, C., and Volkan, V. (2021). 'Introduction'. In A. Hamburger, C. Hancheva, and V. Volkan (eds.), *Social Trauma: An Interdisciplinary Textbook* (pp. v–x). Springer.

Harari, Y. N. (2011). *Sapiens: A Brief History of Humankind*. Penguin.

Harrington, C. (2021). 'What is "Toxic Masculinity" and Why Does it Matter?'. *Men and Masculinities 24*(2), 345–52, https://doi.org/10.1177/1097184x20943254.

Hart, A. (2019). 'The Discriminatory Gesture: A Psychoanalytic Consideration of Posttraumatic Reactions to Incidents of Racial Discrimination'. *Psychoanalytic Social Work 26*(1), 5–24, https://doi.org/10.1080/15228878.2019.1604241.

Hastie, A. (2020). 'Popular Postcolonial Masculinities: Gangsters and Soldiers in Maghrebi-French Cinema'. *Gender, Place and Culture 27*(2), 153–74, https://doi.org/10.1080/0966369X.2019.1596884.

Hastings, R., and Meyer, E. (2020). *No Rules Rules: Netflix and the Culture of Reinvention*. Penguin.

Hearty, K. (2016). 'Legislating Hierarchies of Victimhood and Perpetrators: The Civil Service (Special Advisers) Act (Northern Ireland) 2013 and the Meta-Conflict'. *Social and Legal Studies 25*(3), 333–53.

Heath, C., and Heath, D. (2010). *Made to Stick: Why Some Ideas Survive and Others Die*. Random House.

Heathman, A. (2016). 'Netflix Earnings Up Thanks to Narcos and Stranger Things: 12 Million New Users Signed Up for the Service in Early 2016'. *Wired* (18 October), https://www.wired.co.uk/article/netflix-earnings-increase-stranger-things.

Helmer, W. (2011). *Al Capone and His American Boys*. Indiana University Press.

Henao, V. E. (2020). *Mitt liv med Pablo Escobar* [*My Life with Pablo Escobar*]. Camino.

Herrero-Olaizola, A. (2022). *Commodifying Violence in Literature and on Screen: The Colombian Condition*. Routledge.

Herrity, K., Schmidt, B., and Warr, J. (2021). 'Introduction: Welcome to the Sensorium'. In K. Herrity, B. Schmidt, and J. Warr (eds.), *Sensory Penalities: Exploring the Senses in Spaces of Punishment and Social Control* (pp. xxi–xxxiv). Emerald.

Hoge, W. (1981). 'Colombian City is Corrupted by Cocaine'. *The New York Times* (30 June), https://www.nytimes.com/1981/06/30/world/colombian-city-is-corrupted-by-cocaine.html.

Honneth, A. (2021). 'Recognition Between Power and Normativity: A Hegelian Critique of Judith Butler'. In H. Ikäheimo, K. Lepold, and T. Stahl (eds.), *Recognition and Ambivalence* (pp. 21–30). Columbia University Press.

Houge, A. B., and Lohne, K. (2017). 'End Impunity! Reducing Conflict-related Sexual Violence to a Problem of Law'. *Law & Society Review 51*(4), 755–89.

Ikäheimo, H., Lepold, K., and Stahl, T. (eds.) (2021). *Recognition and Ambivalence.* Columbia University Press.

Jacoby, T. A. (2015). 'A Theory of Victimhood: Politics, Conflict and the Construction of Victim-based Identity'. *Millennium 43*(2), 511–30.

Jamieson, R. (ed.) (2014). *The Criminology of War*. Routledge.

Jankowitz, S. (2018). 'The "Hierarchy of Victims" in Northern Ireland: A Framework for Critical Analysis'. *International Journal of Transitional Justice 12*(2), 216–36.

Jewkes, Y. (2015). *Crime and Media*. 3rd edn. SAGE.

Jorge, M. S. (2021). 'Mulheres em um mundo de homens: *Women in A World of Men* representação feminina em *Narcos* e a ilusão da ficção seriada "universal"' ['Women in a World of Men. Female Representation in Narcos and the Illusion of "Universal" Serial Fiction']. *Estudos Feministas 29*(1), 1–13, https://www-jstor-org.ezproxy.uio.no/stable/48618875.

Jurado Jurado, J. C. (2015). 'Guerra y Nación: La guerra civil colombiana de 1851' ['War and Nation: The Colombian 1851 Civil War']. *HiSTOReLo: Revista de Historia Regional y Local 7*, 99–139.

Kaplan, P., and LaChance, D. (2022). *Crimesploitation: Crime, Punishment and Pleasure on Reality Television*. Stanford University Press.

Karstedt, S. (2010). 'From Absence to Presence, From Silence to Voice: Victims in International and Transitional Justice Since the Nuremberg Trials'. *International Review of Victimology 17*(1), 9–30, https://doi.org/10.1177/026975801001700102.

Khalfaoui, A. (2020). 'Mass Atrocities: Definition and Relationship with Development'. In W. Leal Filho, A. Azul, L. Brandli, P. Özuyar, and T. Wall (eds.), *Peace, Justice and Strong Institutions: Encyclopedia of the UN Sustainable Development Goals* (pp. 1–9). Springer, https://doi.org/10.1007/978-3-319-71066-2_5-1.

Killean, R. (2018). 'Constructing Victimhood at the Khmer Rouge Tribunal: Visibility, Selectivity and Participation'. *International Review of Victimology 24*(3): 273–96.

Klima, A. (2019) *Ethnography #9*. Duke University Press.

Koch, A., Brierley, C., Maslin, M., and Lewis, S. (2019). 'European Colonization of the Americas Killed 10 Percent of World Population and Caused Cooling'. *The Conversation* (31 January), https://www.pri.org/stories/2019-01-31/european-colonization-americas-killed-10-percent-world-population-and-caused.

Koning, H. (1993). *Conquest of America: How the Indian Nations Lost Their Continent*. Monthly Review Press.

Krause, K. (2009). 'Iron Fist Politics in Latin America: Politicians, Public Opinion, and Crime Control'. Paper presented at the 2009 Congress of the Latin American Studies Association, Rio de Janeiro, Brazil (11–14 June 2009), https://biblioteca.cejamericas.org/bitstream/handle/2015/2234/KrauseKrystin.pdf.

Krippner, S., and McIntyre, T. M. (eds.). (2003). *The Psychological Impact of War Trauma on Civilians: An International Perspective*. Praeger Publishers/Greenwood Publishing Group.

Kundera, M. (1980). *The Book of Laughter and Forgetting*. M. H. Heim, trans. Penguin.

Lacalle, C., and Solá, N. S. (2018). 'Judy Moncada: La representación femenina del poder y la ambición' ['Judy Moncada: The Female Representation of Power and Ambition']. In S. G. Luque (ed.), *¿Por qué amamos a Pablo Escobar? Cómo Netflix revivió al narcotraficante más famoso del mundo* [*Why Do We Love Pablo Escobar? How Netflix Brought the World's Most Famous Drug Dealer Back to Life*] (pp. 185–200). Editorial UOC.

Las2Orillas. (2020). 'Las 7 narconovelas que más daño le han hecho a Colombia' ['The 7 Narco Telenovelas That Have Done the Most Damage to Colombia'] (25 February), https://www.las2orillas.co/las-7-narconovelas-que-mas-dano-le-han-hecho-a-colombia/.

Leal Buitrago, F. (2011). 'Militares y paramilitares en Colombia' ['Military and Paramilitary in Colombia']. In E. M. Restrepo and B. Bagley (eds.), *La desmovilización de los paramilitares en Colombia. Entre el escepticismo y la esperanza* [*The Demobilization of Paramilitaries in Colombia: Between Scepticism and Hope*] (pp. 43–68). Universidad de los Andes.

Legerski, J.-P., and Bunnell, S. L. (2010). 'The Risks, Benefits, and Ethics of Trauma-Focused Research Participation'. *Ethics and Behavior 20*(6), 429–42, https://doi.org/10.1080/10508422.2010.521443.

Lennon, J. (2017). 'Dark Tourism'. *Oxford Research Encyclopedia of Criminology and Criminal Justice*, https://doi.org/10.1093/acrefore/9780190264079.013.212.

Lerner, A. B. (2018), 'Theorizing Collective Trauma in International Political Economy'. *International Studies Review 21*, 549–71, https://doi.org/10.1093/isr/viy044.

Lessing, B. (2015). 'Logics of Violence in Criminal War'. *Journal of Conflict Resolution 59*(8), 1486–516, https://doi.org/10.1177/0022002715587100.

Lessing, B. (2018). *Making Peace in Drug Wars: Crackdowns and Cartels in Latin America*. Cambridge University Press.

Levy, D., and Sznaider, N. (2002). 'Memory Unbound: The Holocaust and the Formation of Cosmopolitan Memory'. *European Journal of Social Theory 5*(1), 87–106, https://doi.org/10.1177/1368431002005001002.

Levy, D., and Sznaider, N. (2006). *The Holocaust and Memory in the Global Age*. A. Oksiloff, trans. Temple University Press.

Liévano, A. B. (2018). 'Siete películas imprescindibles sobre drogas en Colombia' ['Seven Movies Not to Be Missed about Drugs in Colombia']. Pacifista! (26 July), https://pacifista.tv/notas/siete-peliculas-imprescindibles-sobre-drogas-en-colombia/.

Loader, I., and Percy, S. (2012). 'Bringing the "Outside" In and the "Inside" Out: Crossing the Criminology/IR Divide'. *Global Crime 13*(4), 213–18, https://doi.org/10.1080/17440572.2012.715402.

Local, The. (2016). 'Colom Heterosexualism and the Colonial /

Lohne, K. (2019). *Advocates of Humanity: Human Rights NGOs in International Criminal Justice*. Oxford University Press.

Lonely Planet. (2020), 'Private Tour: The Life of Pablo Escobar', https://www.lonelyplanet.com/colombia/northwest-colombia/medellin/activities/private-tour-the-life-of-pablo-escobar/a/pa-act/v-28812P1/363323.

Lugones, M. (2007), 'Heterosexualism and the Colonial / Modern Gender System'. *Hypatia 22*(1), 186–209.

Lugones, M. (2014). 'Rumo a um feminismo descolonial' ['On the Way to a Decolonial Feminism']. *Estudios Feministas, Florianópolis 22*(3), 935–52.

Maclean, K. (2015). *Social Urbanism and the Politics of Violence: The Medellín Miracle*. Palgrave.

Malin, B. J. (2010). 'Viral manhood: Niche Marketing, Hard-Boiled Detectives and the Economics of Masculinity'. *Media, Culture and Society 32*(3), 373–89, https://doi.org/10.1177/0163443709361168.

Marcos, A. (2018). 'Why Pablo Escobar Is Anything but Cool'. *El Pais* (3 September), https://english.elpais.com/elpais/2018/08/31/inenglish/1535708632_118999.html.

McCarthy-Jones, S. (2021). 'From Tarantino to Squid Game: Why Do So Many People Enjoy Violence?'. *The Conversation* (27 October), https://theconversation.com/from-tarantino-to-squid-game-why-do-so-many-people-enjoy-violence-170251.

McClanahan, B., and South, N. (2019). '"All Knowledge Begins with the Senses": Towards a Sensory Criminology'. *The British Journal of Criminology 60*(1), 3–23, https://doi.org/10.1093/bjc/azz052.

McEvoy, K., and McConnachie, K. (2012). 'Victimology in Transitional Justice: Victimhood, Innocence and Hierarchy'. *European Journal of Criminology 9*(5), 527–38.

McEvoy, K., and McConnachie, K. (2013). 'Victims and Transitional Justice: Voice, Agency and Blame'. *Social and Legal Studies 22*(4), 489–513.

McGarry, R., and Walklate, S. (2011). 'The Soldier as Victim: Peering through the Looking Glass'. *The British Journal of Criminology 51*(6), 900–17.

McGarry, R., and Walklate, S. (2015). *Victims: Trauma, Testimony and Justice*. Routledge.

McKinney, T. (2020). 'Racial Trauma in Film: How Viewers Can Address Re-Traumatization'. Northwestern University, The Family Institute (2 March), https://counseling.northwestern.edu/blog/racial-trauma-retraumatization-film.

McNamara, M. (2015). 'Review: Netflix's "Narcos" Plays up Pablo Escobar's Menace and Magnetism'. *Los Angeles Times* (27 August), https://www.latimes.com/entertainment/tv/la-et-st-netflix-narcos-review-20150828-column.html.

Medina Gallego, C. (2009). *FARC-EP: Notas para una historia política (1958–2008)* [*FARC-EP: Notes for a Political History*]. Universidad Nacional de Colombia.

Medina Gallego, C. (2010). 'FARC-EP Y ELN. Una historia política comparada (1958–2006)' ['FARC-EP and ELN: A Comparative Political History (1958–2006)']. Doctoral dissertation, Universidad Nacional de Colombia, http://www.bdigital.unal.edu.co/3556/1/469029.2010.pdf.

Mejía Quintana, O. (2018). 'La construcción de una cultura política mafiosa en Colombia' ['The Construction of a Mafia-Like Political Culture in Colombia']. In S. G. Luque (ed.), *¿Por qué amamos a Pablo Escobar? Cómo Netflix revivió al narcotraficante más famoso del mundo* [*Why Do We Love Pablo Escobar? How*

Netflix Brought the Most Famous Drug Dealer in the World Back to Life] (pp. 27–50). Editorial UOC.

Mejía, D. (2011). 'The War On Illegal Drugs in Producer and Consumer Countries: A Simple Analytical Framework'. In C. C. Storti and P. D. Grauwe (eds.), *Illicit Trade and the Global Economy* (pp. 2–29). MIT Press.

Merton, R. (1968). *Social Theory and Social Structure*. The Free Press.

Mignolo, W. (2012) *Local Histories / Global Designs*. Princeton University Press.

Miles, S. (1998). *Consumerism: As a Way of Life*. Sage.

Miller, T., Barrios, M. M., and Arroyave, J. (2019). 'Prime-Time Narcos: The Mafia and Gender in Colombian Television'. *Feminist Media Studies 19*(3), 348–63, https://doi.org/10.1080/14680777.2018.1434223.

Miranda, B. (2018). '25 Years after the Death of Pablo Escobar: The Story Behind the 2 Paintings that Fernando Botero Painted about the Death of the Drug Trafficker'. *BBC* (30 November), https://www.bbc.com/mundo/noticias-america-latina-46298539.

Monleón, J. B. (1990). 'The Dream of Reason'. *Mester 19*(2), 5–20, https://escholarship.org/content/qt0h927883/qt0h927883.pdf.

Morello, H. J. (2015). 'Voiceless Victims in *Sin tetas hoy hay paraiso*'. *Literature and Culture 19*(4), 2–9.

Morrison, W. (2006). *Criminology, Civilisation and the New World Order*. Routledge.

Nakashima Brock, R., and Brooks Thistlethwaite, S. (2020). '#MeToo: The Development of Sexual Harassment Policies in the American Academy of Religion'. *Religion and Gender 10*(2), 205–11, https://doi.org/https://doi.org/10.1163/18785417-01002013.

National Hispanic Media Coalition. (2012). *The Impact of Media Stereotypes on Opinions and Attitudes Towards Latinos*. Latino Decisions, https://www.chicano.ucla.edu/files/news/NHMCLatinoDecisionsReport.pdf.

Neiger, M., Meyers, O., and Zandberg, E. (2011). 'On Media Memory: Editors' Introduction'. In M. Neiger, O. Meyers, and E. Zandberg (eds.), *On Media Memory: Collective Memory in a New Media Age* (pp. 1–24). Palgrave Macmillan, https://doi.org/10.1057/9780230307070_1.

Netflix "Narcos" Billboard'. (15 December), https://www.thelocal.es/20161215/colombia-asks-madrid-to-remove-netflix-narcos-billboard/.

Newman, E., Miro, D., and Bernard, C (2018). 'Foreword'. In Jeff Bond (ed.), *The Art and Making of Narcos* (p. 6). Gaumont Books.

Nimis, J. (2014). 'Introduction: New Media Methodologies in the Global South'. *The Global South 8*(1), 1–6, https://doi.org/10.2979/globalsouth.8.1.1.

Nochimson, M. P. (2002). '"Waddaya Lookin' At?": Re-reading the Gangster Genre through "The Sopranos"'. *Film Quarterly 56*(2), 2–13, https://doi.org/10.1525/fq.2002.56.2.2.

O'Brien, S. (2020). 'Babes and Bullets: The Representation of Gender in Bond Themes and Title Sequences'. In S. Gerrard (ed.), *From Blofeld to Moneypenny: Gender in James Bond* (pp. 103–15). Emerald.

O'Donnell, K. A. (1999). 'Good Girls Gone Bad: the Consumption of Fetish Fashion and the Sexual Empowerment of Women'. *NA—Advances in Consumer Research 26*, 184–9.

Offstein, N. and Aristizábal, C. (2003). 'An Historical Review and Analysis of Colombian Guerrilla Movements: FARC, ELN and EPL'. *Revista Desarrollo y Sociedad 1*(52), 99–142. https://doi.org/10.13043/dys.52.4.

Ordoñez, M. D. (2012). 'Las "narco telenovelas" colombianas y su papel en la construcción discursiva sobre el narcotráfico en América Latina' ['The Colombian "Narco Telenovelas" and Their Role in the Discursive Construction of Drug Trafficking in Latin America']. Master dissertation in Latin American studies, Universidad Andina Simón Bolívar, https://repositorio.uasb.edu.ec/bitstream/10644/3033/1/T1108-MELA-Ordo%c3%b1ez-Las%20narco.pdf.

Orozco Gómez, G. (2001). *Televisión, audiencias y educación* [*Television, Audiences, and Education*]. 2nd edn. Norma.

Pardo Rueda, R. (1996). *De primera mano: Colombia 1986–1994, entre conflictos y esperanzas* [*From First Hand: Colombia 1986–1994, Between Conflicts and Hope*]. CEREC.

Pemberton, A., Mulder, E., and Aarten, P. G. M. (2019). 'Stories of Injustice: Towards a Narrative Victimology'. *European Journal of Criminology 16*(4), 391–412, https://doi.org/10.1177/1477370818770843.

Pilipets, E. (2019). 'From Netflix Streaming to Netflix and Chill: The (Dis)Connected Body of Serial Binge-Viewer'. *Social Media + Society 5*(4), https://doi.org/10.1177/2056305119883426.

Pobutsky, A. B. (2010). 'Deleitar denunciando: La narco telenovela de Gustavo Bolívar "Sin tetas no hay paraíso" marca el pulso de la sociedad colombiana' ['Delight in Denouncing: Gustavo Bolivar's Narco-Telenovela "No Tits, No Paradise" Sets the Tone for Colombian Society']. *Especulo 46*, https://webs.ucm.es/info/especulo/numero46/deleitar.html.

Pobutsky, A. B. (2013). 'Peddling Pablo: Escobar's Cultural Renaissance'. *Hispania 96*(4), 684–99.

Pobutsky, A. B. (2020). *Pablo Escobar and Colombian Narcoculture*. University of Florida Press.

Podraza, M. (2021). 'Forty Years Later: Laurie Strode and the Survival of the Final Girl'. *Horror Studies 12*(1), 133–47, https://doi.org/10.1386/host_00033_1.

Posner, M. (2016). 'The Mafia in Hollywood: The Early Years'. *Queen's Quarterly 123*(2), 178–89.

Presser, L., and Sandberg, S. (2015). *Narrative Criminology: Understanding Stories of Crime*. New York University Press.

Publimetro. (2017), 'Alias J.J.' de Caracol sorprendió: fue la producción más vista por los colombianos'. (9 February), https://www.publimetro.co/co/entretenimiento/2017/02/09/rating-tv-colombia-alias-j-j.html.

Purely Streanomics. (2021). 'Film & TV 2.0: An Industry Transformed'. *Visual Capitalist*, https://cdn.roxhillmedia.com/production/email/attachment/870001_880000/f251ae140e3403be1acd75ac60f1fb4f1747ebc9.pdf.

Quijano, A. (2000). 'Coloniality of Power, Eurocentrism, and Latin America'. *Nepantla: Views from South 1*(3), 533–80.

Quijano, A. (2007). 'Coloniality and Modernity/Rationality'. *Cultural Studies 21*(2–3), 168–78.

Rafter, N. (2007). 'Crime, Film and Criminology: Recent Sex-Crime Movies'. *Theoretical Criminology 11*(3), 403–20, https://doi.org/10.1177/136248060 7079584.

Ramírez R., C. E., and Rodríguez Bravo, J. (2002). 'Pobreza en Colombia: Tipos de medición y evolución de políticas entre los años 1950 y 2000' ['Poverty in Colombia: Assessment and Policy Development between 1950 and 2000']. *Estudios Gerenciales 18*, 81–107, https://www.redalyc.org/pdf/212/21208504.pdf.

Randolph, M. (2019). *That Will Never Work: The Birth of Netflix and the Amazing Life of an Idea*. Little, Brown and Company.

Rao, V. (2009). 'Embracing Urbanism: The City as Archive'. *New Literary History 40*(2), 371–83.

Reiner, R. (2002). 'Media-Made Criminality: The Representation of Crime in the Mass Media'. In M. Maguire, R. Morgan, and R. Reiner (eds.), *The Oxford Handbook of Criminology* (pp. 376–416). Oxford University Press.

Reyes, E. (2013) . 'El gobierno de Colombia reparará por primera vez a una víctima de Escobar' ['The Colombian Government Will Make Reparations to Escobar's Victims for the First Time']. *El País* (17 October), https://elpais.com/internacional/ 2013/10/17/actualidad/1381971825_495193.html.

Riaño-Alcalá, P. (2010). *Dwellers of Memory: Youth and Violence in Medellín*. Routledge.

Rincón, O. (2018). 'No somos Narcos, pero sí Pablo' ['We Are Not Narcos, but We Are Pablo']. In S. G. Luque (ed.), *¿Por qué amamos a Pablo Escobar? Cómo Netflix revivió al narcotraficante más famoso del mundo* [*Why Do We Love Pablo Escobar? How Netflix Brought the World's Most Famous Drug Dealer Back to Life*] (pp. 51–69). Editorial UOC.

Robayo, J. M. (2010). 'Reflexiones en torno al impacto de la Patria Boba: La independencia de Tunja y su provincia 1810–1815' ['Reflections on the Impact of the "Patria Boba": The Independence of Tunja and its Province 1810–1915']. *Historia y Memoria 1*, 11–33.

Robertson, L. (2005). *Conquest by Law: How the Discovery of America Dispossessed Indigenous Peoples of Their Lands*. Oxford University Press.

Robinson, D. (2015). 'Mexico: The War on Drugs and the Boundaries of Crimes against Humanity'. *EJIL:Talk: Blog of the European Journal of International Law* (26 May), https://www.ejiltalk.org/mexico-the-war-on-drugs-and-the-boundaries-of-crimes-against-humanity/.

Robinson, J. (2016). 'La miseria en Colombia' ['Misery in Colombia']. *Revista Desarrollo y Sociedad 76*, 9–88.

Rothberg, M. (2009), *Multidirectional Memory: Remembering the Holocaust in the Age of Decolonization*. Stanford University Press.

Rowe, W., and Schelling, V. (1991). *Memory and Modernity: Popular Culture in Latin America*. Verso.

Saffray, C. (1948). *Viaje a Nueva Granda* [*A Journey to the Republic of New Granada*]. Biblioteca Popular de Cultura Colombiana.

Said, E. (2019 [1978]). *Orientalism*. Penguin.

Sallenave, M. V. B. (2018). 'Construcción de otredad en la ficción: Relato, verdad e identridad' ['Constructing Otherness in Fiction: Narrative, Truth, and Identity'].

In S. G. Luque (ed.), *¿Por qué amamos a Pablo Escobar? Cómo Netflix revivió al narcotraficante más famoso del mundo* (pp. 123–41). Editorial UOC.

Sandvik, K. B., and Lemaitre, J. (2015). 'From IDPs to Victims in Colombia: A Bottom-up Reading of Law in Post-Conflict Transitions'. In M. Saul and J. A. Sweeney (eds.), *International Law and Post-Conflict Reconstruction Policy* (pp. 251–71). Routledge.

Santos, B. de S. (2002). *A crítica da Raçao Indolente: Contra o Desperdício da Experiência* [*A Critique of Lazy Reason: Against the Waste of Experience*]. Cortez Editora.

Santos, B. de S. (2014). *Epistemologies of the South: Justice Against Epistemicide*. Paradigm Publishers.

Sassoli, M. (2019). *International Humanitarian Law. Rules, Controversies, and Solutions to Problems Arising in Warfare*. Edward Elgar Publishing Limited.

Schedler, A. (2013). 'Mexico's Civil War Democracy'. American Political Science Association Annual Meeting Paper, https://ssrn.com/abstract=2299314.

Schiffrin, A. (2000). *The Business of Books*. Verso.

Schiffrin, A. (2010). *Words* and *Money*. Verso.

Schippert, A. C. S. P., Grov, E. K., and Bjørnnes, A. K. (2021). 'Uncovering Re-traumatization Experiences of Torture Survivors in Somatic Health Care: A Qualitative Systematic Review'. *PLoS One 16*(2), e0246074, https://doi.org/10.1371/journal.pone.0246074.

Schwöbel-Patel, C. (2018). 'The "Ideal" Victim of International Criminal Law'. *European Journal of International Law 29*(3), 703–24.

Scott, D. (1997). 'The "Culture of Violence" Fallacy'. *Small Axe 2*, 140–7.

Semana. (2012). 'Lo que no se supo de "El patrón del mal"' ['Things We Did Not Know About "The Patrón del Mal"']. (14 December), https://www.semana.com/gente/articulo/lo-no-supo-el-patron-del-mal/325449-3/.

Shail, R. (2020). 'Adapting the Male Hero: The Comic Strip Adventures of James Bond'. In S. Gerrard (ed.), *From Blofeld to Moneypenny: Gender in James Bond* (pp. 41–51). Emerald.

Shirk, D. (2011). *The Drug War in Mexico: Confronting a Shared Threat*. Council on Foreign Relations.

Silveira, F. L. A., and Soares, P. P. d. M. A. (2012). 'As paisagens fantásticas numa cidade Amazonica sob o olhar dos taxistas' ['The Fantastic Landscapes in an Amazonian City Through the Eyes of Taxi Drivers']. *Revista Brasileira de Ciencias Sociais 27*(82), 153–67.

Simon, J. (2007). *Governing through Crime: How the War on Crime Transformed American Democracy and Created a Culture of Fear*. Oxford University Press.

Skillington, T. (2013). 'UN Genocide Commemoration, Transnational Scenes of Mourning and the Global Project of Learning from Atrocity'. *British Journal of Sociology 64*, 501–25, https://doi.org/10.1111/1468-4446.12029.

Smyth, F. (1998). 'Still Seeing Red'. *The Progressive 62*(6), 23–6, https://franksmyth.com/the-progressive/still-seeing-red-the-cia-fosters-death-squads-in-colombia/.

Solano Cohen, V. (2015). 'Towards a Nosology of the Violence of Drug-Traffic: Literary Topos from the Years of the Plague'. *La palabra 27*, 79–92.

Spallacci, A. (2019). 'Representing Rape Trauma in Film: Moving beyond the Event'. *Arts 8*(1), 8, https://doi.org/10.3390/arts8010008.

Stoneman, E., and Packer, J. (2020). 'Reel Cruelty: Voyeurism and Extra-Juridical Punishment in True-Crime Documentaries'. *Crime, Media, Culture: An International Journal 17*(3), 401–19, https://doi.org/10.1177/1741659020953596.

Sturken, M. (1997). *Tangled Memories: The Vietnam War, the AIDS Epidemic, and the Politics of Remembering*. University of California Press.

Sturken, M. (2007). *Tourists of History: Memory, Kitsch, and Consumerism from Oklahoma City to Ground Zero*. Duke University Press.

Sweet, P. (2021). *The Politics of Surviving. How Women Navigate Domestic Violence and Its Aftermath*. University of California Press.

Taylor, C. (1992). 'The Politics of Recognition'. In A. Gutman (ed.), *Multiculturalism: Examining the Politics of Recognition* (pp. 25–73). Princeton University Press.

Tekin, A., Karadağ, H., Süleymanoğlu, M., Tekin, M., Kayran, Y., Alpak, G., and Şar, V. (2016). 'Prevalence and Gender Differences in Symptomatology of Posttraumatic Stress Disorder and Depression among Iraqi Yazidis Displaced into Turkey'. *European Journal of Psychotraumatology 7*(1), 28556, https://doi.org/10.3402/ejpt.v7.28556.

Todd-Kvam, M., and Goyes, D. R. (2023). 'Dreams and Nightmares: Interviewing Research Participants Who Have Experienced Trauma'. In M. Adorjan and R. Ricciardelli (eds.), *Engaging with Ethics in International Criminological Research* (pp. 130–48). Routledge.

Tokatlian, J. G. (2008). 'La Construcción de un "Estado Fallido" en la Política Mundial: El Caso de las Relaciones entre Estados Unidos y Colombia' ['The Building of a "Failed State" in World Politics: The Case of the Relationship between the United States and Colombia']. *Análisis Político 21*, 67–104, https://revistas.unal.edu.co/index.php/anpol/article/view/46026.

Tomsky, T. (2011). 'From Sarajevo to 9/11: The Travelling Memory and the Trauma Economy'. *Parallax 17*(4), 49–60.

Topping, A. (2022), '"There's So Many Having Major Moral Thoughts": England Fans Conflicted over Qatar World Cup'. *The Guardian* (11 November), https://www.theguardian.com/world/2022/nov/11/england-supporter-conflicted-over-qatar-world-cup-human-rights-record-gay-rights-boycott-tournament.

Toscano, A. A. (2014). 'Tony Soprano as the American Everyman and Scoundrel: How *The Sopranos* (Re)presents Contemporary Middle-Class Anxieties'. *Journal of Popular Culture 47*(3), 451–69, https://doi.org/https://doi.org/10.1111/jpcu.12140.

Trejo, G., and Ley, S. (2020). *Votes, Drugs, and Violence: The Political Logic of Criminal Wars in Mexico*. Cambridge University Press.

Turner, G. (2019). 'Approaching the Cultures of Use: Netflix, Disruption and the Audience'. *Critical Studies in Television 14*(2), 222–32, https://doi.org/10.1177/1749602019834554.

Uhlig, D. (2022). 'How Much is Netflix Worth?'. *GoBankingRates* (21 July), https://www.gobankingrates.com/money/business/how-much-is-netflix-worth/.

Unidad para la Atención y Reparación Integral a las Víctimas. (2018). 'Bitácora diária de eventos: Semana comprendida entre el 12 y el 18 de Octubre de 2013' ['Daily Record of Events: Week from 12 to 18 October 2013']. *Unidad para la reparación integral a las víctimas*, http://www.archivodelosddhh.gov.co/saia_release1/fondos/

co_uariv_1_acceso/36%20Bitacora%20del%2017%20de%20Octubre%20de%202013.pdf.

UNODC (2019). *Global Study on Homicide: Homicide Trends, Patterns and Criminal Justice Response*. United Nations Office on Drugs and Crime, https://www.unodc.org/documents/data-and-analysis/gsh/Booklet2.pdf.

Uprimny Yepes, R., Saffon Sanín, M. P., Botero Marino, C., and Restrepo Saldarriaga, E. (2006). *¿Justicia transicional sin tansición? Verdad, justicia, reparación para Colombia* [*Transitional Justice without Transition? Truth, Justice, and Reparation for Colombia*]. Ediciones Antropos.

Vallejo, V. (2018). *Loving Pablo, Hating Escobar: The Shocking True Story of the Notorious Drug Lord, from the Woman Who Knew Him Best*. Canongate.

van Wijk, J. (2013). 'Who is the "Little Old Lady" of International Crimes? Nils Christie's Concept of the Ideal Victim Reinterpreted'. *International Review of Victimology 19*(2), 159–79, https://doi.org/10.1177/0143034312472770.

Vásquez, J. G. (2011). *The Sound of Things Falling*. A. McLean, trans. Riverhead Books.

Velásquez Vasquez, J. J. (2017). *Surviving Pablo Escobar: "Popeye" The Hitman 23 Years and 3 Months in Prison*. Dipón.

Vicedo, M. M. (2018). 'El fenómeno *Narcos* como serie de ficción ¿Cerca o lejos de la realidad?' ['The *Narcos* Phenomenon as a Fictional Series: Close to, or Far from, Reality?]. In S. G. Luque (ed.), *¿Por qué amamos a Pablo Escobar? Cómo Netflix revivió al narcotraficante más famoso del mundo* [*Why Do We Love Pablo Escobar? How Netflix Brought the World's Most Famous Drug Dealer Back to Life*] (pp. 143–60). Editorial UOC.

Villalba, Y. P. (2016). 'Bicentenario de la Independencia de Colombia: Causas de la Independencia Hispanoamericana y de Colombia' ['Two Centuries of the Colombian Independence: Causes of the Independence in Hispano-America and Colombia']. *Via inveniendi et iudicandi 5*(1), 163–82.

Vincent, C. J. (2008). *Paying Respect to the* Sopranos: *A Psychosocial Analysis*. McFarland and Company.

Volcic, Z., Erjavec, K., and Peak, M. (2014). 'Branding Post-War Sarajevo'. *Journalism Studies 15*(6), 726–42.

Wacquant, L. (1995). 'Pugs at Work: Bodily Capital and Bodily Labour among Professional Boxers'. *Body and Society 1*(1), 65–93.

Walklate, S. (2007). *Imagining the Victim of Crime*. Open University Press.

Walklate, S. (2012). 'Who is the Victim of Crime? Paying Homage to the Work of Richard Quinney'. *Crime, Media, Culture 8*(2), 173–84, https://doi.org/10.1177/1741659012444433.

Walklate, S. (2016). 'The Metamorphosis of the Victim of Crime: From Crime to Culture and the Implications for Justice'. *International Journal for Crime, Justice and Social Democracy 5*(4), 4–16, https://doi.org/10.5204/ijcjsd.v5i4.280.

Wallace, A. (2013). 'Drug Boss Pablo Escobar Still Divides Colombia'. *BBC News* (2 December), https://www.bbc.com/news/world-latin-america-25183649.

Webley, K. (2011), 'Mob Bosses: Pablo Escobar'. *Time* (20 January), https://content.time.com/time/specials/packages/article/0,28804,2043575_2043788_2043569,00.html.

White, R. (2015). 'Environmental Victimology and Ecological Justice'. In D. Wilson and S. Ross (eds.), *Crime, Victims and Policy: International Contexts, Local Experiences* (pp. 33–52). Palgrave Macmillan.

Wilson, J. P. (2004). 'PTSD and Complex PTSD: Symptoms, Syndromes, and Diagnoses'. In J. P. Wilson and T. M. Keane (eds.), *Assessing Psychological Trauma and PTSD* (pp. 7–44). The Guilford Press.

Ystehede, P. J. (2016). 'Contested Spaces: On Crime, Museums, Monuments and Memorials'. In P. Knepper and A. Johansen (eds.), *The Oxford Handbook of the History of Crime and Criminal Justice* (pp. 338–52). Oxford University Press.

Zapata Callejas, J. S. (2014). 'La teoría del estado fallido: Entre aproximaciones y disensos'. ['The Theory of the Failed State: Between Approximations and Disagreements']. *Revista de Relaciones Internacionales, Estrategia y Seguridad 9*, 87–110, https://revistas.unimilitar.edu.co/index.php/ries/article/view/52.

Zelizer, B. (2011), 'Cannibalizing Memory in the Global Flow of News'. In M. Neiger, O. Meyers, and E. Zandberg (eds.), *On Media Memory: Collective Memory in a New Media Age* (pp. 27–36). Palgrave Macmillan.

Index

For the benefit of digital users, indexed terms that span two pages (e.g., 52–53) may, on occasion, appear on only one of those pages.

Collective memory
academic contributions 14–15
barriers for victims 10–11
challenges from global capitalism 91
conversion of violence 6–7
historical violence links 88–89
importance 180
importance of class and social inequalities 138
power of Netflix 144
role of young people 13–14
sense of loss of control 141
struggle for recognition and the cosmopolitan exclusion 157
survivors rather than victims 193
truth and history telling 180, 182, 188–89
Colombia
challenge by Medellín cartel to supremacy of state 35–36
framing drug violence 12–15
high levels of violence 1
history of violence
bombings 1984-1989 25
history of structural oppression under colonial rule 26–28
impact of Global North-Global South divide 26
long-standing conflict connected to drug trade 25–26
overview of key points 20
peace agreement in 2005 33
role of United States as major consumer 31
statistic of casualties 33–34
US war on drugs 31–33
war as a revolutionary tool 28–30
metamorphosis of international perception 2
ource of profit for both local and international actors 190–91
Colonialism
deep-seated cultural perceptions 100–1
exoticising the post-colonial other 109–12
global hegemonic masculinity project 108
hierarchies of victimhood 184
history of structural oppression in Colombia 26–29
impact on history of violence in Colombia 26
neo-colonization of Latin America by war on drugs 32–33
parallel patterns of consumption 196
pervasive impact on victims 11, 16
post-colonial continuities and epistemic differences in power 189–90
post-colonial experience staged for tourist enjoyment 121–23
shaping of knowledge and language 15–16
social critique of Eurocentrism 172–73
Commodification
centrality of gender to Escobar brand 98
commercial appropriation of Escobar's story
birth of narco-telenovelas 70–73
El Patrón del Mal 69

Commodification (*cont.*)
- commercial appropriation of Escobar's story by Netflix
  - globalization of Escobar as a brand 73–80
  - overview of key points 21
  - role of Netflix 80–86
  - violence as spectacle and trauma healing 91–95
  - why do we consume violence 86–91
- creation of Escobar as cultural icon 1–2
- money as a cultural force 6
- trauma economy
  - contrast with light and entertaining tone of global narrative 8
  - dominant global consumerist culture 8
  - impact of media and popular culture 7
  - merging of economic networks around historical events 7–8
  - need to adjust underlying concept 8–9
  - processes of remembrance and memorialization 6–7

Consumerism
- centrality of gender to Escobar brand 98
- commercial appropriation of Escobar's story
  - birth of narco-telenovelas 70–73
  - *El Patrón del Mal* 69
- commercial appropriation of Escobar's story by Netflix
  - globalization of Escobar as a brand 73–80
  - overview of key points 21
  - role of Netflix 80–86
  - violence as spectacle and trauma healing 91–95
  - why do we consume violence 86–91
- commercial exploitation of Escobar museum 196–97
- commercial interests which dominate book publishing 57–63
- dark tourism
  - branding in an unequal society 133–41
  - form of retraumatization 133
  - impossibility of forgetting 119–27
  - shaping of city lives 117
  - shaping of cultural memory 118–19
- Escobar as omnipresent consumer brand 2
- failure to curtail dark tourism and Escobar branding 193–94
- harmful effects within production chain 197
- haunting effect on Medellín 5
- mass-produced cultural items showing Escobar in glamorous light 199–200
- money as a cultural force 6
- photographs
  - menu featuring Escobar-inspired drinks 2–5, 3*f*
  - T-shirt sold in Camden Market, London 2–5, 4*f*
- relation to pain and violence 2–5
- repressed individual and collective traumas 64–67
- role in process of memory construction 198
- role of the global community in fuelling violence 197–98
- role of United States as major drug consumer 31
- social responsibilities of business and corporations 195–96
- trauma economy
  - contrast with light and entertaining tone of global narrative 8
  - dominant global consumerist culture 8
  - impact of media and popular culture 7
  - merging of economic networks around historical events 7–8

need to adjust underlying concept 8–9
processes of remembrance and memorialization 6–7
Cosmopolitan memory 11, 157
Crime control 12
Cultural memory
European cultural memory 157
global economic influence of movies 5–6
inscribed in bodily practices 129
power of Netflix 144
shaping of cultural memory 118–19
Cultural symbols
creation of Escobar as cultural icon 1–2
shift of Escobar's image from disgrace to fame 2
Cultural trauma 9–10, 67

Dark tourism
failure to curtail 193–94
hurtful and disrespectful of the local population 196–97
overview of key points 22
post-colonial experience staged for tourist enjoyment 121–23
profitability of trauma economy
branding in an unequal society 133–41
form of retraumatization 133
impact of media productions 117–18
impossibility of forgetting 119–27
shaping of city lives 117
shaping of cultural memory 118–19
research methodology 18–19
Drug violence
see also **'narco-terrorism'; trauma**
commercial appropriation of Escobar's story by Netflix
violence as spectacle and trauma healing 91–95
why do we consume violence 86–91
conceptual difficulties 12–13
conceptualization 183
connection with politics 184–85
contentious political terrain 12
cultural legacy and role of media 14–15
Global North–Global South divide 189
growth of dark tourism 135
history of violence in Colombia
bombings 1984-1989 25
history of structural oppression under colonial rule 26–28
impact of Global North-Global South divide 26
long-standing conflict connected to drug trade 25–26
overview of key points 20
peace agreement in 2005 33
role of United States as major drug consumer 31
statistic of casualties 33–34
US war on drugs 31–33
hyper-visibility 190
implied causal relationship between drugs and violence 13
legal recognition for victims
drafting of Victims' Law in 2011 163–64
fight for recognition by Federico 164–65
overview of key points 22–23
reflection of globally established hierarchy of victimhood 165–66
transitional justice compared 165
mass drug violence defined 13
Medellín as 'murder capital of the world' 1
Medellín cartel
attacks on journalists 37
attacks on judges 36–37
attacks on police 38
attacks on politicians 37–38
challenge to supremacy of state 34–35
conflict with the M-19 guerrilla group 34

Drug violence (*cont.*)
open war on the Colombian state 35–36
turf conflicts with Cali cartels 35
memories of violence 38–43
newspaper accounts as historic documentation 38–39
obstacles to recognition of trauma 188
relation of consumerism to pain and violence 2–5
role of the global community in fuelling violence 197–98
trauma economy
contrast with light and entertaining tone of global narrative 8
dominant global consumerist culture 8
impact of media and popular culture 7
merging of economic networks around historical events 7–8
need to adjust underlying concept 8–9
processes of remembrance and memorialization 6–7
war seen 'from below', but not 'from above' 173–77

El Barrio Pablo Escobar
photographs
hairdresser's in *El Barrio Pablo Escoba* 123–25, 125*f*
mural in *El Barrio Pablo Escobar* 123–25, 124*f*
portraits of prominent members of Medellín cartel 138, 140*f*
statue of a saint 138, 139*f*
Entertainment *see* **media and enternatinment industries**
Escobar, Pablo
attempt at political involvement 176
centrality of gender 98
commercial appropriation of Escobar's story by Netflix
birth of narco-telenovelas 70–73
El Patrón del Mal 69
globalization of Escobar as a brand 73–80
overview of key points 21
role of Netflix 80–86
violence as spectacle and trauma healing 91–95
why do we consume violence 86–91
cultural icon 1–2
dark legacy through portrayals of his death 198–99
establishment of Medellín cartel in 1976 34
failure to curtail branding 193–94
fear of erasure 200–1
film stills
Andrés Parra as Pablo Escobar in *El Patrón del Mal* 74–77, 76*f*
Brendan Fraser playing Pablo Escobar in *Bedazzled* 106–7, 107*f*
Javier Bardem as Pablo Escobar and Penelope Cruz as Virginia Vallejo in *Loving Pablo* 79*f*
Wagner Moura as Pablo Escobar and Paulina Gaitán as Escobar's wife in *Narcos* 78*f*
Wagner Moura as Pablo Escobar in *Narcos* 101–2, 102*f*
leader of the Medellín cartel 1
mass-produced cultural items showing him in glamorous light 199–200
objectification of women 99
omnipresent consumer brand 2
photographs
of himself 74–77, 75*f*
menu featuring Escobar-inspired drinks 2–5, 3*f*
mug shot in 1976 129–30, 130*f*
Pablo Escobar Muerto by Fernando Botero 198–99, 199*f*
rubble of Monaco building, demolished on order of Medellín's major in 2019 36*f*, 36
souvenirs with the image of Pablo Escobar 130–32, 131*f*

T-shirt sold in Camden Market, London 2–5, 4*f*
tourist showing off Escobar tattoo 130–32, 131*f*
visitors taking pictures at the entrance to the Napoles ranch 122–23, 123*f*
shift of image from disgrace to fame 2
topic of tourist conversation 120
toxic masculinity 97
yearning to live like James Bond 98–99
Escobar's tomb
photographs
pilgrims' offerings at Escobar's tomb 121–22, 122*f*
visitors to Escobar's grave 120–21, 121*f*

Feminist perspectives 106

Gendered stereotypes
Al Capone 98
central role of media 110–11
creation of hierarchies of victimhood 189–90
Escobar's yearning to live like James Bond 98–99
hegemonic masculinity 100–1
immortalization of macho men, submissive women,and exotic others 112–16
narco culture 99–100
objectification of women 99
problematic gender performativity of narco-shows 101–5
shaping of present values 137–38
toxic masculinity 97
Narcos legacy 104–5
objectification of women 100
relationship with violence 97
Global North–Global South divide
additional dimension of gender relations 106–8
consequences for affected communities 184
creation of 'war on drugs' 175–76
differing drug violence victims 189
dominant global consumerist culture 7–8
epistemic power of the North 192–95
failure to curtail dark tourism and Escobar branding 193–94
hierarchies of victimhood
central constitutive element of hierarchies 16
framing of mass drug violence 15
language and models dominated by Global North 15–16
mass drug violence as civil war or an 'ordinary crime' 169–73
shaping factors and responses 189–90
impact on history of violence in Colombia 26
national militarized drug policies 176
orientalism 112
victimhood and cosmopolitan solidarity in a divided world 10–11

Haunting
defined 5
effect of Escobar relics 2–5
emotional impacts of experiencing Escobar's 'resurrection' 93
Escobar's effect on Medellín 90–91, 141–42
impact of commodification and consumer cultures 6
launching of *Narcos* 92
'politics of memory, of inheritance, and of generations' 5–6
Hegemonic masculinity
defined 100–1
gender relations in Global South 106–8
male characters in *Narcos* 103
Hierarchies of victimhood
central constitutive element of hierarchies 16
centrality of innocence 167

Hierarchies of victimhood (*cont.*)
classification as contentious issue 167
framing of mass drug violence 15
further elements beyond the 'innocence paradigm' 167–68
impact of international politics 168
importance 166–67
language and models dominated by Global North 15–16
mass drug violence as civil war or an 'ordinary crime' 169–73
Medellín as reflection of globally established hierarchy 165–66
need to transcend binary distinctions between crime and warfare 191
obliteration of pain 183–85
overview of key points 22–23
relevance of characteristics of conflicts 168–69
seen and unseen victims 177–81
shaping factors and responses 189–90
war seen 'from below' 173–77

Judiciary
Medellín cartel attacks on judges 36–37
memories of violence 43
sense of injustice, voiceless-ness, and revictimization 53–54

Mass drug violence
see also **drug violence**
creation of hierarchies of victimhood
mass drug violence as civil war or an 'ordinary crime' 169–73
overview of key points 22–23
defined 13
difficulty for victims to be heard 13–14
framing marked by three inter-related phenomena 15
shaped by unequal epistemological relations 184
war seen 'from below' 173–77
Medellín
challenge of competing with Netflix 194–95
dark tourism
branding in an unequal society 133–41
form of retraumatization 100
impact of media productions 117–18
impossibility of forgetting 119–27
shaping of city lives 117
shaping of cultural memory 118–19
haunting effect of Escobar 5
hyper-visibility of violence 190
obstacles to recognition of trauma 188
parallel life in media and commercial networks 1
photographs
hairdresser's in *El Barrio Pablo Escoba* 123–25, 125*f*
mug shot of Escobar in 1976 129–30, 130*f*
mural in *El Barrio Pablo Escobar* 123–25, 124*f*
Museo Casa de la Memoria 155*f*, 155
Parque Conmemorativo Inflexión 150*f*, 150–51
replica of James Bond's jet ski at the Escobar Museum 99*f*
rubble of Monaco building, demolished on order of Medellín's major in 2019 *t*2.1 36
souvenirs with the image of Pablo Escobar 130–32, 131*f*
statue of a saint in *El Barrio Pablo Escobar* 138, 139*f*
tourist showing off Escobar tattoo 130–32, 131*f*
politics of resistance
attempt to tell an alternative story 155–57
difficult path to recognition 160–62
project '*Medellín abraza su historia*' 149–50
sense of anger and unease 154–55
recognition of trauma 11

role of consumer items and commercialism in memory construction 198
sensory memories of violence 38–43
strong concern about historic portrayal of events 195
war seen 'from below' 173–77

Medellín cartel
attacks on journalists 37
attacks on judges 36–37
attacks on police 38
attacks on politicians 37–38
attempt at political involvement 176
conflict with the M-19 guerrilla group 34
control of world's cocaine trade 1
establishment in 1976 34
open war on the Colombian state 35–36
photographs
portraits of prominent members of Medellín cartel 138, 140*f*
substantial and enduring power base in city 34–35
trauma of war 45–46
turf conflicts with Cali cartels 35

Media and entertainment industries
see also **narco-shows**
advent of global media companies 67–68
central role in stereotyping 110–11
challenge of competing with Netflix 194–95
commercial appropriation of Escobar's story
birth of narco-telenovelas 70–73
El Patrón del Mal 69
commercial appropriation of Escobar's story by Netflix
globalization of Escobar as a brand 73–80
overview of key points 21
role of Netflix 80–86
violence as spectacle and trauma healing 91–95
why do we consume violence 86–91
commercial interests which dominate book publishing 57–63
creation of glamorous 'narco-aesthetic' 14–15
hyper-visibility of violence 190
immortalization of macho men, submissive women,and exotic others 112–16
impact on dark tourism 117–18
Medellin's strong concern about historic portrayal of events 195
narrative and epistemic power 188–89
newspaper accounts as historic documentation of violence 38–39
North American dominance of motion pictures 109
politics of resistance
portrayal of Gutiérrez's efforts to resist violence 148
role of the global community in fuelling violence 197–98
social responsibilities of business and corporations 195–96

Memory
attacks on journalists 43–44
attacks on judges 43
attacks on police 44–45
attacks on politicians 44–45
battle to control memory 143
centrality to understanding culture and national identity 133–34
collective memory
academic contributions 14–15
barriers for victims 10–11
challenges from global capitalism 91
conversion of violence 6–7
historical violence links 88–89
importance 180
importance of class and social inequalities 138
key issue 91
power of Netflix 144
role of young people 13–14
sense of loss of control 141

Memory (*cont.*)
struggle for recognition and the cosmopolitan exclusion 157
survivors rather than victims 103
truth and history telling 180, 182, 188–89
cosmopolitan memory 11, 157
cultural memory
European cultural memory 157
global economic influence of movies 5–6
inscribed in bodily practices 129
power of Netflix 144
shaping of cultural memory 118–19
dark tourism
form of retraumatization 133
impossibility of forgetting 119–27
shaping of cultural memory 118–19
failure to curtail dark tourism and Escobar branding 193–94
fear of erasure 200–1
need to focus on the silent stories of the people 193
repressed individual and collective traumas 64–67
role of consumer items and commercialism 198
sensory memories of violence 38–43
shaping of cultural memory 118–19
sharing of painful memories 49–52
Monaco building
demolition 150–53
photographs
Parque Conmemorativo Inflexión 150*f*, 150–51
rubble of Monaco building, demolished on order of Medellín's major in 2019 36*f*, 36
Movies and shows about Escobar
Bedazzled
Brendan Fraser playing Pablo Escobar in Bedazzled 106–7, 107*f*
Loving Pablo
Javier Bardem as Pablo Escobar and Penelope Cruz as Virginia Vallejo in *Loving Pablo* 79*f*
Narcos
Wagner Moura as Pablo Escobar in *Narcos* 78*f*
Paulina Gaitán as Escobar's wife in *Narcos* 78*f*
Museo Casa de la Memoria
attempt to tell an alternative story 155–57
photographs 155*f*, 155
replica of James Bond's jet ski at the Escobar Museum 99*f*

Napoles ranch
post-colonial experience staged for tourist enjoyment 121–23
visitors taking pictures at the entrance to the Napoles ranch 122–23, 123*f*
Narco culture 72–73, 99–100
Narco-shows
see also **Netflix**
advent of global media companies 67–68
birth of narco-telenovelas 70–73
branding in an unequal society 133–41
concealment of enabling social and political forces 175
creation of a misguided historic narrative by Netflix 143–47
epistemic power of the North 192–95
globalization of Escobar as a brand 73–80
light and entertaining tone 8
little critical reflection on the role of the U.S.-sponsored war on drugs 111–12
Narcos stills
Wagner Moura as Pablo Escobar and Paulina Gaitán as Escobar's wife in *Narcos* 78*f*
Wagner Moura as Pablo Escobar in *Narcos* 101–2, 102*f*

North American dominance of motion pictures 109–10
popularity 14–15
portrayal of Gutiérrez's efforts to resist violence 148
problematic gender performativity 101–5
role of Netflix 80–86
toxic masculinity 97
transformation of pain to entertainment 189
traumatic memories of war 173
why do we consume violence 86–91

'Narco-terrorism'
see also **drug violence**
framing of violence 174
integral component of political realm 12–13
need for museum of memory 154
use of concept 12–13

Netflix
see also **narco-shows**
commercial appropriation of Escobar's story
birth of narco-telenovelas 70–73
El Patrón del Mal 69
globalization of Escobar as a brand 73–80
overview of key points 21
role of Netflix 80–86
violence as spectacle and trauma healing 91–95
why do we consume violence 86–91
creation of a misguided historic narrative 143–47
Medellín's challenge of competing with Netflix 194–95
new approach with *22 July* 187
power to create cultural memory 144

North-South divide *see* **Global North–Global South divide**

Orientalism 112

Paramilitary organizations
history of violence in Colombia 30–31
labelling of Colombia as 'failed state' 33
Medellín cartel conflict with the M-19 guerrilla group 34
perpetrators of drug violence 12–13

Parque Conmemorativo Inflexión 150*f*, 150–51

Police
Historical Museum of the Colombian National Police 14–15
Medellín cartel attacks 38
memories of violence 44–45
US war on drugs 32, 33

Politicians
Medellín cartel attacks 37–38
memories of violence 44–45
use of war to transform economic, social, and political relations 37

Racial stereotypes
central role of media 110–11
immortalization of macho men, submissive women,and exotic others 112–16
money as the means to transcend racial barriers 30

Repressed trauma 10

Research methodology
bottom-up empirical approach 17
buildings, and streets as a living archive 18–19
exploration of the many forms of social profiting 16–17
interviews 19
privacy and ethical approval from Norwegian Centre for Research Data 19–20
qualitative methods implemented in two stages 18
two individual trajectories 17–18

State actors
gunning down of Escobar 1
perpetrators of drug violence 12–13
US 'war on drugs' 12–13

Toxic masculinity
- *Narcos* legacy 104–5
- objectification of women 100
- relationship with violence 97

Trauma
- commercial appropriation of Escobar's story 69
- cultural trauma 9–10, 67
- intellectual and emotional entrenchment of responses 187–88
- memories of Medellín cartel violence 45–46
- obstacles to recognition 188
- politics of resistance
  - attempt to tell an alternative story 155–57
  - battle to control memory 143
  - creation of a misguided historic narrative by Netflix 143–47
  - demolition of the Monaco building 150–53
  - difficult path to recognition 160–62
  - Gutiérrez's efforts and strategies 148
  - key to achieving a sense of recognition 157–60
  - overview of key points 22
  - project '*Medellín abraza su historia*' 149–50
  - sense of anger and unease 154–55
  - victims and victimhood 151–53
- repressed individual and collective traumas 64–67
- repressed trauma 10
- silent stories 193
- victimhood and cosmopolitan solidarity in a divided world
  - cultural trauma 9–10
  - fractured collective memories 11
  - global interconnectedness and solidarity 10–11
  - repressed trauma 10
  - unequal distribution of recognition 11
- violence as spectacle and trauma healing 91–95

Trauma economy
- contrast with light and entertaining tone of global narrative 8
- dark tourism
  - branding in an unequal society 133–41
  - form of retraumatization 133
  - impact of media productions 117–18
  - impossibility of forgetting 119–27
  - shaping of city lives 117
  - shaping of cultural memory 118–19
- dominant global consumerist culture 7–8
- impact of media and popular culture 7
- merging of economic networks around historical events 7–8
- need to adjust underlying concept 8–9
- processes of remembrance and memorialization 6–7
- profound effect on locals 196–97

Truth-telling 181–83
- argument for truth commissions 182–83
- covering up by authorities 181–82
- importance
  - in achieving a sense of recognition 158
  - central concern 181
- justice, reparation, and guarantees of non-repetition 181
- narrative and epistemic power of the global entertainment industry 188–89
- obstacles created by entertainment industry 188–89
- shaping of collective memory 182

United States
- bombing of Bogotá embassy 25
- epistemic power of punitive, militarized prohibition model 192–93
- example for narco-shows 73–74

North American dominance of motion pictures 109
pervasive impact on victims 11
role as major drug consumer 31
role of Netflix 80–86
societal responses to trauma 187–88
'war on drugs'
criticisms of failing to address internal drug demand 32–33
framing drug violence 12
intensification of efforts 32
labelling of Colombia as 'failed state' 33
little critical reflection in narco-shows 111–12
Task Force One 31–32
training, equipping, and advising local antinarcotics forces 32

Victims and victimhood
cosmopolitan solidarity in a divided world
cultural trauma 9–10
fractured collective memories 11
global interconnectedness and solidarity 10–11
repressed trauma 10
unequal distribution of recognition 11
difficulty for victims of violence to be heard 13–14
Global North–Global South divide 189
central constitutive element of hierarchies 16
framing of mass drug violence 15
language and models dominated by Global North 15–16
hierarchies of victimhood
central constitutive element of hierarchies 16
centrality of innocence 167
classification as contentious issue 167
framing of mass drug violence 15
further elements beyond the 'innocence paradigm' 167–68
impact of international politics 168
importance 166–67
importance of truth-telling 181–83
language and models dominated by Global North 15–16
mass drug violence as civil war or an 'ordinary crime' 169–73
Medellín as reflection of globally established hierarchy 165–66
need to transcend binary distinctions between crime and warfare 191
obliteration of pain 183–85
overview of key points 22–23
relevance of characteristics of conflicts 168–69
seen and unseen victims 177–81
shaping factors and responses 189–90
war seen 'from below' 173–77
hyper-visibility of violence 190
legal recognition
drafting of Victims' Law in 2011 163–64
fight for recognition by Federico 164–65
overview of key points 22–23
reflection of globally established hierarchy of victimhood 165–66
transitional justice compared 165
memories of violence 38–43
need to focus on the silent stories of the people 193
new approach by Netflix with *22 July* 187
obstacles to recognition of trauma 188
politics of resistance
attempt to tell an alternative story 155–57
demolition of the Monaco building 151–53
difficult path to recognition 160–62
sense of anger and unease 154–55

Victims and victimhood (*cont.*)
sense of injustice, voiceless-ness, and revictimization
advent of global media companies 67–68
commercial interests which dominate book publishing 57–63
damage to the self 47–49
overview of key points 20–21
painful practical obstacles to finding self 52–57
repressed individual and collective traumas 64–67
sharing of painful memories 49–52
societal responses to trauma 187–88
struggle for global recognition 196–97
trauma of war 45–46

'War on drugs' policy
criticisms of failing to address internal drug demand 32–33
framing drug violence 12
Global North creation 175–76
intensification of efforts 32
labelling of Colombia as 'failed state' 33
little critical reflection in narco-shows 111–12
need to find different political approaches 191–92
Task Force One 31–32
training, equipping, and advising local antinarcotics forces 32